PRAISE FOR *CARGO OF HOPE*

"A truly inspiring account of a 'mom-and-pop' charity in a 120-year-old wooden vessel. You really feel you are by Shane Granger's side in his plucky little craft bringing succor to some of the world's most remote communities."

—Julian Stockwin, author of the Thomas Kydd novels

"Beneath the author's self-deprecating shipboard wit, there are unexpected dimensions: great courage, to keep risking his boat and crew; incredible resourcefulness, stretching his fuel and food resources to the limit; and exceptional humanity, to try to build futures for the next generation through delivering the basics of health care and education. Without the author and his volunteer crew, and the unstinting support of his sponsors, many people in remote island villages could never hope to find a place in the modern world."

—Earl de Blonville, FRGS; leader of the first Australian arctic expedition

"High seas adventures, remote islands, and the 'art of making a difference' all come together in this fascinating nautical account. Shane and Meggi have seen natural wonders few people on earth have. The reader will feel they are at sea on both fair days and in brutal storms, guided by two highly experienced sailors who have a thirst for adventure and a determination to assist others in need."

—Michael J. Tougias, *New York Times* bestselling author of *A Storm Too Soon* and *Extreme Survival*

"I found this book vivid, candid, poignant, hilarious, and very important—simultaneously a story of love, adventure, and humanity. You'll be fascinated by the exciting ocean voyages, exotic places on the far side of the world, and the sense of true hope that Captain Granger brings to life. I highly recommend this book to everyone who loves the sea, believes in helping our fellow earthlings, and wants a great book that's worth reading again and again."

—Robert N. Macomber, author of the multi-award-winning Honor series

"*Cargo of Hope* is both an exciting sea story and a tale of kindly and compassionate dedication. It's also a deeply *human* book, celebrating generations of those who design ships, those who sail them, and the people who are dedicated to making a difference for those who need a helping hand. A great read in so many ways!"

—Rod Scher, author of *Sailing by Starlight: The Remarkable Voyage of Globe Star* and *The Annotated Two Years Before the Mast*

CARGO OF HOPE

Voyages of the Humanitarian Ship Vega

SHANE GRANGER

Illustrated by Margarete Macoun

Essex, Connecticut

An imprint of Globe Pequot, the trade division of
The Rowman & Littlefield Publishing Group, Inc.
4501 Forbes Blvd., Ste. 200
Lanham, MD 20706
www.rowman.com

Distributed by NATIONAL BOOK NETWORK

British Library Cataloguing in Publication Information available

Library of Congress Cataloging-in-Publication Data

Names: Granger, Shane, 1948- author. | Macoun, Margarete, illustrator.
Title: Cargo of hope : voyages of the humanitarian ship Vega / Shane
    Granger ; illustrated by Margarete Macoun.
Description: Essex, Connecticut : Lyons Press, [2023]
Identifiers: LCCN 2023034391 (print) | LCCN 2023034392 (ebook) | ISBN
    9781493080861 (paperback) | ISBN 9781493080878 (epub)
Subjects: LCSH: Granger, Shane, 1948- | Vega (Sailing ship) |
    Sailors—United States—Biography. | Humanitarian aid workers—United
    States—Biography. | Sailing—Indonesia. | Humanitarian assistance,
    American—Indonesia. | Non-governmental organizations—Indonesia. |
    Indonesia—Description and travel. | Indonesia—Social conditions.
Classification: LCC G540 .G674 2023 (print) | LCC G540 (ebook) | DDC
    915.9804/42092 [B]—dc23/eng/20231023
LC record available at https://lccn.loc.gov/2023034391
LC ebook record available at https://lccn.loc.gov/2023034392

♾™ The paper used in this publication meets the minimum requirements of American National
Standard for Information Sciences—Permanence of Paper for Printed Library Materials, ANSI/
NISO Z39.48-1992.

*To Meggi, who kept it all together and working
while I disappeared into a jungle of words.
To Palgunadi T. Setyawan, one of the finest gentlemen
I ever met, who is sorely missed.
And to all the friends who make what we do possible.*

Contents

Author's Note

Armed with a trusty notebook and pen, I composed most of this story as endless miles passed under *Vega*'s keel during my watches at sea. If you expect one of those boring save-the-world NGO tales, then I can safely say this book is not like that at all. On the other hand, if you want a taste of what it's like at sea on a 130-year-old sailing vessel, loaded to the gills with supplies for some of the world's most isolated islands and enduring every kind of weather; if you want to meet and get to know people who live on remote islands and the unimaginable problems they face just surviving—then this is the read you're looking for. I did my best to pack it with action, adventure, drama, and excitement as it really happened, although I did embellish some events to make for a better read. Occasionally, names have been changed for various reasons.

Rooting out the history of our small wooden sailing vessel, then telling her story, was not an easy task. Fortunately, along the way I had several amazing strokes of luck, each of which brought me one step closer to unraveling *Vega*'s mysterious past.

The first clue came in Durbin, when a Norwegian ship rigger wearing a bright-red boiler suit came strolling down the pier. Upon reaching *Vega* he stopped, eyed her carefully from several angles, then yelled to me, "I know this boat. My great-great-grandfather, he build this boat. This is *Vega*."

Since then I have communicated with a plethora of interesting people, all of whom added to *Vega*'s story. Among them Lars Nerhus, the great-grandson of *Vega*'s builder. A boatbuilder himself, Lars lives on the family farm where the original Nerhus boatyard still stands. Photographs of that two-hundred-year-old house and the boatyard inspired more than one vivid description that appears in this story.

I spent hours captivated by his tales from *Vega*'s beginning and her adventurous past. It was Lars who told of his great-grandfather's famous hat, then showed us *Vega*'s original half model and the 1898 painting done by Jens Nerhus. Little details like the stool and workbench where Ola Nerhus crafted his famous half models, often employing tools of his own making, still exist, gathering dust in the original shed whose door hinge still squeaks.

In Sweden, an amateur naval historian related to Alfred Olsen from Berkavara, where *Vega* spent much of her youth, helped piece together her mysterious demise and rebirth, providing important insights into the people involved and their times. Hardly a month goes by without another interesting piece of the puzzle landing in my inbox. As my knowledge of *Vega* grew, the people who played such an important role in her creation and early years came alive in my imagination, often aided by historic photographs or anecdotes told to younger family members by those who knew *Vega* in her youth.

The depictions of important historical moments in *Vega*'s life are my own, based on known facts and family stories passed down through generations. Ola Nerhus and Captain Niels Vagan may have had that first meeting at the Nerhus farmhouse or down at the local pub for all we know. Johan Carlsson might have hated both scotch and cigars and preferred furry slippers with rabbit ears. I believe it was Mark Twain who once said something along the lines of, "Maybe it happened that way, or maybe it didn't. The important thing is it could have happened that way."

Shipbuilding history aside, this is also a story about adventure and the annual mission that gives life meaning while keeping my partner, Meggi Macoun, and me busy. It's about maintaining *Vega* on a microscopic budget. But most of all this story is about the people you will meet from tropical islands often so remote that when we leave they do not see another outside face until our return, experiences I share with you through the eyes of the teller. Each of those stories is like a portrait, elaborated a bit here and there to convey the ambience and unspoken emotions.

For a guy who successfully failed every one of his English classes, creating this book was not easy. Between the first rough draft and what you now have in your hands stood a learning curve steep enough to frustrate Sisyphus. I owe special thanks to my friend Alan, who patiently guided me along the way, never once reporting my blunders to the Society for the Prevention of Cruelty to Commas. And to a wonderful woman by the name of Brittany who made it happen. As the Irish say, may the good Lord place a flower on their heads.

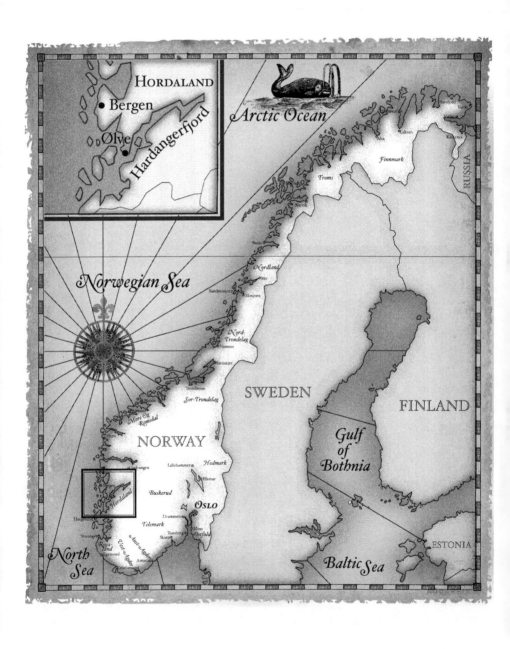

HORDALAND
• Bergen
Ølve
Hardangerfjord

Arctic Ocean

RUSSIA

Finnmark

Troms

Norwegian Sea

Nordland
Mo
Sandnessjøen
Mosjøen

Nord-
Trøndelag
Namsos
Steinkjer

Trondheim

SWEDEN

FINLAND

Sør-Trøndelag

Møre Og
Romsdal

NORWAY

Gulf
of
Bothnia

Lillehammer   Hedmark
Hamar
Gudvangen
Buskerud
Hordaland
OSLO
Drammen
Telemark
Tønsberg   Moss
Skien   Østfold

North
Sea

Stavanger
Rogaland
Aust-Agder
Vest-Agder
Arendal

ESTONIA

Baltic Sea

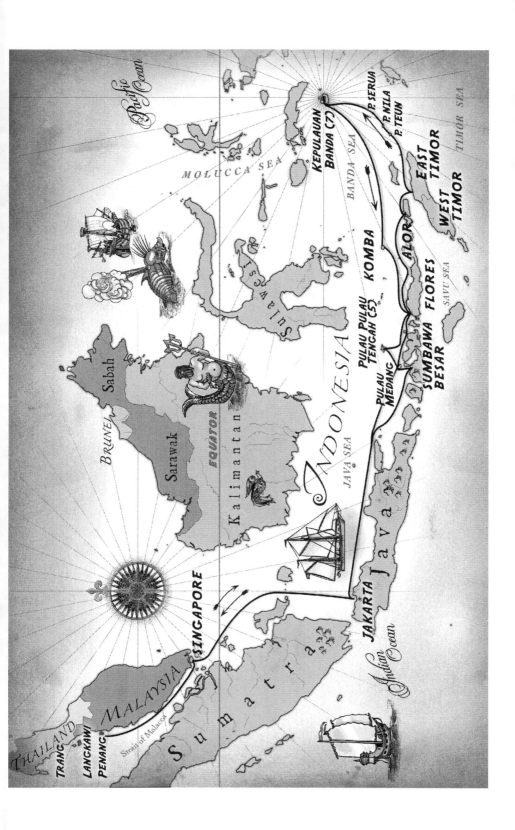

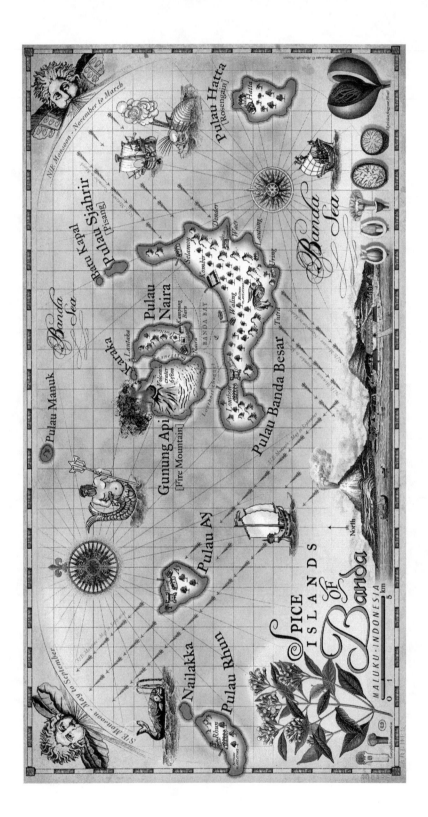

SPICE ISLANDS OF Banda
MALUKU · INDONESIA

Pulau Hatta
[Rosengain]

Banda Sea

Batu Kapal
Pulau Sjahrir
[Pisang]

Pulau Naira

Karaka

Pulau Manuk

Banda Sea

Gunung Api
[Fire Mountain]

Pulau Banda Besar

Pulau Ay

Nailakka

Pulau Rhun

N.W. Monsoon · November to March

S.E. Monsoon · May to September

North

0   1   5
km

PROLOGUE

It would be easy for me to blame it all on "The Book." It was an innocent little book without a single sinister image, unless you consider the page with the shark on it. And, in all honesty, even that fishy mouth full of teeth managed to grin at you in a friendly sort of way. Auntie gave me that book for Christmas when I was seven years old, and it changed my life forever.

The book was filled with images of magnificent sailing ships reaching across gossamer seas, with the sailors all dancing a hornpipe or scanning the horizon in search of a new adventure. From the first page I was captivated, hopelessly enthralled, by the golden age of sail. Eventually that fantasy became the man I am today, with several hundred thousand sea miles under my keel and many more to come.

Long into the night, I huddled under my blankets, clandestine lamp in hand, carefully studying those pictures until I knew the minutest detail each image had to offer. I even gave those old sailors titles and ranks.

I named the shark after Mrs. Clark, a teacher I had at the time who wore severe little glasses perched on one of those long noses that a hawk would be proud of and pulled her hair into a bun so taut her eyes looked oriental. I can still see her standing by the blackboard, dressed like an undertaker's wife come to haunt the front of our classroom. Lips pursed so tightly you could have used them for a ruler, arms crossed and foot tapping the drumroll of doom, while giving me a look from over those glasses so old-fashioned a Neanderthal's grandmother would have been proud of it.

By the time I reached eleven or twelve, I could draw a full clipper ship in all her glory with every detail precisely rendered. I knew the names of each piece of rigging and could bore my friends for hours with trivia about wooden sailing ships. While other kids fantasized about becoming football heroes, I dreamed of commanding a windborne expedition off to the ends of the world in search of adventure. The televised antics of Captain Irving Johnson, Thor Heyerdahl, and others of that ilk only served to heighten my resolve.

The fact is, we all dream of escaping the hectic rat race of today's highly accelerated world. Of a retreat into the leisurely ways of those glorious long-ago days now sacrificed to the twin gods of efficiency and profit. Of escaping back to a time when travel was an art form in itself; a time of discovery, adventure, exotic island destinations, and of course romance. The romance of bark-tanned sails and wooden ships reaching out to far horizons in search of the mysterious unknown, and the great contrast of cultures that made travel so stimulating.

Vivid images of freely roaming the world and enjoying a carefree life-style inspired my fantasies. Not so much from the military aspect, mind you. My admiration was strictly reserved for small cargo boats and the amazing voyages they made with their modest crews of hardy sailors, the winds of fate their only source of propulsion.

There was a time when boats like *Vega*, one of the heroes in this story, could be found trading for cargo in almost every port. After all, at one time Norway had the largest fleet of merchant sailing vessels in the world. North America, the Caribbean, and Africa were common voyages for those tough old sailors of iron who crewed their sturdy wooden ships. Some of Norway's small trading boats even sailed around Cape Horn to load cargos of nitrate-rich guano in Chile. Others may have ventured as far as India and Indonesia.

Carefully designed and built for some of the worst sailing conditions in the world, a weatherly boat like *Vega* would make rounding Cape Horn or Cape of Good Hope not as drastic an endeavour for those old sailors as it seems today. Having sailed over a hundred thousand miles in all types of weather on the old girl, I can assure you that properly maintained, she would have no problem negotiating the average trade routes of those times.

These days, *Vega* and her volunteer crew of intrepid sailors have a new mission: delivering tons of educational and medical supplies to some of the world's most remote island communities. When we furnish a child with the tools to learn, a health worker or traditional midwife with the supplies needed to care for their community, we provide them with a brighter future, and ourselves with a deeply moving sense of accomplishment.

CHAPTER I

The Mother of All Storms

Ripping through an ominous sky blacker than the inside of the devil's back pocket, a searing billion volts of lightning illuminated ragged clouds scudding along not much higher than the ship's mast. An explosive crash of thunder, so close it was painful, set my ears to ringing. Through half-closed eyes burning from the constant onslaught of wind-driven salt water, I struggled to maintain our heading on an ancient dimly lit compass.

This was not your common garden-variety storm. The kind that blows a little, rains a lot, and then slinks off to do whatever storms do in their off hours. This was a sailor's worst nightmare: a full-blown, rip-roaring, Indian Ocean cyclone fully intent on claiming our small wooden vessel and its occupants as sacrifices.

All that stood between us and the depths of eternity were the skill of *Vega*'s long-departed Norwegian builders and the flagging abilities of one man, who, after seventeen straight hours of fighting that hell-spawned storm, was cold, wet, and exhausted.

Using both hands, I turned the wheel to meet the next onslaught from a world ruled by chaos and madness. Should I miscalculate, or lose concentration for a single moment, within seconds the boat might whip broadside to those enormous thundering waves, allowing the next one to overwhelm her in a catastrophic avalanche of white foam: rolling her repeatedly like a rubber duck trapped in someone's washing machine: shattering her stout timbers and violently dooming us all to a watery grave.

The rigging howled like a band of banshees tormenting the souls of sailors long ago lost to the sheer brutality of such storms. Raging wind, fully intent on ripping the air from my lungs, made it almost impossible to breathe. No matter which way I turned my head there was flying water.

Only twenty meters away, the bow of our 120-year-old wooden vessel was invisible in a swirling mass of wind, rain, and wildly foaming sea. With monotonous regularity, precipitous walls of tortured water loomed out of the darkness, rushing toward *Vega*'s unprotected stern. Yet, as each seemingly vertical wall of water raced toward her, its top curling over in a seething welter of foam, our brave little vessel would raise, allowing another monster to pass harmlessly under her keel.

With each wave, the long anchor warps trailing in a loop from our stern groaned against the mooring bits. Those thick ropes were all we had to reduce *Vega*'s mad rush into the next valley of tormented water, their paltry resistance all that stood between us and fifty-two tons of boat surfing madly out of control down the near-vertical face of those waves.

As *Vega* valiantly lifted to meet each successive wave, she dug in her bow: a motion that unchecked might rapidly swing her broadside. Should that happen, the end would come quickly when the next breaking wave rolled *Vega* through 360 devastating degrees. An action that would repeat until nothing remained afloat.

With helm and wind creating a precarious balance against the brutal forces of an Indian Ocean cyclone, our future was contingent upon a single scrap of storm sail stretched taut as a plate of steel, its heavy sheet rigid as an iron bar. Without that sail, steering would be impossible.

While all hell broke loose around us, down below the off watch were squirreled away in their bunks, warm and more or less dry. Little did they realize that at least once every eight to ten seconds I was fighting another giant wave intent on our destruction. Squinting and blinking, I tried to read the wind speed gauge but glimpsed only a meaningless blur of figures.

I should have paid more attention to the old sailor who once advised me never to look down when climbing ratlines or aft during a storm. It might have saved me from almost suffering an apoplexy when somewhere around midnight I glanced astern and saw a wave much larger than the rest come roaring out of the darkness, growing in height and apparent malice with each passing second.

As if that were not enough, another rogue wave came surging out of the night at a ninety-degree angle to our route. Shivers raced up and down my spine, vainly looking for a safe place to hide. Nothing in my years at sea had prepared me for that giant storm-ravaged whitecap bearing down on *Vega's* starboard beam.

Frozen in horror, I watched that watery monster collide with the first giant wave, roaring along its length like a head-on collision between two out-of-control avalanches determined to destroy all in their path. The interaction was explosive. A towering eruption of white water rocketed skyward, an unbridled violence beyond imagination.

Converging on our frail wooden boat from different directions, those twin monsters were a manifest curse from the darkest depths of my worst nightmare. Clearly, they would arrive at the same time. The one would slam into *Vega* like a huge bloody-minded mallet, while the other played the part of a watery anvil, and there was not a damned thing in the world I could do about it.

For a split second that seemed eternal, gut-wrenching fear seized me in its grip. No matter which way I turned the wheel, one of those furious monsters would roll *Vega* onto her beam-ends. Certain destruction would surely follow.

Trembling from cold and fatigue, there was just enough time for me to take a deep breath before water erupted from every direction, transforming my world into a swirling white maelstrom of destruction. I gripped the steering as hard as I could, frantically struggling against inconceivable forces fully intent on sweeping me overboard to turn it against the sideways slide I felt building. Then something struck me a fierce blow to the head. As I began to lose consciousness, my only thought was, *So, this is how it ends.* Then my world turned black.

CHAPTER 2

Birth of a Legend

With a whiplike report, a shower of sparks exploded from a resinous pine log as it collapsed into the heart of the fire, one that blazed invitingly in the ancient stone fireplace, casting its warm glow across the faces of two men sipping from small glasses of fiery Norwegian aquavit. The year was 1890.

A companionable silence existed between them, broken only by the stately ticktock of a grandfather clock standing in the hallway and the crackling of the fire. Although separated by their difference in age, the two men were old friends who also respected each other professionally.

Oil lamps illuminated the comfortable room where they sat. Constructed over many generations from native stone and aromatic Norwegian pine, the Nerhus family farmhouse was ancient. Over the years, its wood had aged to a deep golden-brown luster.

A native of Herøysund, Captain Nils Vagan was a big man with the broad shoulders of a professional seaman whose muscular body tapered to a narrow waist. A strong nose, twice broken in sailing accidents, was set in a wide face weathered by the harsh conditions of his profession. He wore his dark-brown hair long, as was the fashion of the day. That night he had

4

it tightly clasped behind his head in a ponytail held in place by a piece of lightly tanned leather.

What most people noticed first about the captain were his razor-sharp eyes. When he was irritated, something that rarely happened, those diamond-hard orbs seemed to bore mercilessly into the object of his anger. Most of the time, they gave the impression of focusing somewhere just over the nearest horizon.

His full mouth always seemed to curl up slightly at the corners, as if inwardly smiling at some private joke. His powerful voice befitted a man accustomed to making himself heard above the howling winds of a North Sea gale. That night, in the warmth of such a cosy room, he wore an expression of comfortable contentment.

A true man of the sea, at twenty-seven years of age, Vagan was already one of the most sought-after and respected sailing captains on Hardanger fjord. Tracing his lineage directly back to fearsome Viking raiders who originated along Norway's bitter west coast, had he been born in an earlier age Captain Nils Vagan would have made a fearsome seagoing adversary and a master pirate.

Born in 1840, Ola H. Nerhus was a different sort of man, one whose quick, highly observant mind designed and built sailing ships. His hands were large and callused, his reputation for creating strong, swift-sailing cargo vessels unrivalled. Nerhus's designs were so successful that he became a highly demanded shipbuilder, as well as the responsible model builder (the naval architect of the day) and surveyor for many of the most prominent "yard locations" in the Hardanger region of Norway. Nearly a century and a half later, his great-grandson, Lars Nerhus, himself a boatbuilder, discovered his ancestor's name in historic documents, giving reason to believe that most of the famous Hardanger yachts sailed by the men of Tysnes were designed and built by Ola H. Nerhus—an impressive statement considering Tysnes had quite a large fleet at that time.

Age had brought a slight squint to the eyes of Ola Nerhus, eyes that arched down ever so slightly as they branched out into a modest collection of crow's feet. His nose was somewhat wider than normal, suggesting distant Asiatic ancestry, a trait enhanced by his short, stocky stature. One could easily imagine hordes of men like Nerhus pouring out of Mongolia to rage across the great steppes of Asia on their sturdy little ponies, hell-bent on conquest and adventure.

As was his style, Ola Nerhus wore a neatly trimmed moustache above the expressive curve of his lip. A slight dimple creased his strong chin. He had not shaved for several days, giving his normally agreeable countenance a somewhat sinister appearance.

His once intense sapphire-blue eyes had grown lighter over the years but could still flash lightning bolts of displeasure at any worker who dared give less than his very best in the construction of those seaworthy vessels he was famous for designing and building.

Rising from his comfortable leather armchair, Captain Vagan moved over to a window. With one hand, he pushed aside the thick curtain that helped keep the fire's heat in and the intense Nordic cold out. His other hand came to rest on the polished wooden window frame. A glistening world of snow and ice met his gaze. The great fjord's restless water frozen for as far as the eye could see.

Through the window, he could hear the relentless Arctic wind as it roared around the stout stone-and-wood farmhouse. Gazing into the dim whiteness beyond the glass, he mentally reviewed the mission he was on and how best to accomplish it. Ola Nerhus was a busy man, with quite a few ships already under construction. Convincing him to take on another project might be a difficult task. Turning away from the window, he allowed the curtain to fall back into position.

Taking a deep breath, Captain Vagan resumed his place by the fire. Both men knew that his visit was more than a casual social call. What they could not know was that over a century later, decisions made on that winter night in Norway would directly affect thousands of people living half a world away on remote tropical islands in Southeast Asia.

Taking a small sip from his glass of aquavit, Captain Vagan slowly began to explain the motive for his visit. Over the next few minutes, Ola Nerhus listened closely. In his mind, an image began to form. Various well-known shapes combined then diverged, only to merge once again into something slightly different. By the time Captain Vagan finished his proposal, Ola Nerhus knew he could not pass over this strange request the way he did so many others that failed to interest or challenge him.

A small cough broke the spell, reminding both men that Ola's oldest son, Jens Nerhus, was sitting quietly at the room's large wooden table, reading from a leather-bound book he had found in the village. Having overheard the entire presentation, Jens was not to know the deep and lasting impact that meeting would have on his own future.

Rising from his chair, Ola Nerhus refilled both of their glasses then returned to his seat. Over the next few hours, details of this new and exciting project coalesced. When Captain Vagan finally left for his home it was early morning, but deep inside he felt the warm glow of a mission well accomplished. The result of that night's work would be nothing short of revolutionary.

Several months before that auspicious meeting between Captain Nils Vagan and Ola Nerhus, Mr. Johan Carlsson, the successful owner of a cement factory in Degerhamn, Sweden, strolled into his study. Clearly a man's room, the centerpiece was a massive wooden desk made from the deck planks of a trading ship cast ashore during his great-grandfathers' time. The remains of that ship were still visible on the coast close to where Mr. Carlsson's new cement factory now stood.

Unable to sleep, Mr. Carlsson was not exactly the spitting image of a successful merchant as he lit the whale-oil lamp on his desk and settled back into his leather-covered chair. Replacing the lamp's glass chimney, he carefully adjusted the wick until it stopped smoking. Only then did he reach into the top right-hand drawer of his desk for the bottle of light-brown liquid he knew from long experience was safely ensconced there. On the corner of his desk stood a small crystal glass, covered by a hand-embroidered linen napkin.

Johan Carlsson had a problem, and it was starting to affect profits. His new state-of-the-art cement plant produced more, and better quality, cement than the old factory. Of course, that was why he built the new factory in the first place, but it was also the root of his problem.

Although he currently owned several sturdy little sail-powered cargo boats, his factory was making cement, and his agents were selling it, faster than he could deliver. Orders were even starting to come in from faraway England and, more surprisingly, imperial Germany. Business was looking up, if he could only find a way to make those deliveries.

Most of his clients were located in small harbor towns and villages spread along Sweden's lengthy, convoluted coast: ports closed to his larger cargo boats due to shallow water or nonexistent pier facilities. The stopgap solution of chartering boats for those deliveries cut deeply into his profits. After all, cement is sold in tons on tight margins.

Pouring a glass of his special Scotch whisky smuggled from England on one of his own boats, he took a leisurely sip while staring off into space. As much as he hated the idea (Johan Carlsson dearly disliked spending money on things other than himself or his family), he needed a new small cargo boat. The question was where to build the best boat at the lowest cost.

Deeply immersed in thought, myriad facts raced through his mind, blending financial calculations with various available options. As those thoughts became more complex, he unconsciously twirled the almost empty glass between his hands.

This happened at a time when Sweden and Norway were united to form "The Union"—a time when many Swedish owners built ships in Norway, where labor was less costly. Therefore, after exhausting all other possibilities, it seemed only natural that Carlsson should look to the famous, and more economical, shipbuilders of Norway for his newest *jacht*.[1]

Taking a sheet of paper from his desk drawer, he carefully positioned it, then picked up an elegant silver pen, dipped it in ink, and began writing out instructions for his agent in Norway. He also sent a short note to an old Swedish friend and associate in Oslo asking for his advice. With the decision taken and his letters written, Johan Carlsson drained the glass, snuffed out the lamp, and climbed back up the stairs to his bedroom. Happily dreaming of massive profits and huge meals, his deeply resonate snores, the reason his wife insisted on her own bedroom, were soon rattling the windowpanes.

Within a few short weeks, Carlsson had answers from both of his correspondents. For once, his sources agreed with each other. Outstanding among Norwegian *jachts* of the time were those designed and built on Hardanger fjord, a place where the tradition of building strong, swift-sailing cargo boats was already well established in the late 1400s. At the time Carlsson needed his new boat, the finest Hardanger *jachts* were designed and built by Ola H. Nerhus in his Nerhuson boatyard at Ølve.

Carlsson's Oslo associate went so far as recommending that a certain Captain Nils Vagan, of impeccable reputation, act as Carlsson's representative for the project. In late autumn 1890, Carlsson contacted Captain Vagan of Herøysund to act as his intermediary, with special instructions stating Ola Nerhus should design and build the vessel to the highest specifications.

Carlsson wanted the new vessel engineered specifically for heavy concentrated weight, such as cement, bricks, building stone, and even pig iron—cargos most wooden North Sea vessels avoided like the plague. He also specified certification for trade in the Arctic: a classification few wooden boats of the day rated. In a burst of fatherly pride, he decided to name the future boat *Vega*, after his youngest daughter.

---

1. *Jacht*, or *jagkt*, is a generic Scandinavian name for a small cargo boat powered by sail, and the original source of the English word *yacht*.

As autumn advanced into another freezing-cold Nordic winter, Carlsson impatiently anticipated word from Captain Vagan. It was not until late December that a letter arrived from Norway. Hands shaking with excitement, Carlsson slit open the envelope with a solid silver letter opener. Unfolding the single sheet, he spread it out on his desk and began to read.

Almost at once, he found the news he had been anxiously awaiting for the past several months. Ola Nerhus had agreed to design and build the boat, although he stipulated white oak, a wood not normally used in Norwegian boatbuilding, for the keel and frames. Wood that was not available in Norway. Shipbuilding-grade oak would need to be carefully selected locally, then shipped from Sweden to Hardanger Fjord by sea.

Although Carlsson could understand the logic behind this stipulation, procuring and transporting the wood would be a costly exercise. On the other hand, what were friends for if not to help in times of need? With a curt nod, he grudgingly agreed, then did what shipowners throughout the ages have done when faced with similar circumstances: he pulled open the drawer to his desk and extracted the bottle of Scotch. Perhaps a stiff drink would reduce the sting from so much extra cost. At least he could use his own ships to transport the wood.

At the same moment Carlsson was pouring himself a double tot of whiskey, Ola Nerhus felt as if not even a strong drink would solve his problems. Tucked away in a corner of his boatyard's main building shed was his private workbench, well stocked with the precision woodworking tools he employed to make half models.

Many of those tools he had made himself over the years. Each of them was like an old cherished friend. A rare sliver of golden sunlight filtered down through dancing dust motes from a skylight he had installed thirty-five years before to illuminate a pair of work-hardened yet highly sensitive hands holding the freshly carved model of a ship's hull about seventy-five centimeters long and only fifteen or so centimeters wide.

Ola Nerhus designed boats in the tried-and-true traditional manner, by making a miniature model of what the real ship's body would look like. Once approved by the owner, the model was divided lengthwise, saving half for future reference, then Ola Nerhus sawed the other half into slices perpendicular to the centerline. Skilled artisans reproduced those sections full-size on the lofting floor where the ship's frames would be laid out and shaped. Back then, the art of ship design was in making those models, an art at which Ola Nerhus excelled.

Slowly rotating the latest model, he carefully studied each compound curve, first from the stern, then from the bow. His practiced eye quickly spotted tiny faults in the lines, but nothing a scraper or fine wood rasp could not redress. From long years of experience, he easily visualized how that model would respond as a fully loaded ship tortured by some merciless North Sea gale. What he saw was a lovely vessel, one that would sail admirably, yet it was still not what he wanted.

This little ship was destined to carry heavy concentrated weight, a wooden boat builder's nightmare. With all of her load in the center, if the boat hung between two waves it might literally break in half, sinking without a trace in only seconds. But Ola Nerhus was an intuitive naval architect, backed up by a wealth of traditional wisdom long ago earned during his years as an apprentice in Hardanger's finest boatyards. His instinctive understanding of the sea was what made him such a good designer, one whose boats were famous for being fast and safe.

Ola slowly got to his feet. Carrying the latest model a few meters to the end of his workbench, he gently placed it alongside a growing mountain of similar efforts. With a small sigh, he gave it a gentle pat before turning to retrieve another piece of wood from his special store.

With no further sign of emotion, he returned to the well-worn wooden stool. What he needed was a different approach from the standard Hardanger *jacht* with her fine entry and smooth exit run. The problem he faced was not one of size but of carrying capacity. How to make a sixty-foot boat carry fifty-five tons of concentrated cargo and still be safe at sea in the worst of storms? Shifting his position on the stool, Ola Nerhus ran a hand over his chin in that universal gesture men have used to stimulate inspiration for thousands of years. The rasping sound of a two-day beard was all that greeted his effort.

Placing the new piece of wood off to one side, he meticulously cleaned the workbench, then carefully put away his tools. Ola was so deeply engrossed in the complexity of this new design he hardly noticed pushing the stool into its place under the bench or taking his trademark black hat from its peg on the wall. Perhaps a walk along the shore would help. He often solved some of his trickiest problems while walking. Had you asked him, Ola Nerhus would have been the first to admit this project both baffled and intrigued him.

Vega's intended cargo demanded a strong, full-bodied vessel with a high displacement-to-length/beam ratio. Due to tax and harbor pilot regulations, she needed to be a bit short of sixty feet between perpendiculars. Mr. Carlsson was quite insistent his new boat be rated at fifty-five tons to satisfy the demands of his cement, brick, and building stone trade. Additional regulations required the boat be rigged as a traditional cutter. Although effective, the cutter rig demanded a much larger crew than the well-proven two-masted galleass, with its greater sail area and smaller crew requirement.

With these disparate elements spinning around in his head, Ola let himself out through a small wooden door set into the northern side of the boatbuilding shed. As he opened it, the old bronze hinges on that sturdy wooden door gave out a mournful squeak. Threading his way across the busy boatyard, Ola followed a well-worn path that led to the shore, pausing only to answer a question from one of his workers.

Perhaps it was something in the clear clean air of Hardanger Fjord, or the constant onslaught of a powerful master artisan's mind on a difficult problem, but suddenly Ola Nerhus had a flash of inspiration.

Abruptly turning on his heel, he raced back toward the building shed, a hand tightly clamped on his trademark black hat to keep it from flying away. Workers in the boatyard stopped what they were doing to watch in amazement as he rushed by. The master never ran anywhere, nor could even the longest-serving carpenter remember ever seeing him do so.

Back at his workbench, he took up the piece of wood selected for the next model and in a flurry of creative energy began to carve. The new model was radically different from the average Hardanger *jacht*. In a frenzy of intense concentration, the skilled hands and keen eyes of master boatbuilder Ola Nerhus translated his newly inspired vision into a wooden hull model— one that was destined to win an award for design innovations at the great International Fisheries Exhibition of 1898 held in Bergen.

Faced with the age-old conundrum of how to make a small boat carry the same amount of cargo as a much larger one, Ola Nerhus did a splendid job of forming the model that would become *Vega*. To gain more weight-carrying capacity, he employed an old-fashioned buff bow combined with a stern much wider than the traditional heart-shaped Hardanger *jacht*. In fact, *Vega*'s stern seems to have been copied directly from the famous Danish "Marstall *jachts*," then slightly modified into a wider version of the heart shape that was a Nerhus trademark. Humming softly to himself, Ola Nerhus deftly created a full, deep-bodied vessel with graceful tumble home and a sweeping compound curve along her sheer line.

Three hours later, Ola held the master model for a new type of small cargo boat in his hands. Carefully placing it on the workbench, he covered it with a piece of cloth before snuffing out the oil lamp. Now that the hull shape was clear, he could concentrate on building it.

Following another well-worn path from the boatyard and his family farmhouse, Ola mentally began assembling the structural elements that would become *Vega*. His interpretation of a strong wooden boat built for heavy, concentrated loads and service in the Arctic differed from the Swedish. Then again, seas around Norway can be among the most vicious in the world.

Vega's white oak frames are more reminiscent of a naval man of war from the 1700s than any late-nineteenth-century merchant vessel. Those frame sets consist of between four and six grown oak frames tightly trunneled and bolted together with only enough room between each set for ventilation. Nowhere on *Vega* is there more than thirty centimeters (12 inches) between frame sets, and that only at the bow and stern. To insure rigidly and strength, Nerhus gave *Vega* a double hull with interliners even thicker than her outer planking. The result is far from the fastest sailing boat he ever built, but undoubtedly the strongest. That night, he enjoyed an undisturbed, peaceful sleep for the first time in weeks. The following morning, he sent a message requesting Nils Vagan to come examine the new half model.

CHAPTER 3

Battered, Not Beaten

I have woken up in some strange places during my life—everywhere from the boudoir of a French countess to a small-town jail in Louisiana—although none of them compare to being slammed back into consciousness by a few tons of ice-cold seawater while lying in the scuppers of a half-foundered sailing ship. Given a choice, I will happily take breakfast with the countess any day. Right little stunner she was.

Battling up from the depths of unconsciousness is a bit like rebooting a computer; everything starts over again from the here and now, not there and then. I had no idea where, or even who I was, as awareness clawed up through oblivion into the raging violence of a full-blown cyclone. The boat rolled hard to port. Before I could grasp a pin rail for support, another watery fist cascaded over the rail, brutally slamming me back onto the deck. Helpless to resist its overwhelming power, the torrent spun me around, washing me back into the lee scuppers.

Then in a sudden rush of consciousness, reality came hurling back. I was at sea in a vicious storm battling for my life and the lives of my shipmates. Shaking my head in an effort to clear my thoughts, I pulled myself up on all fours. Coughing up seawater and struggling to breathe in that waterlogged atmosphere of savage wind-driven rage, I fought my way back to the wheel. Squinting through salt-encrusted eyes that must have been redder than the devil's business card, I could just make out the compass and our present course. The heading was only a few degrees off our safest route.

Taking a firm grip on the wheel, I turned it three spokes to port. The wheel's resistance felt strangely light. As I waited for *Vega* to respond, the compass obstinately remained fixed on the same heading. When another two spokes to port also brought no result, I began to worry.

Just then, my partner, Meggi, who had been safely ensconced in our aft cabin bunk, stuck her head out of the aft hatch. Screaming to be heard over the raging wind, she informed me an ungodly great rending crack had come from where the steering ram is located just behind our aft cabin bunk.

Leaving the helm to Meggi, I made my way into our cabin. Salt water and blood dripped onto the cabin sole from a deep cut on my forehead as I lifted the steering box cover. What I discovered was straight from a nightmare. Our hydraulic steering ram shaft, made from one-inch-diameter high-tensile machine steel, had shattered like a cheap plastic toy, leaving the tiller arm free to thrash back and forth in those savage seas.

Vega was out of control. Only the drag generated by those long mooring ropes, tightly attached to the stern bits in great loops, and the thrust of our small storm jib held her before the waves. Without steering, there was nothing to stop *Vega* from broaching sideways and being rolled mercilessly into oblivion. The screaming of tortured wood coming from the aft mooring cleats did nothing to relieve my worries. Should one of those cleats give way . . . well, that was a thought simply not worth having.

It was then the real horror of our situation dawned on me: the rudder was not only swinging from port to starboard, fully at the mercy of the sea, but it was also rocking from side to side, a horrifying indication that at least one of the pintles had broken.

If you are not up to date on traditional ship design, rudder pintles are like hinges that attach the rudder to the ship and allow it to rotate when the wheel is turned. *Vega* has two on her rudder and a stout bearing under the rudderstock. Should both the pintles break, there would be nothing to stop our violently gyrating rudder from detaching itself and disappearing into the depths below.

Just then, a sopping-wet Meggi came down the aft hatch, followed by a splash of seawater, to tell me the boat would not steer. Seeing me full on in the light of the aft cabin, the look of near panic on her face suddenly changed.

Feeling helpless, in the middle of a raging storm, on a sailing ship with no rudder, I looked like a macabre escapee from the haunted house of horrors. I was soaking wet, unshaved for days, and squinting at the world through tortured red eyes. Blood trickled from my nose and a nasty cut on my forehead. Add to that the look of pure terror etched on my face, and you can understand why Meggi's mouth dropped open.

CHAPTER 4

The Master's Touch

Soft golden light from a flaming Norwegian sunset exploded across the sky as Ola Nerhus walked around the new little ship slowly taking form in his boatyard. His keen eye perceived every detail. The half-finished boat stood proudly on the building cradle awaiting her hull planking and thick pitch pine decks. Reaching out, his large, calloused hand caressed the curve of a cant frame. Finding it smooth and well turned, he nodded to himself.

Throughout the long days of a Nordic summer that often provided over eighteen hours of daylight for their work, his highly trained artisans and their apprentices had skillfully shaped and fit the many disparate elements that went into creating this lovely frame. It was hard work, the hours grueling. But he knew the cold, hard Norwegian winter would soon return, giving those men several months to relax by the fireside, enjoying the well-earned fruit of their labor.

Far from being the largest or the fastest boat he ever designed and built, somehow this chubby-cheeked little ship had found its way into his heart. So many things about her differed from the usual boats he built. Even her smell—the tangy tartness typical of oak, rather than the rich resin-scented aroma of the local Norwegian pitch pine he normally employed—was different.

Several months before, the long Norwegian winter gave way to the spring of 1891. Flowers bloomed, the fjords thawed. Shipping slowly reappeared. Not surprisingly, one of the first foreign vessels to arrive came from Sweden carrying a consignment of carefully selected and cured white oak. Ola had been pleasantly surprised by the quality of that wood. From long experience, he knew most shipowners constantly cut corners to save a few coins and had expected that from his current Swedish client. But that was not the case. Mr. Carlsson had unstintingly provided first-class, carefully selected wood for the building of his new boat.

Little did Ola Nerhus know of the time Mr. Carlsson spent harassing Alfred Olsen, himself the owner of a small boatyard in Bergkarva, Sweden, to procure the finest boatbuilding wood possible. Nor did he know of how Alfred had scoured the best woodyards in Sweden for the oak Ola was now forming, and to gain a little relief from Carlsson's constant badgering.

As his sharp eye caressed her smooth lines, Ola knew this little boat would never be a fast sailor, although he felt she would certainly be a dependable one, and a very stable boat in bad weather. He was more than a little proud she was to be registered at an unprecedented fifty-five tons, something no Hardanger *jacht* of her size had ever achieved. Overall, he was satisfied with the latest work.

Looking around his busy boatyard, Ola noted the other boats being built or repaired. Off to one side, his crew of serious-looking craftsmen, dressed in their traditional coveralls, were busy repairing the stem of a boat he built thirty years before. They were fine boats, he had to admit, yet from his point of view they shared a common problem. Their owners all wanted racehorses to haul cargo. *Vega* was different. From the very beginning, she was designed as a workhorse that could carry a big load for her size, and do it in all weather without complaining.

Out of the corner of his eye, he noticed someone approaching. Shifting his gaze, he saw it was that man from Oslo, the one selling farm machinery and those newfangled boat engines. He did not blame the man for his constant visits, each with a new approach to the same question. After all, his products were heavy and they needed delivering, often to small islands inside the Arctic Circle. Nor was he the only one to approach Ola with the same proposition. They all wanted to employ *Vega*, with her special capacity for heavy, concentrated cargo, to deliver their products.

In many ways, Ola Nerhus was a typical Norwegian: honest, hardworking, and above all a shrewd businessman, always on the lookout for profitable opportunities. This little boat was not even launched and already people were begging him to carry their cargo with it.

Looking up at the boat growing in front of him, Ola unconsciously removed his trademark black hat. Slowly waving it in front of his face to chase away an annoying fly, he thought of a little boat carrying heavy cargo to isolated Arctic islands. Maybe tonight he would talk with his son Jens about an idea that had taken shape over the past few weeks. If Jens agreed, Ola would write a letter that might just make them both a bit of extra money. Besides, Jens could use the experience, and of course the funds.

Several weeks later Johan Carlsson sat at his massive wooden desk reading a letter from the man in Norway who was building his new boat. That letter from Ola Nerhus was short and to the point.

There were many businessmen in Norway with heavy cargos that needed delivering to out-of-the-way places, many of those places within the Arctic Circle. Few, if any, boats were available to make those deliveries, and those few were booked up far in advance. Their rates were more than double the normal price for cargo. Carlsson's new boat *Vega* would be perfect for those jobs and could turn a handy profit carrying those loads. If Mr. Carlsson agreed, Jens Nerhus would skipper the boat and Ola Nerhus would undertake to manage their joint venture.

The letter then went on to propose various share options and other details of the suggested enterprise. In essence, all Johan Carlsson needed to do was agree, then sit back contentedly collecting his biannual share of the profits.

Carlsson needed few of his shrewd business skills to recognize a very handy profit, at almost no cost to himself. Twirling a silver writing pen between his palms, Johan turned to gaze out the window behind his desk. As he considered this latest business venture, the stately ticktock of a pendulum clock and the pen click-clacking against his finger rings were the only sound in the room.

Times had changed since he commissioned the building of *Vega*. Most of the cement from his new factory now went to Stockholm, or to the fast-growing export trade. Almost all of the exports went in larger ships he chartered when needed. His existing fleet of small sailing cargo boats could easily manage the local deliveries.

Turning back from the window, Carlsson reached down and opened the upper left-hand drawer of his desk. Taking out a piece of notepaper, he carefully placed it on the faded green leather pad in the center of his desk. Moments later, he dipped his pen in a filigreed silver ink well and began to write.

His response to Ola Nerhus was short and to the point, stating that he agreed in principle with Ola's proposal and thanking him for offering it. Being a good businessman, Johan could not resist adding the need to discuss share options in closer detail. He was certain he could get at least another 8 percent out of the deal if he negotiated properly with the crafty Old Norwegian.

Happily chortling to himself at the thought of getting the best of another deal, he sealed the letter, then called for one of his servants. Moments later he heard a door close and, looking out of his window, saw the cook's son racing into town with the letter held tightly in his hand.

CHAPTER 5

Of Tillers and Davy Jones

They say time flies when you're having fun. What they all fail to mention are the moments when time simply shrugs her shoulders and wanders off looking for a cold beer, leaving you in a timeless limbo to get on with whatever you are doing as best you can. Mind you, I can fully understand that attitude. At that moment, if it meant being somewhere else, I would gladly have paid the first round, and maybe even the second—with peanuts.

An insane roll threw me across the aft cabin where I fetched up against the side with a painful thump. Dancing around on the madly gyrating deck, I yelled for Meggi to get out the emergency tiller, while I fought my way back up on deck and retrieved two pieces of stout braided line. Extremely strong and highly resistant to abrasion, that rope was perfect for an emergency rudder repair.

As my head emerged from below, the wind almost blew my hair off. While rigging screamed in torment, raging winds shattered the wave crests into a froth of driven spray before hurling foaming white horses from the wave peaks into the troughs. Struggling to breathe, and reflecting on how Dante would have loved this place, I fought my way forward to the line locker.

Having a bright idea and making it work can be two very different propositions, especially when they involve a wildly gyrating deck and a rudder that violently swings from side to side every few seconds. What in port, on a calm day, would have taken me only minutes to accomplish became an endless eternity of individual seconds, each accented by its own specific danger, and the constant fear of sudden death looming over it all.

Before the emergency tiller could be put in place, I first had to dismount the remains of the shattered steering ram. That involved removing a tight-fitting stainless-steel pin held in place by a reticent split pin. Just getting the locking pin out was a major effort, involving pliers, hammers, bashed fingers and copious amounts of creative profanity. Then the big pin had to be pulled, normally an easy job that became a marathon of horrors. Through all of this, I was relentlessly under attack by a wild flailing rudder and its heavy iron steering arm.

Being in a state fast approaching panic didn't help either. The strange thing about life-or-death situations is how they can focus your mind quite clearly in two different directions. One instinct is to widdle your knickers and hide under the bed with your bum in the air and a pillow covering your head, while another little voice between your ears is screaming at you to do something before you find out if there really is a man with a scythe on the other side.

With the remains of the steering ram out of the way, yet another interesting little quandary presented itself. How to firmly reattach the rudder head to the boat so that when I had the emergency steering tiller in place the rudder would actually pivot and not simply flop from side to side. That is where my two pieces of braded yacht line would come into play, if I could manage getting them in place without losing a handful of fingers—or worse.

Fortunately, there was a space between the steering arm and the rudder head. If I could get the two pieces of line through that space, and bouse them tightly to the sides of the boat, together they would hold the rudder head, more or less, on the centerline so it could be turned.

The biggest problem was getting the two lines through such a small space while retaining all of my appendages and avoiding a short sharp smack on the head from the flailing rudder arm. On shore, it would only have taken a minute or so; at sea in a storm it took ages, each minute filled with anxiety and the stress of impending dissolution as my imagination vividly pictured the boat swinging wildly out of control. How long it really took, I have no idea.

Once I threaded these lines between the rudder head and steering arm, I anchored them firmly behind the beam shelf both port and starboard, effectively wedging them against two stout frames. That done, and after some anxious moments getting the close-fitting emergency tiller slotted over the steering arm, we could steer again. How we were still alive and not well on our way to Davy Jones's locker is still a mystery, for the effort seemed to have taken hours.

While I cursed reticent lines and rudders in general, and sucked on fingers mashed with disconcerting regularity, Meggi duct-taped our hand-bearing compass to a deck pillar so we had something to guide us once steering was restored.

With the emergency tiller in place and a compass to steer by, I gave the tiller an almighty shove to starboard. Nothing happened. Leaning into it with all my strength, I barely managed to shift the blasted thing by a few degrees.

Little wonder the rudder was hard to budge. The original tiller on a boat like *Vega* would have been between four and five meters long and required one and sometimes two standing men to shift it. The emergency tiller our lives now depended on was a little over one-meter-fifty long, and can only be operated from a sitting position.

Calling our two young crewmen, I put one on each side of the tiller and gave them a course to steer. It is amazing what fear can do for your strength and endurance. Considering the wild gyrations our boat was making, just staying in one place was a major effort, much less applying force to steer. Yet somehow, those two intrepid lads managed to get us back on course.

Leaving them to grunt and groan over the tiller, I went searching for a few pulleys and some line to rig up relieving tackle, a devious sailorly invention consisting of four blocks rigged on a single line in such a way that when half the tackle pulls the other half pays out. In our case, the four-to-one mechanical advantage I cobbled together meant one person could steer the boat, more or less.

Just then, lightning illuminated the aft cabin, quickly followed by an almighty explosion of thunder so close that it rattled my teeth. We might have steering again, barely, but our fight for survival was far from over.

CHAPTER 6

A Devious Change of Flags

The scene might have inspired a rural painting by one of the great masters. Seated in a stiff-backed wooden chair was a tall man wearing only black trousers and a plain woolen shirt with the sleeves rolled back almost to his elbows. The long, expressive fingers of his right hand held an artist's paintbrush, the wooden end of which he unconsciously tapped against his front teeth. In his left hand was an artist's palette displaying a rainbow of colors.

Clear azure-blue eyes gazed intently at the small oil painting propped on the table against a heavy candleholder. The painting he had diligently spent the past few weeks working on portrayed a scene he never tired of seeing.

The light from another short winter's day was quickly fading. The voice of his wife came from the kitchen. She would be busy helping his mother prepare the family dinner. Soon darkness would force Jens Nerhus, the oldest son of Ola Nerhus, to stop for the day.

Reaching over, he placed the paintbrush in a small jar of turpentine. Swishing the brush around until satisfied it was clean, he then wiped it on an old piece of cloth. Tomorrow he would paint a flag at the top of the little ship's mast. A flag that would proudly announce her name as the *Vega*.

The winter of 1898 was harsh, even by Norwegian standards. To help pass those long winter hours, Jens decided to paint a portrait of the small cargo boat he skippered, a hardworking little boat that was designed and built by his father, one he dearly loved and took immense pride in commanding. After all, her design had recently won an award for technical innovations at the 1898 International Fishing Exhibition in Bergen, something his father was extremely proud of, even if he tried, unsuccessfully in most cases, to conceal the fact.

Jens had been captain of the *Vega* from the day she was launched in the spring of 1892. Under his command she become one of the most successful little cargo boats on Hardanger Fjord. From the moment winter ice first thawed until the winter storms returned, he and his little boat were constantly on the move.

To quote Lars Nerhus, Jens's grandson: "When I was very young my grandfather told me many wonderful tales from his sailing days. The boat he loved to remember most was always the *Vega*. He would tell me stories of her famous voyages, wonderful adventures of sailing her deep into the Arctic to remote islands and even further around the top of Norway loaded with heavy machines the other bigger *jachts* could never dream to carry. Many of the very first generators to reach the northern islands, and engines for much larger boats, were delivered by *Vega*."

This happy state of affairs continued until 1904–5, when the political Union of Sweden and Norway foundered. Each country once again became independent. Overnight, boats built in Norway could no longer be exported to Sweden or have Swedish owners.

Suddenly finding himself in the difficult position of owning a cargo boat in Norway he could not legally bring back to Sweden, Johan Carlsson was not a happy man. Over the previous twelve years, that little boat had paid for itself several times over. It was one of the best investments he ever made. Now, what with the Norwegians calling it a Swedish boat and Swedish officials calling it Norwegian, the little dear was sitting idle at the dock costing him money, while there was honest work it could be doing in Sweden.

Johann was busily damning all meddlesome politicians, and their ancestors, to the deepest pits of hell as he stomped into Alfred Olsen's bustling boatyard. The fact it had rained the night before and the yard was still muddy only served to fuel his anger at the world. By the time he reached the office door, Johann was actually looking forward to venting a bit of frustration on young Alfred.

Alfred Olsen was a big, easygoing mountain of a man with broad shoulders and a bushy blonde moustache only a walrus could love. He was a boat-builder, a man content with his place in life who dearly loved his wife and was as proud as any man could be of their two lovely children. As he watched Johan Carlsson approach the office door, Alfred Olsen was also an unhappy man. After all, it was not his fault Norway and Sweden had broken apart, again. In fact, he was rather pleased they had. Of course, the new shipping rules were nothing short of pure madness. Everyone knew that. But, as with most silly laws, there were ways around them. Fortunately, for Alfred, human ingenuity tempered with a dose of devious scheming had come to his rescue.

Putting on his best face, Alfred politely opened the door for his guest. A tray stood on the corner of the main desk with a decanter of whisky and two glasses prominently on display. Perhaps the scheme he'd concocted with the local harbormaster and the ship surveyor would do the trick. He dearly hoped so. His life would be a lot more peaceful if it did.

Roughly one hour and two stiff tots of whisky later, Johan Carlsson left Alfred's office. Chortling happily to himself, he could not help thinking that perhaps young Alfred was not so useless after all. If this plan worked, Johan might just give him the cement needed to pave over the boatyard. There was always the batch from last month that was a bit off. He would never dare sell it to any of his customers, but it should be good enough for paving.

All that remained was for Johann to send his instructions to Norway. The rest would be easy enough, once the boat arrived.

Later that summer, the *Vega* left Ølve lightly loaded with a cargo of hides and dried fish destined for Bergkvara, a small town on the west coast of Sweden—close to Kalmar. Up until the First World War, Bergkvara was one of Sweden's three most important harbors. It was also renowned for shipbuilding.

The passage, on what would become her final voyage under the newly reinstated Norwegian flag, was uneventful, with fair winds and calm seas. On arrival, her cargo was quickly offloaded. Later that same day, the boat went round to a pier beside Alfred Olsen's boatyard. On the next high tide, *Vega* came out of the water. Once high and dry, a gang of shipwrights randomly removed several hull planks, exposing the boat's inner structure for inspection.

Early the next morning, the local surveyor and the harbormaster made an official visit to Olsen's boatyard. Places like Bergkvara are mostly large villages where the entire population know each other and are usually interrelated. With a nudge and a wink, due to some mysterious internal damage the local surveyor solemnly declared *Vega* an unrepairable total loss. The harbormaster and Mr. Olsen duly signed and sealed the surveyor's report as witnesses. That done, the three men retired to Alfred's office for a well-earned glass or two of aquavit and a cigar, both cheerfully provided at Alfred's expense.

Later, when the two men left Alfred's office, each carried a cloth bag containing two large bottles of Johan's Scotch whisky and an envelope filled with banknotes. That night, Johan celebrated with a glass of real single-malt Scotch whisky, not the cheap stuff he so generously gave the two officials. Sipping the golden liquid, he puffed contentedly on an imported cigar. Perhaps it was time to send Alfred the first batch of cement.

Based on the surveyor's official declaration, duly registered and witnessed by the local harbormaster, *Vega* was removed from the Norwegian Registry of Shipping. As far as officialdom was concerned, another tired little boat had reached the end of her working life and would soon be broken up for firewood.

To quote Lars Nerhus, "I was always told *Vega* was the best and strongest *jacht* he [Ola Nerhus] ever built, and all I could find out was that she went to Sweden in 1905 and never returned. This would be told to me in a sad voice by my grandfather, and it always made me sad, as if some important part of our family had been lost."

On May 10, 1906, Alfred Olsen's boatyard was a busy place. Not only were a large gang of construction workers industriously paving over the yard with cement, but a newly built boat was scheduled to be launched for Mr. Johan Carlsson. There were flags flying and colored bunting strung around the yard, giving the place a festive air. Later, Johan's daughter Vega launched the new boat as *Vega af Bergkvara*, with Swedish Registration No. 6532. Well, what she actually did was launch a lovely little boat that was more or less new.

As Mr. Carlsson's boat slipped into the water, the town band tootled and squeaked while the official party busied themselves drinking and celebrating. No one noticed—or at least no one commented—that with the exception of fashion pieces added to her bow and stern, this new boat was identical to the one condemned in Alfred's yard only months before. Johann was so pleased with himself he reached into the wrong pocket and gave both the surveyor and harbormaster one of his expensive imported cigars.

From that unusual resurrection, *Vega* continued life under the Swedish flag, eventually becoming the famous *Vega of Bergkvara*. Much later in life, *Vega* was assigned the radio call sign *SEUY*. She faithfully transported cement, building stone, bricks, and other heavy loads up until 1938, when Olands Cement AB of Stockholm purchased her from Johan's son. Olands operated her until 1949.

In 1928, *Vega* was equipped with a one-cylinder, twelve-horsepower diesel engine, later upgraded to a mighty fifteen-horsepower single-cylinder engine in 1939. Today we laugh at such small horsepower ratings, yet those engines pushed the fully loaded boat every bit as fast as her current six-cylinder, 250-horsepower Perkins engine, and at about one-fifth of the hourly fuel consumption. Apparently, horses have become smaller these days, while consuming a lot more feed than they did back then.

As the demand for small wooden cargo *jachts* declined, *Vega* soon found herself employed as a "stone fisher." Stone fishers haul a steel dredge bucket across the bottom of the shallow North Sea, collecting the round glacial stones that litter the sea floor for construction projects. A hard and dangerous profession, stone fishing is a notorious "ship killer."

The work is brutal, the profits small, while wear and tear on the boats is enormous. Most stone fishers end their lives on the bottom of the North Sea, having been broken by the concentrated weight of a load they were never designed to carry.

Conceived and built for precisely that type of cargo, *Vega* survived. Still carrying a modest sailing rig, she became the last wooden sailing boat working as a stone fisher. In the late 1960s, still strong but showing the scars of her long, hard life, alone and forgotten, *Vega* was left to sink in fifteen meters of water while on anchor in the bay outside Tyresö Castle.

A group of local divers eventually raised *Vega*, then undertook the effort to make her seaworthy again. After almost a decade in their care, she was once more abandoned until a new owner purchased her.

Harboring a dream to sail around the world alone, he undertook a complete restoration of *Vega's* hull and rigging. The refurbishment of her hull was a success; however, that of her rigging (she was rerigged from a cut-down galleass to a cutter) left much to be desired. As the renovation progressed, many experienced old salts warned *Vega's* latest owner that it would not be possible to sail her single-handed, yet he doggedly pursued his dream.

In the summer of 1996, *Vega* set sail from Stockholm to Falmouth, England, stopping at eight Swedish cities along the way for farewell ceremonies. Those festivities were extensively covered by Swedish media. The main celebration was held in Bergkvara. While old salts wagged their heads at the foolishness of youth, the entire town turned out—school band, official speeches and all—to proudly celebrate the last surviving Bergkvara sailing *jacht* setting out on such an epic adventure.

Dreams are wonderful things, often inspiring the most amazing events and inventions, but, that said, it never pays to ignore those with generations of hands-on experience behind them. Day sailing between towns along the route is one thing. Negotiating the notorious North Sea or the Bay of Biscay on a deep-sea passage is something else altogether, as *Vega*'s owner soon learned. Somewhere between England and the Canary Islands his dream faltered, then died. Having motored most of the way to Grand Canary Island, *Vega* was unceremoniously hauled out on the hard, where for the next five years she suffered under the scorching Spanish sun—forgotten, ignored, and neglected.

Red sails in the sunset, set flying from the tall masts of a traditional wooden ship, never fail to invoke fantasies of escape from today's highly accelerated world back to a time of discovery, adventure, exotic destinations, and the romance of wind-powered vessels reaching out to far horizons in search of the mysterious unknown and contrast of cultures that make travel so stimulating.

For my German partner, Meggi Macoun, and me, that dream became a reality in 2001 when we found *Vega* in the Canary Islands, where she had been abandoned on the hard for half a decade. After several abortive attempts, we finally managed to buy her. "As is. Where is."

At the time, I had tens of thousands of sea miles in my wake, much of that alone on a small square-rigged brigantine I salvaged from a beach in West Africa—a vessel I once single-handedly sailed across the Atlantic without an engine or functioning rudder.

Meggi, a gifted graphic designer and creative director who had frequently explored the wilds of East Africa alone in her trusty Land Rover, found the prospect of blue-water sailing on a hundred-year-old boat both exciting and intimidating.

I'll let Meggi continue the story:

"I will never forget our first night on *Vega*. It started to rain early the next morning and every deck seam on the boat leaked. We covered our bunk with a tent of plastic trash bags and wound up having breakfast sitting under the skylight, since that was the only dry place on board. Not the most auspicious beginning for a new lifestyle.

"Neglect is a boat's worst enemy, and *Vega* had suffered from inattention for over five years. Blocks were frozen, and most of her systems no longer functioned. It was weeks before she could be brought to minimum seaworthiness. On launching, two weeks passed before the planking swelled to size, sealing the hull properly. While waiting, we worked from dawn to dusk catching up on long-neglected maintenance.

"In those days crossing the salon at sea was frightening. Without proper handholds, we were soon covered with bruises from sharp corners. Also, there were no portholes; the skylights could not be opened. No one had considered natural lighting or ventilation. What we had was a hodgepodge of wasted space and a potato farmer's idea of how to lay out cabins.

"It is never a good idea to jump into major refitting without lots of forethought. Things that might not look right at first are often that way for a reason. Bearing this in mind, we decided to wait and watch. We wanted to learn all of *Vega*'s "little ways" before making any meaningful changes.

"Sailing from the Canary Islands via Cape Verde, Salvador de Bahia, and from Cape Town to Durban gave us a deep insight into both the strong sea-kindly qualities and deficiencies of *Vega*. Although our 'wait and learn' logic was sound, so many problems emerged during those voyages that long-term planning had to be set aside in favor of 'right now' solutions. Many of those we accomplished in Durban.

"The first time we took *Vega* out for a sail we discovered her rig was radically out of balance. Later we learned that for the cutter rig she then carried her mast was roughly one-meter-thirty (4 feet, 3 inches) too far forward—still in the proper position for a two-mast galleass rig, yet not at all suitable for a cutter. With her mast so far forward, when she came up into the wind the force of her head sails quickly pushed her off the wind, requiring more rudder to hold her up to the wind. That rudder would push her stern downwind. Together those forces caused her to sadly sag to leeward on anything more than a close reach.

"That clearly explained the problem we had tacking and her inability to make reasonable progress to windward. On most other wind angles, she was an honest, dependable sailor. At that point all *Vega* really needed was some knowledgeable love and attention to rectify the many past mistakes inflicted on her.

"Arriving in Malaysia, we soon realized there is more to owning a boat than possession and maintenance. If we tie *Vega* to a pier, she will die in a year. Like Shane and I, *Vega* must keep busy to stay in shape. We needed a purpose that included *Vega* constantly moving, one that added meaning to our lives. Poised on the cusp of living our dream, we had no idea what to do next."

CHAPTER 7

Sun, Stars, and Hope

A wave slammed against the hull, snapping me out of my exhausted trance with a start. It was my turn on the emergency steering tiller, and I was ready for the knacker's yard. Falling over with hunger and fatigue, I desperately needed sleep. My ribs hurt from a fierce crack against the wheel. Dried blood matted my hair. The small hand compass I was steering by had become little more than a blur that faded in and out of focus a meter or so away. Constantly blinking my eyes and wiggling around on the shelf where I sat, it was all I could do to keep my eyes open.

Somewhere south of the Seychelles a full-blown Indian Ocean cyclone by the name of Gafilo had mercilessly battered our small wooden boat for three endless days and nights of second-to-second existence, punctuated by one life-threatening emergency after another. Even though we had survived those stress-filled days of constantly fearing for our lives, the danger was not yet over.

Considering the vast number of experiences you can happily do without in life, a big storm at sea must surely rank right up there with root canals and tax audits. And people wonder why I have so much white hair. Cyclone Gafilo provided us with the kind of days that build character, or so I'm told. If you ask me, times like that are enough to have Popeye the Sailor selling his boat to buy a date farm in the Gobi Desert—on top of a mountain. Many large ships and fishing boats were lost in that tempest, yet thanks to her builder's skill and proven North Sea heritage, *Vega* survived.

In normal circumstances, we only need one person on watch, with a second down below in the salon on standby—a polite way of saying "sound asleep on the sofa." Now, with the steering broken, we needed two people for every watch. One up on deck trimming sails while keeping a lookout for ships and any other dangers, and a second crewmember down below to manage the tiller.

Even with relieving tackles rigged, the emergency steering demanded so much physical effort it was simply impossible for one person to steer for more than an hour at a time. Even by rotating stints at the tiller and on deck every hour, four hours on and four hours off left us with precious little time to eat and sleep.

Severely bruised and battered from the storm, all four of us were suffering from painfully sore muscles brought on by the intense effort needed to steer. As the cyclone progressed, we downed paracetamol tablets as if they were candy and in general lurched about like zombies.

At the height of the storm, we discovered there were only three minutes of credit remaining on our satellite telephone. That phone was our only means of communicating with the outside world. Our only way of calling for help should the boat begin to sink. Of course, in an emergency, we would also try the VHF radio, but its limited range was not encouraging.

In desperation, I dialed up the Iridium Help Center, because those calls are free, and explained our situation. Perhaps it was tedium, an honest desire to help others in distress, or a combination of both, but those lads came to our rescue. Throughout the storm, they checked in with us every hour on the hour, never missing a call to track our position and update us on the latest weather prognosis. It may not seem like much, but just knowing someone was actively following our progress was a huge boost to morale on board *Vega*.

Thanks to the weather reports and advice relayed from London, we altered course to avoid the worst of the storm's violence. Those reports also gave us hope. Knowing the best course to steer and when we could expect the cyclone to pass made suffering through the present an easier burden to bear.

Those lads pulled out all the stops, tracking us hour by hour on a big map they found somewhere, downloading the latest satellite images, and even enlisting the advice of an expert on tropical cyclones from the World Meteorological Organization at Bracknell. I doubt we would have survived without those two amazing young men in their small East London apartment. As the Irish say, "May the good Lord set a flower on their heads."

There was also information they did not share with us: the gigantic bulk carrier that broke up and sank not far from where we were, the offshore ferry that was lost, or the many other vessels screaming Mayday at the time. They knew, and we thankfully did not, that Cyclone Gafilo was the most violent cyclone to hit the Indian Ocean in over ten years. A real monster that was as busy breaking records as it was tormenting us.

As the wind and seas began to abate, I changed our course more toward the north, a direction that agreed well with the wind and reduced the load on our crippled steering gear. Covered in bruises, cuts, and scratches, we were all struggling on the last of our energy reserves—and those were fast running out. By putting the four of us together, we might have been able to muster one competent crewmember and the cat, just.

What we desperately needed was a safe port, to repair our shattered hydraulic steering ram and rudder. A place to rest and recover from the storm. Dead on our feet, if a troop of pink elephants had ridden by on unicycles they would have fit right in.

The closest safe haven was Victoria harbor on the island of Mahe in the Seychelles. With the fragile state of our steering, winning those few hundred miles would be a difficult task—perhaps even impossible. Once again, our friends in London came to the rescue. Deciding that Victoria in the Seychelles was our best option, they contacted the port authorities and Coast Guard in the Seychelles, advising them of our location, current course and speed, and our intention to enter their port. They also advised that we had serious steering problems, which might make maneuvering in tight places difficult, if not impossible. It was a good thing they did.

Three days later, we arrived off the entrance to Victoria Harbor. By then we had established contact with the port authorities and Coast Guard using our VHF radio. Both services proved very professional and extremely helpful. The Coast Guard sent out a boat to meet and guide us through the reefs at the harbor entrance. When they saw how bad our steering was, they decided it would be safer to tow us in. That decision made sense to me but still did not solve our steering problem.

Entering Victoria harbor was stressful for everyone on board *Vega*. With the head of the rudder loose, our ability to steer was hit-and-miss at best. Try to imagine: pushing the tiller a few degrees to one side or the other was no guarantee the actual rudder would move. Most of the time the rudder head would cant to one side, but the actual rudder did not pivot. So, when nothing happened after an adjustment, we would add even more correction until all of a sudden the rudder actually turned, usually much more than desired. The result was *Vega* zigzagging her way between the reefs like a drunken snake. It was a miracle we made it through the channel without running aground.

Once inside the harbor, our troubles were just beginning. First, we had to dodge around an enormous yellow oil-tanker mooring buoy, which we managed to miss by about five meters. I swear at one point the fellow on the back deck of the Coast Guard boat ducked down with both hands grasping the top of his head in that universal sign of impending disaster.

Fortunately, there was only a single fiberglass sailing sloop in the small boat anchorage. As we approached, a man came up from below to urinate over the side. At first, he did not notice the rather large, heavy boat headed directly at him with apparently no intention of turning away. But when he did, the fellow gave such a start he must have jumped half a meter into the air.

Mind you, at the time I was having apoplexy yelling down at Meggi to turn the tiller. At the very last second our rudder flopped over and *Vega* sheared off to pass safely behind the yacht. After that sure cure for constipation, I hope the fellow's laundry still accepted his linen.

The Coast Guard cut us adrift in a nice spot where we dropped the anchor and heaved an enormous communal sigh of relief. Once we thanked the Coast Guard lads for all their help and established anchor watches, the rest of us promptly fell into our long-neglected bunks, dead to the world. Anchor watch aside, I slept thirty-six hours straight. When I finally made it back to the land of the living, one quick look around convinced me the Seychelles might not be paradise, but is close enough to fool me.

How easily sailors forget. Bad memory must be a prerequisite for the job. One day—after seas rough enough to make a whale puke—you're swearing to all and sundry that once back on land you will never set foot on another boat again, not even a rowboat at the county fair. Then the wind drops and the sea calms. Minutes later, all is forgotten, and it's back to business as usual. As crazy as it may seem, that is exactly what happened on board *Vega*. After such a harrowing experience, we were all so pleased to be alive that the previous week of hardship seemed unreal.

We spent almost a month in the Seychelles, making repairs and in general recovering from our nautical tribulations. Mind you, there are few places on earth better suited for the rest and recuperation of storm-battered sailors than the Seychelles Islands. The sunny climate and friendly, easygoing people were precisely what we needed. If you add to that the fact their women are generally some of the most attractive you will find anywhere, little wonder the place is famous. I saw more than one island beauty who could curl the toes on a plaster saint with little more than a smile.

I forget what I was looking for at the time—it could have been anything from the local supermarket to a public toilet—when several days after we arrived I stumbled into the local newspaper office. In any case, once there I had the bright idea to ask if there was some way to publicly thank the port authorities and Coast Guard for all their help.

The editor jumped on my idea. It must have been the slowest news week on record. Next thing I knew, it was me giving a full-blown interview and a photographer roaming the boat, snapping pictures of everything, including the cat box. A few days later, there was *Vega* right at the top of the front page, followed by half a page full of my ramblings. That same afternoon we had the local television station out for another interview where we praised the local port control and Coast Guard, then thanked the island population in general for being such nice people.

The result of those two articles was amazing. Everywhere we went, people approached to commiserate over the storm or make suggestion on how to fix our damaged rudder. Most of them called each of us by name and in general acted like they had known Meggi and me for years. Strolling through the town, people on the street smiled and bid me, "Good morning, Captain Shane!" It was almost enough to have me wearing sunglasses.

Several days later, the local boatyard hauled us out, at a hefty discount. When the yard manager saw the state of *Vega*'s rudder, he shook his head. After a long slow whistle, the man looked up at me and said, "God must love you." Thanks to his help, our rudder was soon better than new and several other small problems resolved.

Since in one of those interviews I mentioned our pockets being so empty that we could rent them out for storage space, and how it would most likely be beans and rice from Seychelles to Malaysia, a group of employees from the Seychelles Commodity Board all chipped in to make up a care package containing food and other necessities. They even remembered toilet paper and toothpaste. It was a jovial crew that took turns rowing back and forth bringing those supplies out to *Vega*.

That same evening we hauled up the anchor for a monthlong odyssey on mostly calm seas under clear blue skies, but with little or no breeze. Since none of our nine sails, originally designed for the North Sea, were suitable for the light wind normally found close to the equator, we spent much of that time aimlessly drifting around the Indian Ocean. We might still be there were it not for the equatorial current.

You see, there is no such thing as a sail for all conditions, and that trip was the perfect example. Sails are designed for different wind states, ranging from big gollywhobblers built from very light cloth for the lightest of airs to tiny storm sails, the latter constructed from heavy canvas stiff as cardboard and overengineered to take anything Cape Horn might throw at them. The reason for this has more to do with how sails work than anything else. After all, a sail is nothing more than a vertical wing made from cloth; how you present that shape to the prevailing wind is what generates a sail's driving power.

In most cases, it is not wind pushing on the back but "lift" created by air flowing over the front of the sail that causes a boat to move. In light air, if the sail is too heavy, it just hangs there looking like damp laundry, and is just about as useful. Light cloth assumes the proper shape in less wind, providing drive long before a heavier sail. Size also plays a big part in sail design. But that rant is best saved for another time.

One night I overheard a crewmember singing to pass the time on watch. His little ditty summed up that trip quite nicely: "Drifting, drifting, over the flaccid main, the skipper says to get it up, but all it does is hang. . . ." He composed several additional verses, and most inventive they were. His vivid descriptions of various anatomically impossible sexual acts were quite ingenious. But those must wait for the X-rated version of this book—soon to be available in a plain brown wrapper. If you ask me, the lad had been too long at sea.

But there were also highlights on that journey. Take the day we drifted into a school of dolphins. Imagine hundreds of those graceful creatures cavorting around *Vega* as we all turned out to watch their playful antics. Always the curious one, Meggi grabbed her snorkeling gear and quietly slipped into the water. Within seconds, several large inquisitive dolphins surrounded her. Tilting their heads from side to side for a better view, they came so close she could almost reach out and touch them. Since dolphins communicate with high-pitched whistles and squeaks, perhaps they found the squeals of delight filtered through her snorkel amusing. When she finally climbed back on board, had the grin on her face been any wider the top of her head might have fallen off.

CHAPTER 8

Calm before the Tsunami

Fortunately, like all sailing voyages, our odyssey from South Africa to Malaysia finally came to an end. We were more than ready for a few of land's luxuries when we finally limped into the Royal Langkawi Yacht Club. I for one was dreaming of something long and tall with ice in it and a massive plate of fried potatoes.

With the boat safely moored, it didn't take us long to find the bar and restaurant. Lounging on the terrace with a cold Bombay Sapphire Gin and Tonic in one hand and a triple-decker club sandwich in the other, I was surrounded by the sweet-smelling aroma of tropical flowers, mixed with a salty tang from the sea. A golden fish eagle soaring above the marina suddenly stooped. It barely touched the water only meters from where I sat before several beats from those mighty wings effortlessly bore it aloft again. Dagger-shaped talons tightly gripped a small fish.

All things considered, life looked good. From where I lounged in a comfortable chair, with a nicely padded cushion, the past weeks felt like a dream. Had we really just arrived in Malaysia from a rather boring monthlong journey across the Indian Ocean? What the other patrons of such an august establishment thought of the bedraggled, somewhat scruffy and whiffy new arrivals successfully imitating recently rescued castaways, they politely kept to themselves. Although one or two tactfully shifted themselves upwind.

With a cold drink in one hand, towel and soap in the other, after scoffing down my lunch, this little boy set off at a trot looking for the nearest shower. Still clutching my drink, I found a comfortable-looking shower stall, stripped, turned the water to its hottest setting, and lay down on the floor with my feet propped up against the opposite wall to luxuriate in my first hot shower in over a month. I was in paradise, that is until the hot water ran out. When you consider what washed out of my hair alone, it's a wonder the drain still worked.

You may find that a boring way to end our Indian Ocean odyssey, but bearing in mind what fate had in store, I will gladly take tedium any day. You always know where you are with boredom, whereas with excitement anything can happen, and usually does, especially at sea.

Meggi and I spent almost a year in Langkawi, sorting out various urgent problems such as the fresh water and toilet systems and making temporary improvements to *Vega*'s living quarters. When we first acquired *Vega*, her interior was a cross between Afghan goat shed and African chicken coop. I still believe the chickens were winning.

During that time, Meggi spent long days in front of her computer, diligently creating drawings and manipulating ideas for *Vega*'s living space. Being Meggi, she was determined to get the maximum use from every centimeter of space. Often when she had a bright idea for one end of the boat, those changes rippled all the way to the other end. More than once, she complained that a boat interior is nothing more than one big complicated piece of furniture.

While Meggi argued with bevels and curves, I stayed busy with rigging and the myriad other things demanding attention. The electrical system alone would have sent an Italian spaghetti chef into fits of rapture.

In reality, the task we faced was no less daunting than a complete refit of the interior and a rerigging, including a new mizzenmast with its accompanying spars, sails, rigging, and irons. I won't even go into all the various systems and electronics that needed overhaul or replacement. Every time I managed to scratch something off the top of my to-do list, three more items magically appeared at the bottom.

CHAPTER 9

The Great Tsunami

Right in the middle of that seemingly endless struggle, a natural disaster occurred of such colossal proportions that it completely changed the direction of our lives and *Vega*'s future. The afternoon of December 26, 2004, brought an inundation of sudden death and destruction that resounded around the world. In Langkawi, it started out as another lovely day set against a deep-blue sky with only a few scattered clouds riding the gentle breeze. It was impossible to imagine the normally placid marina becoming a maelstrom of vicious swirling currents.

While we enjoyed another tropical day, hundreds of miles away colossal waves battered the island of Sumatra with devastating force. Unstoppable killers, often over ten meters high, thundered ashore without pity, slaughtering over a hundred thousand people within minutes. Entire cities were destroyed. Those murderous waves were felt as far away as East Africa, Sri Lanka, and Thailand.

As luck would have it, we were in the Langkawi Yacht Club. As the first surge struck, Meggi and I were preparing for a well-earned siesta when, without warning, *Vega* slammed against the pier. Her mooring lines screamed against the bitts as the first of several massive tsunami waves, generated by an undersea earthquake, struck.

And so began one of the most unusual afternoons of my life. Rapidly repeating tides vacillated from extreme high to extreme low in only minutes, filling the marina with raging currents and whirlpools. The air was filled with a cacophony of sounds: a bedlam of banging halyards and tortured mooring lines overlaid with the urgent calls of sailors fighting to save poorly moored boats. Meggi and I scrambled to double our mooring lines until we had a cat's cradle of ropework only a drunken spider could love. As we struggled from moment to moment, there was one all-encompassing question: *What the hell is happening?*

With half the coastal population of Southeast Asia scurrying for their lives, our greatest fear was damaging the Yacht Club pier. I am still convinced they would have made us pay for it. At one point, I had *Vega*'s engine running, ready to slip our lines as the floating pontoon came within half a meter of lifting free from its piling.

To understand my alarm, you need to consider how a modern marina is constructed. Floating piers ride up and down with the tide on massive pilings driven deep into the seabed. The height of those pilings depends on the highest predictable tides. Based on that, the designer adds a safety margin so the pontoons cannot escape. Should the water level exceed the height of the piling, the pier—boats and all—can float off and drift away.

We were lucky to escape with only a few scratches to *Vega*'s paint and one or two broken mooring lines. Many were not so fortunate. The tidal surges created that day were *twice* the height of a normal high tide. The other marinas on Langkawi were devastated when piers came adrift from their pilings and over a hundred boats were washed out to sea. Some of those boats survived. Others, driven by giant tidal surges, were washed ashore, hopelessly grounded well above the normal high-water level.

Through it all, chaos and confusion reigned. You see, although we could see *what* was happening at any given moment, no one knew *why*. A subtle but important difference. When I switched on our marine radio, it came alive with frantic calls for help and the latest disaster reports. That was a day of pure bedlam as bystanders and boat owners did their best to assist each other and rescue yachts whose owners were not on board at the time. A heroic effort that saved quite a few boats, even though many others were lost.

Over the next few days, as the magnitude of that monumental natural disaster and its toll of human misery filtered in, people from all over the world volunteered to help alleviate the suffering.

Having seen firsthand the damage inflicted on their own island, many people on Langkawi came forward to help others who had lost homes, families, everything—in a few brief moments of devastating horror. Race or nationality no longer mattered. No one cared if you were Christian or Muslim, Chinese or European, or even purple with bright green stripes. We were all human beings, and some of us urgently needed help. The more fortunate rendered assistance as best they could. The problem was how to transport and distribute that support to those who needed it most.

Since *Vega* was one of the few boats capable of carrying enough to make the thousand-mile return trip to Sumatra worthwhile, and willing to volunteer, we quickly found ourselves the focus of an ad hoc relief effort.

Between the Chinese business community in Langkawi, the Sikh community on the mainland, and a multitude of willing Malaysian shop owners, we soon had almost twenty-two tons of food and medical supplies committed for what became our first Mission of Mercy. Over the next few days, a constant stream of donated supplies poured into Langkawi on fast ferries from mainland Malaysia. In a show of solidarity, ferry companies transported and stored those provisions free of charge.

The plan was a simple one. We would deliver our relief supplies to the Island of Pulau Weh, located just north of Banda Aceh. Although severely damaged by the tsunami, Pulau Weh still had a functioning port where we could transship those goods onto local cargo boats that would distribute food and medical supplies along the devastated west coast of Sumatra.

To those of us sitting on Langkawi in an air-conditioned office we had dubbed "The Chaos Control Centre," that plan made a lot of sense. What it failed to consider were the vicious seas around Sumatra's northern coast—some of the nastiest waters you will find anywhere outside the seventh circle of hell. That Greek lad in *The Odyssey*, the one who was always getting in trouble, would have been right at home there.

Our brilliant plan also failed to consider how lightly built Indonesian cargo boats are. They may look big and have impressively thick planking, but those boats are not designed for the same consistently rough seas as *Vega*. Then again, at sea you can never forget the element of luck.

CHAPTER 10

Loading the Beast

If you picture *Vega* parked alongside the dockyard pier with a constant stream of food and medical supplies streaming into her cargo hold, then add Meggi holding a clipboard where she busily notes each item loaded by a merry band of muscular Malaysian sailors, and let's not forget the vessel's jolly captain puffing his salty pipe and getting in the way of those with real work to do—you'll at least have the latter part more or less correct, although I never smoke a pipe.

Looking back, the truth was a mixture of chaos and bedlam blended with tons of rice, sugar, and other assorted eatables. If anyone knew what was happening from one minute to the next, I never met them. The only thing missing was the rabbit in a top hat inviting us to his tea party. At least the medical supplies were easy to log and store.

You see, we couldn't just ring up the local supermarket and order several truckloads of food, even if we did miraculously find the money to pay for it all. On the contrary, those supplies arrived in so many various shapes, forms, and quantities it was almost frightening. Everything from pallets of rice and sugar from Penang to individuals bringing in small bundles or bags containing a few assorted items. Everyone helped to the best of their ability.

What I remember most are the unsung heroes, bless their hearts. The small shopkeepers, gardeners, lorry drivers, farmers, and ditchdiggers. Although we preferred things in case lots, or the rice and sugar in full bags, many donations arrived as a modest box of mixed provisions, or a cloth folded and knotted around several handfuls of rice and a small tin of tomato paste. Even though that forced us to spend hours repacking small bundles of bulk items like rice or sugar, or sorting canned goods into more easily managed boxes, we knew those contributions came from the heart, each according to that person's means.

Of course, just about the time we started patting ourselves on the back to celebrate getting it all stowed away, our friends from the unofficial Chinese business community arrived with their contribution. Every Chinese counter jumper on the island participated in that whip-round. I thought Meggi would have an apoplexy when they proudly showed us two tightly packed panel trucks loaded with supplies.

People like to joke about tight-fisted Chinese. And it's true. They *are* sharp businesspeople who can drive a hard bargain or methodically squeeze a coin until the sultan's nose bleeds. On the other hand, I find the Chinese are damn good at organizing things and quite generous when it comes to helping others less fortunate than themselves.

As I stood there, eyes bulging and mouth agape, one of the Chinese shopkeepers made a comment I shall never forget: "We Chinese do not like donating to big charities. They might use our money for anything. With you, we know our help will go straight to those who need it most." I didn't realize it then, but his summation changed our lives.

We soon had all five yacht club trollies trundling back and forth delivering boxes and bags to *Vega*. Meanwhile, as the mountain of cargo grew, Meggi muttered and mumbled about needing a trailer to stow it all in. Those two-and-a-half-ton panel trucks may not look very big, but it is incredible how much they hold when tightly packed. Then again, *Vega* does not look very large either, yet somehow Meggi managed to stuff it all in. Thirty years together and that woman still amazes me.

Two days before we departed, *Vega* was so full you could barely move down below. All of the cabins and even the toilets were stuffed with bags of rice and sugar, boxes of canned goods, cases of baby formula, and of course medical supplies. With our salon packed to the beams, the only clear space consisted of a path leading to the chart table, galley, and engine room. We would sleep out on deck, praying it wouldn't rain.

Packing *Vega* until her seams bulged was only part of the problem. Our navigation kit was a disaster waiting to happen. Well, you try finding charts for Sumatra, which is in Indonesia, while on a small island in Malaysia, and see how easy it is. Then there was another important question: Were those charts still accurate? What we saw as a tortuous series of gigantic waves was the result of a colossal undersea earthquake not far from the northern tip of Sumatra. Nature only threw in the tsunami as an amusing afterthought.

Experts were already speculating on what effect that massive shift of tectonic plates had on the surrounding islands. According to them, the land was either raising, or sinking, or out for a cup of tea, depending on which talking head you happened to catch. Trying to understand all that pseudoscientific babble was enough to have stone statues begging for the paracetamol.

Our destination was a small port on the island Pulau Weh, whose entrance was already complicated enough without sunken fishing boats and collapsed piers. Possible changes in the seafloor meant water depths would differ from those shown on our charts. Considering our depth sounder only worked when the cursed thing felt like it, you can imagine what that did for my blood pressure.

More than once, I thanked my lucky stars we would not be going down the west coast of Sumatra, where the geological changes were more pronounced. I could easily visualize the few safe anchorages now fouled by earthquake-generated landslides or the detritus of whole villages.

While we were getting the boat ready, our friends from Sikh Aid dispatched an envoy to Pulau Weh whose task it was to prepare for our arrival. Overall, Richie, our Sikh Aid representative, did a great job navigating the maze of rubber-stamp-o-paths, chartering two local cargo boats to distribute what we delivered and in general making himself useful.

Seven days after the tsunami struck, we had *Vega* loaded and ready for departure. I wish I could say the town orchestra turned out to see us off, although having heard that band I would prefer a few dancing girls, a bit of flag waving, and a short speech by the mayor. The fact is, we just decided it was time to leave, cast off our lines, and set a course for northern Sumatra.

CHAPTER 11

A Mission of Mercy

With *Vega* so heavily loaded, that voyage from Langkawi to Sumatra took longer than expected. Through a miscalculation on my part, we loaded her down by the bow rather than the stern. This made her sluggish and slow to steer. As we puttered along at between four and five knots, our hastily scraped-together crew proved to be champions.

Randy, an inveterate British adventurer, had years of experience at sea. Of medium height with gentle brown eyes, Randy was always in motion, radiating a disgusting abundance of energy and intense curiosity for any and every new experience life has to offer. The first thing he did was take charge of our binoculars.

John, a Singaporean, was launching his career in photography. With black hair and an expressive face, John always sported a smile. He joined us at the last minute, eager for a chance to photograph the aftermath of that great tsunami close up and in person.

In those days, everything that could float, and many things that shouldn't, was drifting on the ocean. Whole trees, overturned fishing boats, even a complete roof of a Thai house with several forlorn chickens and a duck perched on top soon ceased to be of interest, other than as objects to be avoided.

For me those long nights, darker than the halls of doom, were the most nerve-racking part of our journey. With no moon and half the detritus of Southeast Asia drifting around, the risk of a serious collision was real. Any second there might be an almighty crunch. Within minutes, we could be standing off in the dinghy watching *Vega* disappear beneath the waves. We joked about it, as people will in such circumstances, but the reality was never far from our thoughts.

I was on watch that sunny morning, with nothing more exciting to keep me company than the odd flying fish and the rumble of Mister Perkins, the name we lovingly gave the fuel-guzzling monstrosity infesting our engine room, when a helicopter came roaring over the horizon heading straight for *Vega*. It was a bizarre-looking contraption festooned with rockets, guns and a strange assortment of pods that might have contained anything from chewing gum to nuclear weapons. As it came to a hover in front of us, I could just make out the pilot and gunner all kitted out like Arian Gods of War. A load hailer ordered us to contact them on VHF channel 16. Which I did.

As the radio came on, a commanding voice informed me *Vega* was entering restricted waters and must turn north at once. We were headed west and having a hard enough time of it without going out of our way, so I politely informed them our boat was loaded with food and medical supplies on an emergency relief mission and traversing Indonesian waters along a clearly defined international shipping lane. One of the busiest in the world. Since they were not the Indonesian Navy, or Coast Guard, or even the Society for the Prevention of Cruelty to Animals, I fully intended to maintain course and speed along my lawful route.

Again, they demanded we turn north. So, in the best spirit of international relations, I tried a different tack.

Oh, dear, says I in an innocent voice, if they were so afraid of a one-hundred-year-old wooden sailing boat, going so slow it would have trouble catching a cold, perhaps a rethink of their defensive measures was in order. I also informed them, in an offhand manner, that the whole conversation was being filmed by the BBC. Which is when John, taking his cue like a good 'un, went up on deck and pointed a video camera their way.

Somewhere someone must have had an attack of uncommon sense. Perhaps one of the cooks, or a plumber, was wondering through their radio room at the time. In any case, without another word, that great fuel-wasting monstrosity did a rapid turnabout before lumbering away, not to be seen again. We never did spot their famous warship or figure out what country it came from.

There are times when Fate springs strange surprises. Some are pleasant enough, although if experience is anything to go on, the majority are merely her playing another practical joke. And Fate always plays with loaded dice.

Randy was up in the bow amusing himself with the binoculars when he suddenly turned my way and screamed. "Turn! Turn hard to starboard! There is an overturned fishing boat in front of us." Cursing like a true sailor, I spun the wheel hard to starboard. By then I could clearly see a huge, gray, barnacle-encrusted obstruction directly in our path. With *Vega* so heavily loaded there was no way she could veer away in time.

Just then, John came racing out on deck with his video camera to begin filming. That video says it all. Only seconds away from colliding with something even bigger than *Vega*, that massive obstruction moved, hoisting an enormous tail skyward before disappearing into the depths and taking a good ten years off my life with it.

CHAPTER 12

Into the Jaws of Hell

It was early morning when we arrived at the lovely old colonial town of Pulau Weh. Picking our way around sunken boats and other debris, we tied up to one of the few still serviceable piers. No sooner had we arrived than Richie, our Sikh Aid liaison, came to meet us. Richie, a big jovial man, sported the obligatory Sikh turban and beard. Although clearly one who spent a lot of time smiling, that morning he was not in a cheerful mood.

Both of the local cargo boats he hired to carry our supplies down the west coast had been so badly damaged by the rough seas on a previous attempt that they were forced to turn back. Neither captain was interested in trying again. We could offload our cargo into a nearby warehouse, but he was not sure how those supplies could be delivered. He then went on to brief us on the local situation. In a nutshell, the hardest hit communities were along the west coast of Sumatra.

Television had the entire world convinced Banda Ache was the center of devastation. The truth is all the journalists were huddled together in Banda Ache's two remaining hotels, where they could enjoy air-conditioning, hot meals, and a bar with iced drinks. Few if any ventured further than the city limits. None went down the west coast. Those who know Banda Ache soon realize the most famous news footage was shot from the roof of the town's best hotel. Don't look at me; I never said those highly paid disaster journalists were dumb—just overpaid.

While Richie was explaining the situation, I noticed a dugout canoe slowly paddling our way. Out of the corner of my eye, I saw Randy, who speaks a little Bahasa, go to the side. Then John disappeared down below on the run, quickly returning with a bottle of water that promptly vanished over the side. Curious, I excused myself to see what was happening.

Tied to *Vega*'s port side was an ancient wooden canoe containing one old man and a young boy dressed in rags that were more a collection of holes held together by random threads than clothes. They both looked dead tired as they passed the water bottle back and forth between them.

After the usual half hour of hi, hello, and how are you the local culture requires, Randy figured out their village was destroyed by the tsunami while they were out fishing. Being the only boat to survive those monstrous waves, they had set out looking for help. Since then, the two of them had paddled their small canoe through some of the world's most difficult currents and waves, passing one devastated village after another in search of aid. As we talked, the boy passed out in the bottom of the canoe from exhaustion.

These were not beggars. They were proud, honorable people who had been peacefully going about their lives when fate thrust them into a natural disaster far beyond their wildest nightmares. Dehydrated, scared, hungry, and bone tired, yet still pushing on, they had made it this far. Could we possibly refuse to at least *try* going down the west coast to deliver the food and medical supplies we had on board? That was, after all, more or less exactly what we'd come to do. We just had to ignore the bit about rough seas, riptides, five-meter tidal bores, whirlpools, and standing waves.

Vega was built to withstand the North Sea and violent Arctic storms fully loaded with heavy cargo. We had already seen her doggedly fight through a cyclone in the Indian Ocean. If any boat could make it, she could. The real question was could we? I readily admit the prospect of such a voyage frightened me cross-eyed.

You see, I never claimed to be one of those heroes always ready to stand tall and courageous in the face of dastardly hardship. If my country was at war and called me, they would get the answering machine saying I had moved to Port Stanley in the Falkland Islands (beep, beep). Meanwhile I would be on my way to a remote tropical island in the South Pacific, on a tramp steamer, with a broken radio. The thought of sailing through one of the nastiest little stretches of water on our planet, in a boat loaded almost to her limit, fairly gave me the screaming meemies.

On the other hand, there are times when you almost saunter your way around the corner to a place where you can leg it to safety when life taps you on the shoulder with a task only you can do. Should you decline, well, that just doesn't bear thinking about. Not if you want to continue looking other people straight in the eye, the most important being those eyes you see in the mirror each morning.

There are people who could easily turn a cold shoulder on such suffering. Me? I pride myself on not being one of them. I'm not the bravest person around, but I still have a few strains of humanity left, some lingering sense of responsibility as a human being—or in this case a serious attack of temporary insanity.

Even though this might be the dumbest thing I ever did, the only choice was to put on a brave face and get on with it, hoping and praying for the best.

While the old man and the boy, who turned out to be his grandson, scoffed down their rations on board *Vega*, I called a crew meeting. I usually do not subscribe to democracy at sea, unless it's one man, one vote, and I'm the man with the vote. On a well-run boat, there is only one captain who makes all the decisions. Right or wrong, I am responsible for the outcome. I listen to suggestions if there is time, but when the chips are down it is my call, and my head on the block.

In this case, the decision was so momentous and the hazards so great, I felt if *Vega* were to continue down the west coast to deliver our cargo we should all agree. With the four of us gathered on the cabin roof, I explained the conditions, the dangers as I saw them, and what I thought of our chances.

Just so you know, I was not the only one ready for a hatter's ball. We all agreed to go. So, early the next morning, with the skipper's knees merrily knocking out a symphony of apprehension, we set off on what became one of the hardest voyages I have ever sailed. Riptides, standing waves, currents, cross-seas, whirlpools, and tidal bores all waited to ambush us as we set out. The old man and his grandson wisely elected to stay behind with family on Pulau Weh and recover from their ordeal.

I am not going to preach about the rampant devastation and suffering we observed. If you were there and saw it, then you know and are scarred for life by those visions. If not, then be glade you missed it. Suffice to say, we made it down the west coast and delivered our supplies. A voyage that saved lives and helped a few people get back on their feet.

I will never forget all those stunned blank faces. People so overwhelmed by events that they could not fathom what had or was happening to them, much less put a why to it. Talk about a landscape from the gardens of hell. Families ripped apart, whole communities destroyed, futures obliterated, and the survivors so badly traumatized I doubt they will ever fully recover.

They say war does that to people, but so can nature. The only difference is that nature doesn't look to profit from all the suffering and waste. She just does it because, well, that's nature for you.

CHAPTER 13

Of Standing Waves and Whirlpools

In all my years at sea, I have never encountered such an intense concentration of nautical horrors, all busy infesting one small stretch of water. Coming back, we spent almost four days trapped in nautical nastiness that would have given an optimist on valium nightmares. Even now, sitting in the safety of a calm, secure harbor, I still get shivers just thinking about our return around the northern tip of Sumatra.

Mind you, the seas were just as bad on the way down, although with wind and waves coming from astern the effect was less pronounced. Heading north, the whole miserable boiling conspired against us. With the engine roaring away and guzzling fuel like a thirsty camel, between slamming into head seas, struggling over standing waves, whirlpools spinning us in every direction, and the ever-constant wind holding us back, there were times we cheered when our speed over ground surpassed one knot. It could take long minutes for the boat to fight her way over a single standing wave.

If you never had the pleasure of sharing the same stretch of water with standing waves, let me explain why you haven't missed much, that is, unless you are a seagoing masochist. Standing waves form where two strong currents meet head-on, forcing up a steep hill of water that usually stays in one place. The fact they are not moving is what makes them so difficult for a boat to manage.

Normally waves are in constant motion, traveling at a speed propor-
tionate to their height. A moving boat simply goes up and over them. Or, as
frequently happens, if a vessel waits around long enough, the wave gets bored
and goes away of its own volition.

Encountering a standing wave is like hitting a watery wall. Since the
thing is not moving, a boat must power its entire weight up and over the top
unaided. Reaching the crest, it becomes like a plank on a seesaw, balancing
there with the propeller out of the water. If your floating palace, complete
with screaming engine, lacks enough inertia to make it over the top, it slides
back and the whole nerve-racking process begins again. Oh, and did I mention that once the little dear finally does tip over the top she drops down
the other side like some demented ten-year-old with a new skateboard on
a big hill?

The stresses and strains this puts on a ship's structure are enormous,
the screams and groans of tortured wood deafening. Broaching becomes a
very real danger. Each standing wave demands the utmost care and personal
attention. Little wonder those two large pinisis were so badly damaged. Fortunately, big standing waves are rare, even along the west coast of Sumatra.
Then again, even one as small as two meters can be a right gut twister. And,
just to make it more interesting, standing waves form where two powerful
currents meet, one of which is always against you.

Wherever two strong currents meet, you also get whirlpools. Nasty little
devils that can spin the boat in a full circle faster than you can say Hollywood. And best not forget riptides shaking the fillings out of your teeth.
Given a choice, I would gladly choose a seaside resort with pretty girls in
skimpy costumes serving me cold drinks, and perhaps a relaxing massage. As
I said, just thinking about that trip still gives me the willies.

Truth be told, those days and nights are only a blurred memory of
disparate panics and general misery carefully sealed in one of those mental
compartments with ten padlocks and a sign on the door saying, "Warning to
self, DO NOT repeat this experience, never, not even on a bet, honest, I'm
not kidding me."

When we finally limped into Pulau Weh, both our little ship and her
crew looked like recently rescued castaways. We were swathed in bruises, our
variable-pitch propeller had jammed, the exhaust elbow in our engine was
cracked, and more than one part of the rigging needed urgent attention. Yet
all things considered, we survived and *Vega* was still floating: a feat that must
count for something.

Over the next few days, we did our best to get *Vega* seaworthy again. We repaired the rig and had the exhaust elbow wielded. But the variable-pitch propeller defeated Randy and me both. It simply needed parts we could not even hope to find. John, being Singaporean, was about as useful as a priest in a brothel. Great person, mind you, always ready and willing, but the Singaporean idea of fixing something usually consists of finding the phone number for a nearby technician.

It took us four days to sail from Langkawi to Pulau Weh while fully loaded. The return voyage required almost a week. Shortly after leaving Pulau Weh, the exhaust elbow broke again. That, coupled with the frozen variable-pitch propeller, which of course jammed in course pitch, meant the engine constantly belched black smoke. Most of which happily deposited a dark oily film on every available surface in the boat.

The propeller pitch was so course that it restricted me to slightly more than idle speed. I could advance the throttle but only gained denser exhaust fumes. And just about then the Northeast Monsoon set in against us, bringing with it short steep head seas.

All in all, we were once again reduced to urging *Vega* along by sheer willpower and cheering when the speed surpassed two knots. It was impossible to sleep down below due to the exhaust fumes, and cooking became drudgery. Our food tasted of exhaust, our clothes smelled of exhaust, and we all four looked like coal miners coming off the night shift. As I said, lovely little voyage that was.

On the plus side, Meggi and I had discovered how a boat like *Vega* can make a difference for people living on remote islands. By the time we struggled our way back to Langkawi, a plan had evolved. Granted it was rough around the edges and would take years to refine, yet evolve it did. And twenty years later, it's still what we do.

CHAPTER 14

The Art of Making a Difference

During our years living in Africa, Meggi and I learned what actually helps people, and how to spot projects designed for aid workers and their agencies to worm more money out of innocent donors. You would be amazed how much hard work that lot put into ensuring their job security, paying themselves exorbitant salaries with incredible benefit packages, and wasting money in general—all tax-free by the way.

Over the ensuing months, we developed a simple, straightforward plan. As a small "mom and pop" charity, we cannot save the world, but we can make one small part of it a little bit better. Indonesia is a nation with more than 17,500 islands where many of those small islands have fallen through society's cracks and been neglected, or are so difficult to access it is impractical for government to support them. Those are the forgotten people we assist.

Meggi and I volunteer ourselves and *Vega*, since that is all we have. A large group of friends, who want to make a difference but wish their assistance to go directly into the hands of those who need it most, donate the tools and supplies for our yearly deliveries based on lists from teachers, midwives, and health workers on those islands. Like a glorified DHL, we deliver the educational and medical supplies received from our friends or purchased with donated money.

That simple system ensures someone is waiting for, and needs, every item we bring. On a boat the size of *Vega*, we cannot afford to waste valuable space on trivial things. Hence, we never take old clothes. We far prefer to carry antibiotics or teaching supplies.

You see, no one understands the needs and priorities of a remote community better than the people living there. So, if you really want to help, you have to start by asking *how* you can help. Based on that simple premise, the year after the tsunami we visited several islands in Eastern Indonesia, where we talked with village leaders, teachers, midwives, and health workers. The most important question we asked was this: What do you need to do your job and improve your community? From their answers we made a list.

Passing through Singapore and Malaysia on our way north again, we approached the same friends who helped during the tsunami, asking if they could help with the things we needed. The response that first year was modest but encouraging. Returning to our first two islands the following year, *Vega* had many of the items they requested on board.

While delivering those materials, we collected new lists, then visited two new islands, adding their requests to our list for delivery the following year. As our capacity grew, we added more destinations to our route.

That first year we delivered two bags of expired medical supplies and twelve boxes of basic school material; the year before COVID-19 struck we distributed roughly twenty-four tons of donated medical and educational supplies directly to those in need, including more than 120 comprehensive midwife and health worker sets weighing an average of twenty kilograms each. Every year we resupply and upgrade those kits.

Whenever possible, we have a volunteer Indonesian doctor along on our deliveries to hold clinics for the remote communities we visit and provide training for traditional midwives and health workers. Some of the places we go had never seen a real doctor until *Vega* brought one to their island. Not at all bad for a little boat struggling along on budgets you need an electron microscope to find—if there is even anything there to be found.

CHAPTER 15

The Trang River and Bird's Nest Soup

Upon completing our first mission, before we could go further, *Vega* needed to be hauled out of the water and given a thorough going-over. I wanted to completely sand her down to bare wood, replace all of her caulking, then do a first-rate bottom painting job on her. And that was just for starters.

After asking around, it became obvious that the area's best, most reputable wooden boat yard was located on the Trang River in Thailand. So Meggi and I took a ferry from Langkawi, then a long taxi ride to check the place out. What we saw was impressive. An old family-owned yard with three slips and a well-found metal shop, Mister Vims's yard had everything we needed. But what I found most impressive were the jobs they had in hand and the professional, no-nonsense, manner in which obviously highly skilled workers were going at them. Replacing the stem on a one-hundred-foot wooden fishing boat comes to mind. While there, we arranged to slip *Vega* in two weeks' time. That would be the best tide for coming up the river and hauling out.

I readily admit being a confirmed shellback who is only comfortable with lots of blue water under the keel. Close to land there are too many rocks and reefs just waiting to cause mischief. Just imagine my state as we worked our way up the Trang River that first time on a rising tide. There are places where the navigable channel is not much wider than *Vega* is long, so you can easily envision what my blood pressure was like by the time we reached the boatyard.

We spent six very productive weeks in Mister Vims's boatyard that first time, and wound up going back annually until the place closed ten years later.

Two years after that first visit, *Vega* was back at Mister Vims's yard to have her bottom painted. We were only out of the water for a few days, mostly puttering with little things while the paint dried. It always amazes me how those Thai ladies can paint straighter lines by hand than most of us manage with masking tape. Must be all those years of practice.

I was busy with some little repair when the yard manager came along to say we had a visitor at the office. Strange news that, as almost no one on our "A" list actually knew where we were, or would have been able to find the place if they did. Perhaps I should mention that Kantang is about as far off the tourist path as you can get and still be in Thailand. Thinking it must be the long-lost freezer repairman, who by the way never did show up, I asked the yard manager to let our visitor in.

Much to my surprise a nice new, somewhat shinny combo van pulled up beside *Vega*. Seconds later, a well-dressed young man with a big smile on his face climbed out. That's when it dawned on me that he must be our friend Udom from Bangkok. Along with a group of his close friends, Udom had been gathering items for our health worker and midwife kits. I had last heard from him on Facebook, when he asked where we would be in Thailand so he could deliver the stuff they collected.

Let me make clear that Bangkok is a long way away from Kantang on roads I wouldn't wish on my worst enemy. Better make that second or perhaps third-worst enemy—just to be safe. Still, there was Udom standing beside *Vega* looking bright and happy half a country away from his home.

Udom's story serves to underline how far some of our friends, bless them one and all, go to help us help others. If they really do give out credit for good deeds, then Udom earned enough to get away with almost anything and still make it into paradise through the express VIP door, with bells on.

Udom was accompanied by a beautiful young lady. We did shake hands, but I admit being too busy admiring her to catch the woman's name. In case you have never been to Thailand, some of those Thai girls are enough to have saints drooling in their soup. Together they had made the ten-hour drive from Bangkok to Kantang to deliver the supplies their group gathered for us. That in itself was an amazing feat. But when he started unloading what they brought, my mouth dropped open.

Udom and his friends had taken a big bite out of the medical expendables list and managed to find all of it. There in a growing mound behind his van were hundreds of boxes of surgical gloves, thermometers, tongue depressors, surgical clamps, and tweezers. Along with a whole load of other hard-to-get items, here was a treasure trove of badly needed, in-date medical supplies slowly being revealed as he unloaded box after box.

I thought Meggi was going to faint. You see, those are the expendables needed for day-to-day operations in any clinic or health post, basic supplies that midwives and health workers need for doing examinations and performing deliveries, and we have such a hard time sourcing them. What he was unloading would provide a solid core for the new midwife kits we had planned for that year.

Convinced they would spend the night with us, to rest up before starting the long arduous drive back to Bangkok, Meggi was already planning dinner when Udom announced that they must start back at once. It seems he needed to be at his office for an important meeting the following morning.

After we thanked them profusely, then poured a dose of cold, fresh-squeezed mango juice down their throats, off they went. That man is either very dedicated to his work or slightly nuttier than I am. Which says a lot. In any case I wouldn't have wanted to be him when he arrived at work the next day. I just hope the bag of dark-roasted coffee beans we gave him helped to mitigate the "road lag." Udom's sacrifice ultimately made a meaningful difference in a lot of people's lives. As we happily loaded his donation onto *Vega*, Meggi commented it was a great way to start our yearly collection.

Once freed from the claustrophobic confines of the Trang River and out on open water again, we made straight for two small islands that lie just in front of the river mouth. We have been using these lovely little islands for several years as a favored rest-and-relaxation anchorage. Luckily they fall just in front of the Trang River entrance, so they are perfect for a stopover on the first night out of the boatyard.

Actually we have two favorites right beside each other. One is the twin islands of Ko Lian Nuea and Ko Lian Tai. Then a few miles farther south is the spectacular island of Ko Phetra. Mind you, all three are lovely places that provide good anchorage and protection from all but a westerly squall.

We usually anchor close in to the massive limestone cliffs. Typical of Thailand's western coast, all three karst islands are riddled with caves and overhangs just begging to be explored. For scenic value, Meggi and I both prefer Ko Phetra, but if it's peace and a private anchorage where clothes are optional, then give me the twins every time.

CHAPTER 16

Jakarta

Whoever said, "I used to muck about in boats, but now I boat about in muck," must have come from Jakarta. The road traffic alone is enough to bring on nightmares worse than a late-night dinner of lobster in blue cheese sauce. A cloud of brownish-gray smog obscures the place, and the burnt electrical smell reaches over twenty miles offshore, but since the land is sinking and sea level raising—both at an alarming rate—air pollution may soon be the least of their worries.

The seawater is so dirty no one ever volunteers to clean *Vega*'s prop, a job we usually draw straws for. As Meggi once commented, the almost total lack of visibility under that disgusting liquid may be a disguised blessing. At least you cannot see what you are sharing the water with.

Once finished, whoever finally gets stuck with that exasperating job runs for the shower like all the fiends of hell are after them. If by demented demons you mean a vast assortment of viruses and germs, then maybe they really are.

One thing is for sure: no one opens his or her mouth in that water. One small sip might lead to weeks in the intensive care ward. Doctors with clipboards looking serious while shaking their heads and a whole troop of attentive young medical students come to see the latest developments. Or more likely, to check if you turned cyan or fuchsia overnight, or perhaps are sporting pink polka dots with green stripes that day. For sure, they would compose a new write-up or two for the medical journals.

Jakarta is a place without a single marina, or at least a marina not falling apart or half flooded every time the tide goes a little above normal. Fortunately, our friend Pak Jusli invites us to use his private pier on the exclusive island of Pantai Mutiara.

That pier forms part of his charming Jetski Café, the "in" place on an island with what looks like the highest concentration of wealth per square meter found anywhere in Indonesia. Jusli's place is also home to the Pantai Mutiara Harley Davidson Motorcycle Club. This is a spot where almost every night we see Ferraris, Maseratis, and every custom-made form of personal transport you can imagine. Although I must admit, the Sunday morning Harley Davidson Motorcycle Club meetings are my favorite.

Imagine a row of lovely motorbikes, all polished to the nines. Everything from sleek cut-down choppers to what can only be Harley's answer to the space shuttle, all lined up on display as their happy riders take a break from running Indonesia to go riding in style. I am sure you can also easily picture me wondering about guzzling free coffee and drooling on the chrome work. If only I was twenty-four again and had the keys to one of those magnificent monsters.

The thing is, although dressed in scruffy leathers and steel-toed boots, many of those rowdy-looking characters, who happily give the biker's hand-shake, are some of Indonesia's most powerful business executives. During the week, they occupy top-floor offices with acres of expensive carpet and desks you could host a football match on, while a small army of beautiful secretaries run around making coffee and doing all the work. Some of the men are famous for noses so hard you could sharpen knives on them. But dressed in their "colors" for the biweekly Harley Club meeting, they are some of the friendliest people you will ever meet. Over the years more than one has become an ardent supporter of our work.

For us Jakarta is an important stopover where we buy all the medical supplies, seeds, tools, and most of the educational materials, which need to be in the Bahasa Indonesian language. We purchase the pharmaceuticals there to ensure the Indonesian Ministry of Health approves and the instructions are in Bahasa. It also helps that one of our Harley-riding friends owns the largest wholesale distributor of pharmaceuticals in Indonesia and sells to us at cost, when not outright donating.

Jakarta is our final chance to stock up on provisions for the long months ahead, when we will be thousands of miles away from the next supermarket. Jakarta is also a place where I usually wind up giving talks on practical ship design at the University of Indonesia, addressing women's clubs and schools, and in general singing the song and dancing the dance. Or as one friend puts it, blatantly mooching and begging.

My main rant at the university is usually along the lines of, "Ships are tools meant to do a job. So how can you possibly hope to design a proper tool if you have never used one?" Of course all of those intense young engineering students consider me ready for a padded room, complete with sleeveless dinner jacket, but then again who knows. Maybe one of those bright young people will get the idea and some poor sailor will have an easier life for it.

As much as we enjoy the lovely place where we moor and our many friends, it is always a pleasure to escape that great seething mass of humanity. When we leave Jakarta, the boat is loaded to the deck beams. Every cabin and even the toilets are packed solid with supplies destined for the islands we support. A claustrophobic path between boxes and bags provides access to the galley, chart table, and engine room. With *Vega* so well stuffed, this is a time when we all sleep out on deck, fervently praying for dry weather and calm seas. Prayers that are seldom answered.

CHAPTER 17

Rough, Wet, and Wild

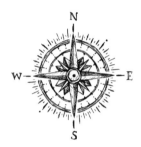

Our yearly slog from Jakarta to Pulau Medang takes place against a rare insight into the world as it must have been when still new and raw. Indonesia is one of the most geologically active places on Earth, a land still being born, where earthquakes, mudslides, belching volcanoes, flaming lava flows, and tsunamis are commonplace occurrences.

If the sobriquet Ring of Fire conjures images of volcanoes curving away into the distance for thousands of miles, the reality is even more impressive. Three tectonic plates are still busy forming the Indonesian archipelago, pushing and shoving one another like dowager duchesses locked in a small closet.

A look at the underwater geography of eastern Indonesia shows a mass of swirling arcs where vast underwater rifts plunge to depths over seven thousand meters and gigantic volcanic mountains, well over eight thousand meters high, thrust up from the seafloor.

Damned impressive place, if you want my opinion. Just try not to be around when one of those volcanic brutes goes boom, as Krakatoa did some years ago, or that big bruiser on the island of Bali that lost over seven hundred meters from its top like a champagne cork going *pop!* during one impressive detonation. One day there was this pointy mountain minding its own business, and the next a few hundred meters went missing from the top. Mind you, there was a mind-boggling *BANG!* somewhere in between.

This vast panorama of natural beauty slowly slipping into the past along our starboard side helps break the monotony of that long journey, a time when we either sleep out on deck or huddle below on top of the cargo, wishing we could sleep out on deck, where it would be much cooler. The seas are not the roughest, nor the biggest, but they are the most uncomfortable. Short choppy waves breaking across *Vega*'s bow, sending sheets of spray flying back along the deck, may have something to do with it, but I always find that stretch the harshest part of our year.

We really have no other choice than banging away against the wind, current, and head seas for days at a time, enduring speeds that often fall below three knots with the engine howling away as it swills fuel like a thirsty drunk in a brewery, until finally the long thin island of Madura slips astern and we turn into the Bali Sea. You may laugh, but we often cheer when our speed over the ground goes from two to two and a half knots.

Forget romantic images of sailing that stretch. With the Southeast Monsoon often blowing dead against us, the miles we win are all thanks to Mister Perkins chugging away down in the engine room. I can imagine what it must have been like in the days of pure sail when square-rigged ships forced their way along this stretch of contrary wind, currents, and seas. Of course, they would never have been mad enough to try it at the turn of the monsoon, as we are usually obliged to do.

The first indication of glorious salvation comes within an hour of passing through the Raas Straits, a narrow passage between the islands of Pulau Sapudi and Pulau Raas that separate the Java Sea from the Bali Sea. There are times when two seas have different names simply due to their location or some ancient geographer's fantasy, but in this case, the Java Sea and the Bali Sea are so different in consistency and nature they deserve distinct monikers. Passing into the Bali Sea, the water magically transforms from murky dark green to clear deep blue, with a much friendlier swell. Rarely do we transit the Raas Straits without being welcomed by flying fish and dolphins.

The Bali Sea usually has wind we can sail with. Nothing to get excited about, mind you, but it does give everyone on board some honest exercise, along with a chance to start learning how that mystical spider's web of lines and sails work. By the time we reach Medang Island, the sea has changed dramatically. And a welcome change it is. From that point onward, there might be days when the weather is disagreeable or the seas a little uncomfortable, but at least we have the consolation of knowing the worst is behind us.

CHAPTER 18

Her First Day on the Job

A small fishing boat, redolent with the smell of ancient fish and rotting seaweed, slowly approached the dilapidated wooden pier on Medang Island. Around his head, the owner wore a brightly colored headscarf. Tightly wrapped in the traditional Bugis fashion, his sarong provided a vibrant contrast of color. With the skill born from a lifetime on the water, he nudged his small boat closer to the rickety wooden structure. At thirty-four-years-old, Ahmad Fajir has spent most of his days fishing, but he prefers the easier task of playing ferry should a fare be on offer.

The pier's only other occupant, a modest wooden cargo boat badly in need of paint, was offloading a consignment of mixed goods. From deep in its hold, colorful bundles and bales flowed ashore along a chain formed by well-muscled sailors clad only in their wraparound sarongs and a head cloth. Their golden-brown bodies glistening with sweat under the tropical sun, the cargo handlers teased and joked with each other as they worked. A group of happy youngsters raced along the beach, deeply intent on the serious business of being children. An old man sat in the shade of a mangrove tree repairing his fishing net. A wide-brimmed hat woven from palm fronds lay on the ground beside him.

Wiping sweat from his eyes with the tail of his headscarf, Ahmad looked to the bow of the boat where a rather attractive young woman stood. She wore a modest white blouse and long, comfortably loose black pants. As he watched, she tied back her hair with a bright-green hairband, then donned the traditional Muslim headscarf local women prefer for traveling.

Her husband and two children huddled together under a blue plastic awning in the middle of the boat. Ahmad had borrowed that ragged plastic sheet from his friend Habib, knowing from long experience that during the often-boisterous crossing from Sumbawa to Medang without protection his customers and their meagre possessions would be drenched by splashing waves and flying spray. Today the seas were unusually calm, the passage a comfortable one. Even so, he suspected the youngest girl was mildly seasick.

Standing in the bow, a small frown creased the young woman's brow. Here she was, a fully fledged midwife and nurse arriving at her first official posting. She should be proud of such an accomplishment, yet she could not help feeling a twinge of anxiety.

Mitha smiled to herself. She grew up on an island like this, well aware of how small-community politics work. At the foot of the pier, under a shady tamarind tree, a group of older women sat companionably on a large green plastic sheet, ostensibly sorting seaweed and preparing plastic water bottles to be used as floaters for their seaweed farms.

Mitha knew those were not just any women. They were the island matrons, come to inspect the new midwife. Although this was her unofficial reception committee, unless she spoke first those women would studiously ignore her while doing their best to sneak surreptitious peeks.

As daunting as her initial meeting with those powerful old women might be, she must first negotiate the rickety wooden pier that swayed and shook every time one of the sailors carried a load across it, a prospect Mitha found frightening. There did not seem to be a single nail in the entire construction. Drawing a deep breath, Mitha wished there was another way ashore, one less likely to dump her in the water. She chuckled to herself. What a memorable entrance that would be.

As her little family emerged from under the plastic cover, Mitha heard the children exclaim excitedly on their new surroundings. Her husband would quietly take it all in without comment. She turned to search him out. As their eyes met, he nodded slightly. Supportive as always, he began to hoist out their meager belongings, passing them up to willing hands on the swaying pier.

Taking another deep breath, Mitha did her best to scramble onto the pier in a dignified manner. With a toss of her head, she adjusted the headscarf and then, after a silent prayer, headed for the women sitting in the shade. With a slightly forced smile illuminating her face, Mitha called out, "Salamat Pagi." The women cheerfully answered her greeting.

Shifting ever so slightly, they opened a spot for her in their circle. Settling into her place, Mitha unconsciously began sorting seaweed, a chore she had grown up with and could do in her sleep. Out of the corner of her eye, she saw one of the women give a slight nod of approval. Within minutes, Mitha found herself the focal point of a lively conversation. Although the questions seemed innocent enough, Mitha knew she was being tested.

What the matrons of Medang saw was a polite, vibrant young woman with raven-colored hair and sparkling brown eyes radiating a friendly, no-nonsense confidence in herself and her abilities. They already knew much about her from the last midwife. A certified nurse and midwife, this new girl had graduated from her official Ministry of Health training shortly before being assigned to their island.

For Mitha, the next few hours became a blur. Taken on the official round, she diligently met all the island elders and drank the appropriate cups of tea, surprised yet inwardly pleased to discover she liked the people she met; they made her feel important. Young as she was, these respected officials accepted her as an important addition to their little community.

While Mitha was busy shaking hands and swilling tea, her family and their baggage were conveyed to the official clinic and midwife's residence. Taking one look around the place, her husband stoically shook his head, then set out to borrow a shovel and some tools from their nearest neighbor.

The children he assigned to sweeping the front yard with an old broom. Within minutes, other youngsters joined them, quickly forming a happy brigade diligently chattering and sweeping. Judging by the dust raised, each of them came with their own broom.

Exhausted from her official rounds, Mitha arrived at her new home only to encounter the sad reality of life on a remote island. The further you are from the main population centers, the easier it is for the ministry to ignore you. Her small rural clinic consisted of an empty three-room building, the interior of which was now covered in dust. The front yard was neatly swept, but her husband had forgotten to close the front windows. Knowing he meant well, she smiled and shook her head.

At a stretch, that building might accommodate her family. A broken storage cabinet in what had once been the examination room stood eaten by termites and starkly barren of supplies. Its door dangled at a forlorn angle from a single hinge. When she went to open the back door, it fell off in her hands.

Dedicated and well trained, Mitha had been sent to a place where there was absolutely nothing to work with. Standing where a back door should have been, she hung her head and sighed. This was not how she imagined her first posting. Her husband reached an arm around her waist and hugged her. Turning to lean her head against his chest, tears begin to form. Tears she valiantly fought to hide.

On her own, with an entire community now dependent on her for medical care, she felt powerless. Looking up into the kindly eyes of her husband, she allowed a tiny smile to curl her lips. Frequently, Mitha's parents had called her stubborn, willful, and even proud. Fortunately for the people of Pulau Medang, those accusations were somewhat true. Faced with an impossible task, Mitha squared her shoulders, took a deep breath, and never looked back.

While her husband repaired the back door, she would need a bucket, bleach, and lots of soap. The ceramic wash basin was almost beyond salvation and the floors thick with grime. That first night they slept on a clean bare floor.

Squeezing her small family into one of the three chambers, Mitha dedicated the front two rooms to her "clinic." What should have been the family's parlor became the waiting place. The front bedroom became her examination and delivery room. Although her family had only mattresses on the floor, with the help of those stately village matrons, she managed to furnish the examination room with a wooden bed, a stool, a small table, and a cabinet to store the meager supplies she brought with her. Supplies purchased with her own money.

A year rolled by and still Mitha struggled to do her job. There were times so deeply frustrating she swore she would quit, but her inner strength and strong stubborn streak refused to let her. On Pulau Medang, she was respected and needed. And here she would stay doing her best. Then, one day, two foreigners from an old sailing ship appeared at her modest clinic and a miracle occurred.

CHAPTER 19

Befriending Paradise

Arriving by sea, one quickly notes how every island has its own distinctive aroma. Volcanoes with their strong smell of sulfur and steam, often in stark contrast to the verdant scent of land and forest. On more settled islands, the rich fragrance of tropical flowers mingle with the smell of cooking fires and exotic spices.

Once on land, it is no longer the fragrance we notice but the sound of an island—a polyphonic orchestra ranging from a deep geological rumbling to high-pitched birdcalls, the wind in the palm trees, surf on the beach, all blend to form each island's distinctive song. An all-pervading undertone to village life.

After slugging our way around Java, through water that could do with a good flushing—followed by a healthy dose of toilet bowl cleaner—the island of Medang is a welcome sight. Located northwest of Sumbawa between the Bali and Flores Seas, Medang is so small it rarely appears on maps. Here the seabed gently slopes upward, forming a crescent-shaped bay surrounded by white sandy beaches bordered by coconut palms. A peaceful anchorage where we can relax and enjoy the pleasures of life afloat in one of the world's most beautiful maritime regions.

There are two communities on Medang Island, although Bugis and Bajo are really just one long village with two distinct ends merging somewhere in the middle. The islanders claim each community has its own distinct culture and traditions. As you stroll down the only road, the architectural style abruptly changes as one village suddenly becomes the other.

Bugis are Indonesia's traditional boatbuilders and seafarers. They tend to be fishermen and sailors. For thousands of years these hardy people built and manned Indonesia's trading craft and larger fishing boats. Someone once said Bugis sprang from a cross between cats and fish. Seeing how at home they are on the water, I can imagine some truth to the story.

Historically, those inveterate sailors were also the most adept pirates. Bugis pirates were the origin of the term *Boogieman*. Although they were never much for hiding in closets or jumping out at naughty children, they did invent the traditional black sails Hollywood now installs as standard equipment on every well-kitted-out pirate vessel.

From time immortal every Bugis boat had two occupations, each based on an age-old cultural tradition as well as the size of one's boat and its crew. If the other boat was smaller, those on the larger craft instantly became pirates. If the other boat was bigger or had a larger crew, the smaller vessel suddenly became innocent traders going about their lawful business, fleeing for dear life as fast as those big black sails would carry them, since by then the bigger boat would be busily chasing them according to traditional job description number one. In many ways, they were almost like the British.

Lovely lot those old-time Bugis sailors were, just the thing to scare reticent kiddies into bed at night or make them eat their greens. Mind you, they still have that rugged, well-muscled look with long black hair, flashing black eyes, and stringy beards.

It requires no great leap of imagination to visualize today's local fishermen dressed in a tightly wrapped head cloth and colorful sarong; they do that anyway. If you add screaming bloody murder while leaping aboard some innocent—read smaller—boat while flourishing one of those horrible wavy kris knives, the only thing missing would be a jolly afternoon of ravaging, pillaging, and plundering.

The Bugis we meet today are direct descendants from the intrepid slave hunters whose very name had the dreaded, jungle-dwelling headhunters of Borneo taking to their heels—with their whole brood in tow. It is not hard to picture those merciless headhunting savages legging it for the deep jungle or the relative safety of an active volcano. Which, by the way, the male headhunters considered less of a menace than Bugis slave-trading pirates. What their women thought about it all no one ever bothered to document.

The people of Bajo, Medang, are the stay-at-home land-lover type and inhabit the southern end of the island. Mostly from Sumbawa, they man the shops, cultivate gardens, herd cows, make palm wine, and in general keep the island from drifting away while the Bugis are off fishing or trading.

Knowing *Vega* typically arrives in late June, a lookout is posted, most likely a student excused from classes in return for sulking around the beach keeping an eye out for our arrival. As a result, usually no sooner do we drop anchor off of Medang Island than a young boy goes racing down the beach, spurts of sand flying from his bare feet. By the time we arrive ashore, a welcome committee is waiting for us.

We land on a lovely beach located between two clumps of mangrove trees and backed by a stand of coconut palms, a place where the protection of mangrove roots and slight tidal current created a small lagoon. There we can safely tie the dinghy to overhanging mangrove branches.

Just up the beach is a small, rather dilapidated building on pilings that was once painted bright red. I find it reminiscent of a chicken coop. Leading away from this picturesque little building with its disintegrating thatch roof, the footpath meanders through a palm tree plantation to the village of Bajo.

The local architecture consists mostly of traditional wooden houses built on stilts, painted in dazzling colors that would have caused Gauguin to give up on the South Pacific and Van Gogh to thumb his nose at southern France. Moving to Pulau Medang, they might have set up housekeeping together and painted to their hearts content.

The islanders are quite friendly. Young boys paddle out to *Vega* in borrowed dugout canoes, full of curiosity and excited at the prospect of practicing their English. Happy just to exchange a few words with whoever happens to be on deck, given half a chance they will cheerfully hop on board and infest the place for hours. You see, for them learning English is an important step toward a well-paid job in the tourist industry.

On our first visit to Medang, when we enquired about the island midwife or health worker, everyone we spoke with steered us to "Guru Amir" at the school. Later we discovered they did this not because there was no midwife but because Amir put out the word for them to steer all foreigners to him. The reason he ambushed passing visitors was to provide new

English-speaking voices for the children. In short, having no books or other teaching aids, he needed practice dummies for his students.

That first morning as we strolled down the path leading to his school, we were guided by two enthusiastic young girls who magically appeared from nowhere cheerfully yelling, "Guru Amir, Merry Christmas, Good Morning" and "God save the King" for all I remember. Happily dancing along beside us, one of them had Meggi by the hand, diligently dragging her toward the school. Having taken a shine to me, the other girl chattered away in Bahasa with the odd "My Name Is Good Morning Happy New Year Mister" inserted from time to time.

And so, at the head of a small noisy convoy, we arrived at the primary school where Guru Amir taught English. When we first met him, Amir was a volunteer English teacher without a single textbook, or any English materials at all for that matter. He taught by repetition. Originally from Medang, Amir is typical of many young teachers in Indonesia. His salary is modest, the benefits few.

Dedicated to their profession yet part of a system struggling to provide services for a fast-growing population equal to Europe scattered among more than seventeen thousand islands distributed over an area the size of Canada, he and his fellow teachers do an admirable job, often with little to work with. From our perspective, the cheerful young man we met that day was exactly what we were searching for.

On another visit, as our dinghy approached the shore, I could see Amir and his friends waiting to welcome us. Waving back, I knew we had a secret. On board *Vega* were the three desktop computers they had requested. When the head teacher first asked us for those computers, his logic was impeccable. To prepare children properly for the future, they must learn to use computers. Even the lowliest forms of employment require computer skills these days. But the teachers must learn how to use them first.

Also, carefully wrapped in plastic and tucked away safely on board *Vega* was the LCD projector they begged us for the previous year. On the list of what they needed, that projector had been underlined twice—in red. Why an LCD projector was such a priority baffled me, but we had found them one.

It always takes a while to arrive properly. Once we shake all the hands, drink enough tea and soda to float a battleship, and enjoy more than one home-cooked delicacy, we are usually well into the second day, happily burping our way from ceremony to ceremony and trying not to fall asleep during the speeches. Aside from the fact it isn't considered impolite, having the guest of honor snoring away during his speech can put even the most diehard politician off their stroke.

It was not until the third morning after we arrived that offloading began. Boxes and bags of medical and educational supplies were brought up from below, checked, then loaded into our dinghy. Three trips later, we offloaded the computers and projector.

The whole upper class from Amir's school turned out to help carry things from the beach to their school. With an abundance of energetic youngsters, we never lacked willing hands. As soon as the loaded dinghy arrived, an entire classroom descended on it. Each student cheerfully took up a package, then set out for the school.

The final load contained what they were all waiting for. When we began offloading computers and monitors, along with bags containing cables, mice, and keyboards, a little cheer went up along the beach; more than one impromptu dance broke out. That exuberant display not only came from students but from teachers as well.

As our little parade of computer-laden students proceeded through the village, more than one parent came out to see what the excitement was about. Most of those curious bystanders soon latched onto one of the teachers, who then proudly passed along the latest gossip. It seems having computers in the school raised the status of their entire village. It wasn't long before we had everyone including the town drunk coming up to us saying, "Terima kasih," which means "Thank you" in Indonesian. More than one insisted on mauling my paw, while others tried to shake my arm lose from its socket. Some of those burly fishermen are stronger than they realize.

By lunchtime, the whole island was aware their children were one step closer to learning the mysterious, mystical art of computers. Over the next few days, wherever we went people thanked us for helping the school. I must say, we were also proud of that accomplishment, although their computer problems were far from over.

Like many small islands, Medang only has electrical power from five to ten each night. Although that minor technical detail did not seem to worry anyone, I could see where it might prove disconcerting for students wanting to learn computer skills during the day. Fortunately, the teachers and village elders foresaw the problem and found a typically Indonesian solution. We soon discovered how important the mysterious LCD projector was.

CHAPTER 20

A Miracle for Mitha

When we first visited the island of Medang and inquired about the island midwife, Mitha timidly welcomed us into her home. When she showed us her examination room, I was dumbfounded. Out of that small three-room house, she was providing medical care for well over a thousand people. Meggi and I realized at once that although she had the training and skill, she sorely lacked the equipment, expendables, and pharmaceuticals needed for the job.

Sitting in her waiting-room-cum-parlor, sipping the mandatory cup of tea, Amir described our mission to her. While he was busy explaining, I had a surreptitious look around. Right away I noticed the clock over her examination bed was not working. Hefting a plastic container designed to hold a thousand paracetamol tablets, I found it empty. Catching Mitha's eye, I could see she was ashamed, not for herself but for the sad state of her small clinic.

As Amir continued his explanation, Mitha was leery at first, then slowly I saw her face begin to register signs of hope. Reflecting that glimmer of optimism, she sat up a little straighter and her eyes began to sparkle. When she fully realized what Amir was saying and the objective of our mission, both hands flew to her mouth followed by a little gasp.

Mitha looked over to where I sat. Torn between doubt and hope, her dark eyes bored into mine. When I gave her my most encouraging smile and nodded in a friendly manner, tears slowly flowed down her cheeks.

After a short discussion concerning the problems she faced and how best to solve them, we asked Mitha for a list of the supplies and equipment she needed to do her job properly. At the top of that list was a neonatal resuscitator, followed by a few other basic yet important items. Looking at her requirements, I knew that dedicated young woman's life was about to change. We already had most of what she needed on board *Vega*. In fact, each of our standard midwife kits contained much more than what she put on her modest list.

Toward the end of that first meeting, we agreed Mitha and her husband should visit *Vega* later that afternoon, which they did. When we dragged out both a midwife and a health worker kit for her, I thought the woman was going to widdle her knickers.

One of my fondest memories is of Mitha sitting on *Vega's* cabin roof cradling that neonatal resuscitator as if it were a newborn baby, unrestrained tears of happiness streaming down her face as she sorted through both a complete health worker kit and a midwife kit. Her squeals of delight at discovering another treasure in those bags more or less made my year.

Earlier in the day, Meggi and I had augmented those two kits with additional supplies we felt might be helpful. Every year since that emotional first encounter, we have returned to resupply Mitha.

CHAPTER 21

Hot Air, Nails, and Noise

The day after delivering our supplies to the school, one of the teachers came paddling out to *Vega* in his canoe requesting we attend a special community "event" to be hosted at the school that evening. He seemed rather excited about it, asking repeatedly if we would be there.

Late that afternoon *Vega*'s entire crew, minus the anchor watch, went ashore to see what the excitement was about. Arriving at the school, we found the quadrangle packed with people. I venture to say half the village was there, milling around and looking pleased as punch with themselves. There were flags flying and colorful bunting hung all over the shop. Children squealed as they chased each other around the chairs, under the tables, and between innocent people's legs. I never imagined a few computers and other school supplies would get the whole island so excited. They even built a temporary stage lined with folding chairs and backed by two large bamboo poles with a sheet stretched between them.

Every chair in the school was out and filled with happy villagers. The entire setup radiated an air of festivity, with women gossiping and men standing around smoking while surreptitiously downing nips of *sopi*. Mind you, should the urge ever strike to set up a company selling battery acid, paint remover, or toilet bowl cleaner, I suggest you bottle that homemade

Indonesian hooch, then sit back and watch the cash roll in. At the rate things are going these days, you would soon be the only one around with a product that really works as advertised.

I was in the process of asking my way to a toilet when some big shot spotted the day's special guests of honor and insisted we be paraded to the stage and duly seated. As Meggi and I solemnly took our seats, my only interest was in finding a tree, a potted plant, or even a dimly lit wall close to hand. Instead, I wound up trying to surreptitiously bounce up and down with my legs tightly crossed while bravely enduring speech after speech.

Somewhere in the past, I managed to dominate my fear of speaking before large groups, at least to the extent it involves me looking sincere while mumbling platitudes and boring everyone to tears. The firm decisive expression is normally me wondering if there will be free food, or perhaps an acute attack of gas. The expression I wore that evening was mostly due to a bladder charged well beyond its nominal capacity, informing me in no uncertain terms that if I did not soon relieve the situation, I had best plan on standing in a puddle.

Now you know why by the time my turn to speak came around I did so wearing a smile any undertaker would quickly recognize. I am also fairly certain my eyes were turning yellow. I followed the mayor and a few other long-winded dignitaries, who rambled on like good little public officials seeking reelection.

If you want a tricky task, try speaking to a large audience in a language they do not understand, then waiting until an interpreter translates what you just said, all the while covertly wishing you could bounce up and down with your legs crossed. I find the hardest part is remembering what I want to say next while someone translates what I just said. The real trick is keeping it down to very simple sound bites. That way if you get lost, no one notices.

The other trick is knowing when you have said enough. Make it too short and people feel you are not taking them seriously. Make it too long and they fall asleep. What I do is watch the audience until I see people raptly staring at their fingernails or keenly exploring a nasal passage, which is usually as good a sign as any that it's time to say thank you and go looking for the free food.

No sooner did I finish my bit and have my hand mangled by various dignitaries than an energetic troupe of students began clearing the stage. Taking that as my cue to sneak away, I had just enough time to make a quick dash for the toilet, where my keen sigh of relief must have been heard on the next island.

Returning to the crowd, I saw that our chairs had been removed from the stage and placed with great care right in the middle of the front row, from where it would be almost impossible to escape with dignity. As we waited, I noticed a posse of teachers roaming the crowd shoving small woven baskets under everyone's nose.

Here, here, thinks I. This looks just like the plate going round at a "Save Your Soul for $10" tent revival. The reality was even worse. If I had known what the immediate future held in store, I would have been down on all fours crawling under tables and between chairs, gibbering in a frantic dash for the nearest exit. Dignity be damned.

Once the collection brigade was back in front, and after a few quick words from the head teacher, someone killed the lights. Music, reminiscent of a chain saw hitting a tenpenny nail, blared from the school's aging sound system. On the sheet behind the stage an image flickered to life.

Trapped like rats in a barrel with no possible means of escape, we were mercilessly subjected to an ancient DVD copy of a copy of *The Sound of Music* dubbed in Bahasa. Well? You try sitting through 174 minutes of Julie Andrews babbling away in Bahasa and see how long it takes before brain cells start committing suicide and dribbling out your ears.

I am proud to say Meggi and I sat there, sporting diplomatic grins, through the entire thing, intermission and all. I later learned it was part of a plan employing the new computers and LCD projector to raise money for a small generator.

The scheme was simple. They would show movies once a week and take up a collection. The money would go toward buying a small portable generator. Once they had their new generator, the proceeds from those movies would be used to purchase the fuel. Their ultimate dream, mind you, is a satellite internet connection so they can watch live football matches. Talk about community-based education and cultural development programs.

I found it a rather good idea, and the school did eventually raise enough money to get themselves a generator so students could use the computers we brought during school hours rather than having to come back at night. Personally, I applaud that kind of initiative, but I could easily have done without *The Sound of Music*. Then again, it could have been *Mary Poppins*. Forget hot knives and waterboarding, halfway through that one I would have confessed to anything.

As it turned out, Meggi had a better idea. Why not make computer labs from laptops that can be used during the day and then left to charge at night when the island has power?

Luckily, Pulau Medang is blessed with a natural-born geek by the name of Fadli, who is also a teacher. He dove into the technical side of computers with a passion. It did not take long before he was tearing down broken CPUs and using the parts to make ones that worked.

The next year we brought fifteen almost new HP laptops to establish the school's first official computer lab, with Fadli in charge of course. Since we also brought lots of networking cables and several gadgets Fadli considered treasures, he and Amir stayed up all night creating an integrated classroom network.

When we returned the following year, the first thing Fadli said was, "We have internet now." Had the grin on his face grown any wider his hair might have fallen off. The system was a simple island-style solution to an island problem. To show me, he placed his cell phone in a plastic bag and, using a piece of clothesline, hauled it to the top of a palm tree. From there he could tap into a cell phone tower about five miles away on the bigger island of Moyo. The speed was nothing to boast of, but the thing is it worked—more or less, sort of.

Starting several years ago, all final exams in Indonesia became online, a disaster for students from small islands without computers. When it came time for exams, parents would take up a collection and send their kids to be tested on a bigger island. Since those students had never seen a computer, much less used one, they failed.

When we replaced desktops with laptops at the school, Fadli asked if he could use the old ones to establish a free night school for anyone who wanted to learn computers. He soon had students from all the surrounding islands pitching up on his doorstep.

Back in Jakarta, we busied ourselves pestering friends both high and low to get a cell phone tower for Pulau Medang. We must have done something right since on our next visit Fadli proudly showed us a newly installed, solar-powered cell phone tower. There had been other changes as well. The school now had an official program where students from other islands on their way to be tested could spend a week on Medang learning about computers. They even had sample tests to practice on.

The year that COVID-19 struck we received an email from Fadli and Amir. The attached photo showed them grinning like Cheshire cats high on nitrous oxide, while students beavered away in the background on laptops.

The text was short and to the point. "Pulau Medang is now an Official Testing Center." No wonder they looked so proud. Now students from the outer islands come a week early to learn about computers, practice with sample tests, and, when the time comes, take their final exam online using the same machines they learned on.

Pulau Medang has come a long way since we first discovered the place. Although the people there give us thanks for those accomplishments, all we did was provide the tools for others to work with. The real heroes are Fadli and Amir, who took what we provided and made more than anyone ever expected from it. I still laugh at Fadli's hand phone hot spot dangling from the top of that palm tree. But it worked.

CHAPTER 22

Who Wants Another Adventure?

"What is it like being hundreds of miles from the nearest land?" is a question I have heard in various iterations for years. Most of the people who ask are hoping I will regale them with yarns of death-defying feats performed in the face of raging storms, when no one in their right mind goes to sea looking for perilous adventure and excitement. Why they insist on confusing my passion for the beauty of old sailing ships with some demented desire for a precarious lifestyle is completely beyond me. You see, to date, I have suffered through more than enough tempestuous excitement at sea to last me three lifetimes, at least. The last thing I want is more. What I really pray for, every time we cast off the lines, is a nice dull, monotonous voyage; the key operative word in that wish being *dull*.

Looking back over all my adventures, as some people insist on calling them, it's enough to have me searching the yellow pages for remote mountain monasteries. You know the kind of nightmarish recollections that usually come back to you after a late-night meal of dubious grease burgers and deep-fried potatoes, complete with cheap oil in the sauce just to muddle your digestion.

That Indian Ocean cyclone alone was enough to provide me with a lifetime supply of palpitations and soiled linen. When you add the likes of Hurricane Albertos and the Great Tsunami of '04, along with the entire wretched congregation of meteorological and oceanographic calamities I somehow managed to wriggle through with a whole skin, little wonder my hair has turned gray.

What I treasure most at sea are those monotonous moments when the most exciting thing happening is a gentle breeze and perhaps the odd flying fish. Mind you, keep a weather eye on those flying fish. They can be vicious little devils. More than once, while innocently minding my own business, one hurled itself directly at me. You try having a malevolent half kilo of piscine kamikaze launch itself at you out of the darkness. Talk about a walloping surprise. Of course, Scourge, our ships cat, considers them the feline version of Pizza Express. The freshest meal imaginable, delivered right into her paws.

Ah yes, those cherished moments of dullness enhanced by the shear bliss of drifting aimlessly through another watch anesthetized by the study hum-drum-hum-drum of boredom. That's the happy ticket for this lad. In fact, if you ask me, anyone who goes to sea looking for excitement might just as well take up bull baiting or lascivious molestation of Bengal tigers. Either one would be a lot cheaper, and most likely safer in the long run.

I was enjoying a peaceful off-watch kip when out of nowhere a resounding report that small cannons would have envied shook the entire boat. Within seconds the wildly flapping thunder of an uncontrolled sail had me out of my bunk and up on deck so fast I forgot my pants.

I saw right away that our twelve-meter-long, often spliced main yard had shattered at the gantry iron when the starboard brace failed. One side was still held by its rigging and at the center by the iron. But being only attached by its rigging, the other half was swinging madly. Every time the boat rolled, that six-meter piece of pine arced out over the starboard side then swung back to strike the main mast with all the force of a malevolent battering ram. Between times, the blasted thing was doing its best to shred the 120-square-meter running sail still attached to it.

Muttering a foul imprecation that seemed suitable to the moment, I grabbed a hank of line and raced to the foredeck. Along the way I yelled for Meggi and Jo (an old friend from Singapore who was sailing with us that year) to get the square sail down before we lost that also. While they argued with jammed halyards and twisted lines, I set out to stop that piece of flailing spar from doing any more damage.

By then all the rigging attached to its yardarm collar was hopelessly twisted into a cat's cradle that would take forever to sort out. No wonder Meggi and Jo were having a rough time getting the square sail down. That also meant we could not simply slack the lift and lower the broken spar to the deck.

Considering its weight, I quickly discarded the idea of grabbing the thing as it went swinging by. I might have stopped it that way, but then what would I do? And, the fact is, I did not fancy being hit by the thing. That could be downright painful, if not deadly. But if I could get a line around the lift line, then lash that to the forward shroud, sorting out the rest would be easy.

I shot up the starboard ratlines to a place just above where the yard's rigging was attached and the fun began. You see, I had to pass a loop of line around the lift in order to haul it in tight against the forward shroud. That may sound like an easy task, but the arc of swing was over a meter away from my perch. And, just to keep the game interesting, the line I needed to trap was in constant motion. Ah the joys of a jolly life at sea.

There I was, halfway up the ratlines with one end of my line tied to the shroud. All I needed to do was pass the free end around that errant line and haul it in tight using only one hand. Simple, right? Using a whiplike action, I could throw my line out and it would duly wrap itself around the line. But when I tried to ease it back to where I could grab the end, it always slithered lose. By using a slightly different method, I could get the thrown line to go out and around the lift then whip back toward me. But that meant throwing with my right hand, then instantly switching to a position where I could catch the end before it slipped past. But every time it came within reach, the devious thing was already below my reach and falling away fast.

Without effective sail to keep her on course, by then *Vega* had swung broadside to the swell and was doing her best to roll me off the shrouds. There was no way I could use two hands for the job. Half the time I needed them both just to hang on. Once Meggi and Jo sorted out the square sail they could set the inner and outer jibs to stabilize us. But for the moment they had their hands full fighting reticent halyards. One of which led to a snake's nest on top of the broken piece I was trying to snag.

I tried every trick in the book to seize that lift line. Nothing seemed to work. I even had my hand on the cursed thing at one point, then *Vega* decided to take a hardy roll, forcing me to release it and grab hold of the shrouds. It was either that or go swimming. At times like those you have no other choice than to take a deep breath, curse the air blue, and get on with it. The wise old wag who once said close only counts in horse shoes and pregnancies must have been a sailor.

To cut a long half hour of misery short, about the time I was starting to tear my hair, *Vega* decided to pitch into an errant wave, sending the broken spar arcing directly at me. That cursed thing hit the forward shroud so hard it almost had me off the ratlines and in for a dunking.

Little wonder I am convinced there are gods wandering about with nothing better to do than amuse themselves by tormenting us poor mortals. Deities with a sense of humor almost as sick as Juan de Torquemada at his best. When the ruptured yardarm iron tangled with the main topsail halyard fall just long enough for me to get a paw on it, I assumed the local cloud sitters had grown tired of mucking me about and mooched off to plague some other poor lad. I'm thankful they didn't throw a dose of cold wind and rain into the mix just to make things more interesting.

Within seconds I had the spar secured and from my lofty roost was able to help Jo and Meggi untangle the square sail halyard. Once we had the sail down, we slacked the lift and hauled the broken spar down on deck.

In short order, we had *Vega* settled down on her original course under an array of fore and aft sails set to harvest the quartering wind. Of course, by the time we managed to clear up the mess it was my watch again. And people wonder why I'm such a fan of boredom at sea. Finding a replacement for that yard proved difficult. You see, good spar wood is not readily available in Southeast Asia. They have all the hard, heavy wood you could ever want but do not have wood that is light and strong. After searching for over a year with no results, we finally found a solution on the tiny island of Nila.

CHAPTER 23

A Volcano-Powered Hot Tub

Located in the middle of the Banda Sea, hundreds of miles from the nearest neighbors, the tiny volcanic island of Nila is so remote we were the first boat to stop there in ages. Zooming in on our electronic charts indicated the most recent soundings were from 1934, which did little to inspire confidence. I later discovered the island is slightly more than two miles south-southeast of its charted position. So either the surveyor's clock was off by about ten seconds or the island went walkabout during the previous eighty years. It was a good thing I planned our arrival for midmorning or we might still be looking for the place. Reefs aside, Nila is a beautiful little place, about two miles wide and three miles long.

It was early morning when we hove to off that remote island in the Banda Sea. A light scattering of crisp white clouds streamed from the volcano's peak, highlighting intensely green tropical foliage. In the lee of that lovely island the seas were calm, the wind a gentle zephyr laden with the exotic fragrance of a tropical landfall. In contrast, the bedraggled crew of *Vega* was still rather well shaken, stirred, and perhaps a little green around the gills from the previous night's experience.

Not wishing to arrive in the dark, we spent the previous night plodding along at three knots. A miserable long hard slog through turbulent seas that had *Vega* constantly pitching and rolling. Unable to come to terms with waves from several directions, and with only a few small sails to stabilize her, *Vega* could not settle into her usual gliding rhythm. The kind of night where the whole crew heartily wished they were somewhere else. Inspecting the Great Wall of China where it crosses the Mongolian desert is one of my favorites.

This small island, formed by a single volcano, is only the tip of an ancient tectonic ridge running from southwest to northeast. Ascending almost 7,800 meters (24,000 feet) from the ocean floor before broaching the surface, this massive fault line formed by two of the earth's most active tectonic plates supports only a few widely scattered islands. These semiactive volcanic islands harbor some of our planet's most isolated communities.

For most of us, picturing life with no electricity, internet, telephone, or television is almost as difficult as imagining life where money has no meaning, there being no shops to spend it in. The islanders just take it in stride and look at you in an odd way if you talk about the importance of cash. Being far from wealthy, I found their approach to coinage quite refreshing.

As long as the whole place doesn't go bang, there are distinct advantages to living on a semiactive volcano in the middle of the Banda Sea. One of those, at least for people on the island of Nila, is a constant supply of hot running water. The mountain is only semidormant and still steams from various vents around the island. It also seems quite happy percolating hot mineral water out through various vents. One of those can be found about halfway up the northern face in a shady glen overlooking the anchorage.

That particular hot-water spring bubbles cheerfully from the mountainside, forming a small stream that flows into a natural stone pool. Shrouded in myths concerning its magical abilities to heal and encourage fertility, although the water is hot, it is also fresh and sweat to the taste. According to older islanders, back during World War II, Japanese soldiers completed the last major improvement to the Nila Island Hot Tub and Spa Club.

Our first wild mountain hot tub break happened on the same day we went scouting for a piece of bamboo large and long enough to make a new main yard for *Vega*'s square running sail. It was Meggi's idea to replace the often-spliced old main yard that had recently broken with bamboo. Using light and immensely strong bamboo as a replacement instantly appealed to anyone who had ever hoisted that old yard into its place.

Meggi's solution was taken from the Chinese sailing ships that use bamboo for most of their spars. The problem was finding a piece straight enough over almost twelve meters and with a seventeen-centimeter average diameter.

Our friends on Nila assured us there was a plentiful supply of big bamboo available just a short stroll up the mountainside. So early one morning the great bamboo adventure began when Meggi, Jo, and I set out accompanied by several friends to find a new main yard.

Forty-five grueling minutes later, we were assured the best bamboo was only a little farther up. *Pant-pant, gasp, moan, pant-pant, groan.* That volcano is steep. And the path leading through dense tropical jungle barely deserves the title of goat track. Fortunately, there are not many mosquitoes on Nila. Of course what they lack in mozzies is more than made up for by a hundred other blood-sucking monsters. I must have lost a half kilo to those ravenous winged beasts. And another few kilos in perspiration. Not that I couldn't easily afford the loss.

You would be amazed how many different opinions there can be about one pole. It took over three hours to locate and fell the bamboo we all agreed would make a proper yard. In the end a twenty-meter specimen was cut, trimmed to size, cleaned of leaves, and hauled out onto the trail ready for its journey down the mountainside.

We suggested transporting it the way most of you would, by interspersing a few of us along the length to share the load. Once everyone was ready we started off down the path. Sounds like a wonderful plan, does it not? The problem was, it didn't work the way we thought it would. The trail was full of twists, turns, dips and crests where the one in the middle would go from being crushed to hanging on for dear life in only a few paces. Either that or simply let go until the pole came within reach again.

Our local friends put up with this for roughly fifty meters. I assume they were being polite, either that or laughing themselves silly on the inside while maintaining straight faces for the world in general. In any case they decided it was almost lunchtime, so best hurry back to the barn for a feed. Politely nudging us out of the way, two of the boys hefted our twelve-meter pole between them and took off running down the mountain at top speed.

Being sticky, sweaty, bug-bitten, and tired, we had no complaints. I actually enjoyed watching that massive piece of nature's best disappear down the path, cherishing the thought I no longer had to lug it. Just about then my reverie was disturbed by the lad who stayed behind to act as our guide suggesting we have a look at the hot spring just nearby.

After the long dusty climb, complete with itchy scramble through thick brush to find a pole, then cutting it down and cleaning the limbs off, and the sweaty labor of manhandling it onto the path, a quick sluice down sounded like heaven. The best part was that after careful questioning we discovered this amazing spring was only one hundred meters or so away.

So off straggled our hardy band of intrepid adventurers trying to put brave faces on another trek through the jungle. I for one was dreaming of an air-conditioned bar with an ice-cold drink in hand where I could comfortably watch some other poor bugger being eaten by bugs—on Discovery Channel, of course.

We followed our guide along a small path through the bush and, sure enough, only a few minutes later found ourselves in a shady glen whose feature attraction was a pool of crystal-clear water surrounded by those smooth stones you usually only see in tourist brochures or the bathrooms of expensive houses. The perfect setting to wash off after a sweaty day of traipsing through the bush. There were even smooth flat stones carefully positioned to sit on.

It did not take us long to shed what clothing decency allowed. That idyllic-looking little pool was so enticing after our long morning of hot sweaty jungle that we completely forgot it was full of hot water as we raced to be the first in.

The water did not look hot. No steam wafted from its surface. There was just an innocent looking mountain pool in a shady glen inviting us to jump in and enjoy its cool mountain waters. As we made to wade right in, with no thought of how hot it was, I saw our guide cringe. Then the squeals and squeaks began. I was fortunate. Having chosen a lovely flat stone at the water's edge to sit on, I planned to slowly slide in, luxuriating in cool fresh water as I went. When the first toe touched water, my plan changed.

We all know there is only one way to enter a hot tub. Slowly. You start with the feet and progressively immerse yourself until the point where everyone inevitably hesitates for a few seconds before plunging farther. At that point, exclaiming "Ouiiii" or "Eeeeek" is considered normal practice. Once past the tricky halfway point, a slow sensuous slide up to neck level is usually followed by the standard-issue "Ahhhhhhhh" of contentment.

All pretty standard stuff, as long as you know in advance it's going to be hot. In this case at least one of the girls was so carried away she jumped right in. Lucky for her, the water is less than waist deep. In any case she came flying out with an amazing turn of speed, appearing to walk on water in her haste to get back on land.

The three of us luxuriated in that natural spa bath until just before sunset, when we emerged like three well-pickled prunes. And best of all, that piece of bamboo provided an excellent main yard for our square running sail that, so far, has outlasted the original wooden one.

CHAPTER 24

The Finger of Fate

A lone figure, dressed in ragged khaki shorts and a faded blue T-shirt, strolled along the shoreline, occasionally glancing out to sea. He had been born on this island over fifty years before, back when the island still had a government health worker, an official teacher, and of course the preacher to polish souls, in between marrying and burying the islanders, a job made difficult by his steadfast refusal to respect the ancient island customs. All three were gone now, recalled in a fit of economy thirty-five years before, by a government that scarcely knew his island existed.

A dignified man of medium height, with broad shoulders hardened from a lifetime of fishing and garden work, his rugged features accented a face formed by years of experience and the confident acceptance of responsibility. Streaks of gray highlighted his curly black hair. That evening, Baba Eki Marantika was in a pensive mood, reflecting on his life's diverse successes and failures.

As a small boy, he played on this beach chasing crabs or helping with the fishing canoes. The small cave where he and his friends had shared their secrets was still there, only a stone's throw from where he stood. Even then, he had been a leader, chosen by the other boys as their headman. Now he was headman of the island, and his people's only source of medical care.

Seating himself on a rough-hewn palm log bench, he watched the sky dim through various shades of evening. Deep in thought, he failed to notice the myriad stars as they appeared, stark against the velvet background of night or the Milky Way spreading its faintly luminescent cloud across the sky. He was more than thirty years away, on a day long ago when the island health worker offered him a job as his assistant. Back then, there had been an official ferry, a ship whose monthly visit everyone on the island anxiously anticipated.

The first health worker was a cold, reserved man from Jakarta. Frequently passed over for promotion, his posting to such a remote island made him resentful and bitter. An incompetent alcoholic, he remained an outsider among the villagers until the day he left. Under him, Baba Eki learned little, other than how to sweep and mop the health post, run errands, mix hangover cures, clean up vomit, and meekly be yelled at. When that man left, the entire island breathed a sigh of relief.

The next health worker fell in love with the island and its people. Quick to make friends, he worked hard to earn their trust through dedication and his honest respect for island traditions. Discovering in his young assistant an inquisitive, willing student, he taught Baba Eki the basics of health care. For Baba Eki these practical lessons were a revelation. As time passed, his knowledge and experience grew. Then, after a single radio message from Jakarta, his whole life changed.

Remembering that day Baba Eki shifted his position on the log bench. Flexing his toes in the warm white sand, he could still visualize the sorrowful look worn by the health worker as he broke the news. The government would no longer support Nila. The next ferry would be the last. He, along with the teacher and preacher, had been ordered to leave on it.

Getting to his feet, Baba Eki turned onto the path leading to his home. It was almost suppertime and his wife, Ibu Lala, would not appreciate tardiness. As he climbed the path, Baba Eki revisited that final morning. With the ferry waiting offshore, all three government officials boarded the ship's launch and departed. Having spent the previous night drinking themselves into a stupor of celebration, the teacher and preacher never looked back. The health worker kept his eyes firmly fixed on his friends ashore, frequently waving goodbye.

As he watched them leave, Baba Eki slid a hand into his pocket where keys to the health post and supply room—with its modest stock of bandages, sutures, and a few medicines—now resided. With a tear in his eye, the health worker had implored Baba Eki to use those supplies for the people. That night Baba Eki cried himself to sleep, tightly clutching the health post keys in his hand.

Two days later, Ekus the boat maker managed to cut his foot rather badly while digging out a new canoe. His friends naturally brought him to the house of Baba Eki, who sewed him up and bandaged the wound. From then on there was no turning back. Baba Eki became the island health worker. With no official training, a cheerful young man suddenly found himself thrust into a succession of life-or-death situations simply because there was no one else to do the job.

Over the next thirty-five years, Baba Eki matured. He married his childhood sweetheart, Ma Lala, and became headman of the island. He also struggled to keep his community healthy. A difficult battle, fought without drugs or other medical supplies. Today the islanders call him "The Needleman" and firmly believe that if a person has not already passed over into the land of their ancestors, then Baba Eki can save them. Coming from countries where medical care is often taken for granted, we can only imagine what it must have been like for him as he faced the ailments and traumas of a small, remote community alone, with no medical supplies and no one to consult with.

CHAPTER 25

A Cargo of Hope

Upon arriving at Nila, once in the lee of the land we all breathed a sigh of relief before heaving to begin preparation for anchoring. It was not long before every available canoe on the north side of the island was scurrying in our direction, each of them loaded to the tipping point with friendly well-wishers, all waving and in some cases singing.

First up the side was the island headman, Baba Eki, with his wonderful sense of humor and more dignity than a busload of bishops. Within minutes our deck resembled a tramp interisland ferry, covered with smiling faces and the cheerful banter of excited people.

Over the next hour or so, that many visitors did serious damage to our meager store of concentrated fruit juice and sweat biscuits. Not that we minded, it all being shared among friends. Even the island drunk managed to make it on board, where he took one look around, yelled something like "Yippee," and proceeded to pass out under the aft awning.

When you consider ours are the only outside faces those people see from one year to the next, *Vega*'s annual arrival is an important event in a community where excitement consists of catching a big fish or getting drunk on the local hooch and watching palm trees grow.

Lucky for us, the next smiling face to climb on board was Pak Jak, the best reef guide on the island. Having him to steer me safely through that nightmare tangle of coral to a safe anchorage is always welcome. Better than a double dose of Valium or a tot of rum as we slowly make our way in.

The entrance to Nila's anchorage is a twisted channel between coral reefs full of sharp-toothed coral traps, just waiting to rip the bottom out of an unwary vessel. Nila is one of those places where even with four anchors out behind coral heads, I still worry about dragging. The thing is, once inside, if the anchors do drag there is only one place to go. And that is the stuff of every sailor's worst nightmare.

On Nila we supply educational and medical supplies for three small communities, as well as other important items such as tools, vegetable seeds, spare parts, fishing gear, nails, bolts, screws, thread, sewing needles—you name it. You see, we are their only contact with the outside world. Their only source of those important supplies.

When we arrived, the tide was rapidly falling. Therefore, I decided to wait until it turned before making our entrance. Even with the guidance of someone like Pak Jak, I always prefer to enter tricky places on a rising tide. That way if we run ground—again—there is every chance the tide will quickly lift us off.

You may have noticed that being a sailor is often an exercise in wariness. The reason for that is simple. At sea anything that can go wrong, will go wrong, eventually—and usually at the worst possible moment. Yet frequently even a healthy measure of paranoia is not enough. Which constantly has me wondering, "Am I being paranoid enough?" As one of my mentors once said, "It's never the emergency you prepare for that happens." Mind you, he also said, "It's your job to worry about everything that can go wrong, then once you've done that, start worrying about the things you forgot to worry about the first time round."

Waiting for the tide to change, we filled our time with general gossip from the island, new babies born, canoes launched, fish caught, the myriad things people on a small island find important. I find their idea of news being about real things that have an effect on people's lives refreshing. Makes you wonder about all the "crises" the rest of us call news. Most of it is media rubbish, which has little or no effect on people's daily lives—other than keeping journalists busy causing more stress and worry among the general population. Little wonder I never watch television.

Several hours later, we slowly worked our way in through the coral-infested entrance. Even with Pak Jak guiding us, I had one of our crew up on the main top watching out with a handheld radio, while Meggi perched on the bowsprit doing the same. Slowly, very slowly, we picked our way into the anchorage. I was chewing my mustache the whole way. Twisting and contorting *Vega* through that narrow channel is not easy.

The final turn that disgorges into the lagoon is so tight I can only make it by backing and filling, judiciously using *Vega*'s notorious prop walk to twist her around the bend. All this in a channel that may have been as broad as the Suez Canal but, from my position at the wheel, seemed only slightly wider than *Vega*.

Getting our anchors down and safely lodged behind large coral heads seemed to be an unspoken cue for the wind to pick up for the next two days, making it impossible for our small boat to land on the beach.

Fortunately, the main reef extends almost a mile out to sea, effectively protecting the shallow northern anchorage from the massive swells we watched break with astonishing force along the reef's outer face. Unable to go ashore, we waited, fixing a few things and cleaning up the boat. Happy to have arrived safely and excited about our upcoming adventures among a community living free from outside influences exactly as their ancestors did. Lucky devils. It still amazes me such lovely little pieces of unspoiled paradise continue to exist.

Another ripe nut hit the sand with a solid *kathunk*, vividly reminding me never to sit under trees with coconuts on them. Laugh all you want, but here is what the experts say. "A coconut falling from height will cause serious damage, no matter where it hits you. Granted a hammock stretched between two gently swaying palms may look enticing in a beach resort brochure, then again everything looks good in those advertisements—even the food. What they never tell you is how aggressive palm trees can be when agitated. If you really must park yourself under one, first determine if it is armed" (excerpt from *A Dummies Guide to Surviving in the Tropics*).

I was enjoying one of those days straight out of a fantasy adventure novel, where a gentle tropical breeze tickles the local palm trees while errant fluffs of cloud meander their way across a cobalt-blue sky. Several children played in a small canoe close to the beach: two fishermen stretched their hand-woven net across one side of the lagoon. In the distance, *Vega* seemed content to gently tug at her anchor.

Meggi was off with the local ladies' sewing circle, most likely discussing the latest island fashions or the price of bananas in Singapore. Judging from the boisterous peals of laughter erupting from that direction every few minutes, they were enjoying themselves.

I sat on a raised bamboo platform, roofed over with a thatch of split palm leaves, marveling at my current predicament and feeling sorry for the people in big cities who will never know such perfect peace and tranquility. I am sure there are better ways to pass your time than relaxing on a rustic tropical island, hundreds of miles from the next landfall—but not with your clothes on.

We were the first outsiders to stop at this lovely little island in over thirty years. And to top it off, we arrived on a hundred-year-old sailing ship bearing gifts of donated medical and educational supplies, as well as an assortment of knives, fishing gear, and vegetable seeds we were willing to trade for cloves and cinnamon. We even had a few good-quality cast-iron pots and pans with us that year. Which, considering the occasional clatter of metal and squeals of delight, were going over a treat with Meggi's group.

To appreciate what our arrival means to those people, just imagine a place where no goods at all arrive from the outside world, forcing them to be self-sufficient in everything. No nails, fishhooks, fishing line, knives, axes, cooking pots, lamp wicks, cloth, or even matches had come to the island in almost two decades. Medical necessities were a distant dream. School supplies nonexistent.

I must admit, Trader Meggi's Traveling Emporium was one of her better ideas. What with there being no other source of everyday kitchen utensils, sewing supplies, or other domestic knickknacks, her scheme provided a much needed service. The idea was not to make a profit but to provide what is needed in a way that respects people's pride and dignity.

Since randomly donating such treasures to some villagers and not to others was a sure formula for animosity, and with cash money being almost unknown on those islands, Meggi hit on the use of local foodstuffs, handicrafts, and spices as a form of barter currency. We later sell what she garners at boat shows and open-house events, then use that money to restock the shop.

Being an artist from the hair on her head to the tips of her toes, Meggi can be worse than a magpie when it comes to collecting island handicraft and artwork. I usually go along with her creative quirks, if for no other reason than to maintain domestic harmony. Mind you, I drew a line at the two-meter-high carved wooden statue reminiscent of several severely constipated gargoyles perched on each other's heads. The thing was almost as big as I am. Well, you try finding space for something like that on a boat. In any case,

Meggi's general store gives her a wonderful chance to get to know the village ladies and collect local gossip while they haggle.

You may laugh, but that gossip is our best source of information about what each island needs and how best we can help. The funny part is that to this day neither Meggi nor I speak Bahasa, other than the few polite phrases one needs to scrape along. Mind you, Meggi is quite proficient with numbers and what she needs for shopping. Amazing what hand gestures, drawings in the sand, and willing minds can accomplish.

CHAPTER 26

An Arrow through Time

Two hunters made their way along a familiar jungle path in utter silence. Their tall handmade hunting bows are powerful enough to drive razor-sharp, meter-long arrows through the thick hide of a wild boar. Once deeply embedded, the arrow is held tightly by its twin barbs. Without thought, their bare feet followed the well-known trail. A gentle breeze tickled the forest canopy, lacing the air around them with a ballet of sunlight and shadow. As they climbed higher, the carpet of dead leaves and dried moss grew thicker, causing a slight crunching sound with every step.

From the time they were small boys playing at mighty hunters, those young men grew up with bows and arrows. Both had spent long hours making their prize hunting bows and special iron-tipped arrows, designed so that once embedded in a target the arrowhead quickly detaches from the shaft.

On coming of age, each boy diligently performed the secret rituals, known only to the men of the island, so their weapons would be blessed and their hunting always successful.

Arno was eighteen years old and slightly taller than his year younger friend Pilli. Both shared the typical black hair and dark-brown eyes of islanders. In the peak of health, their muscles rippled under a sheen of sweat as they silently stalked through the jungle, their well-formed bodies work-hardened by a life spent roaming the steep sides of a volcano, diving for lobster in the lagoon, or rowing the heavy dugout canoes used for fishing. Although not an easy existence, life on their remote island was healthy and the people content.

From high on the volcano, Arno had an unparalleled view of the surrounding ocean. There were no ships in sight, only the deep blue of the open ocean. Not that this surprised him. In his entire life, no ship had stopped at the island. The old people said no outsiders had visited Nila since the government recalled the health worker, teacher, and priest in 1978. Since then the islanders had been on their own, completely isolated from the outside world.

For Arno and Pilli, their entire universe consisted of a small island barely three miles from north to south and two from east to west, most of that taken up by the precipitous flanks of a semiactive volcano. A world where everyone is related and the most exciting event is the giant fish caught by uncle Jaap last year or the squabble between Ma Rosa and Ma Lala, a scandalous feud that had been going on for so long no one can remember how or when it began.

Quietly stalking elusive wild boar on a steep volcano covered with lush tropical jungle is difficult work. Therefore, it was not surprising when later that morning Pilli—always considered the lazier of the two—decided to have a rest. He would wait in the shade while Arno climbed a nearby clove tree. From that lofty, well-hidden vantage point, Arno would keep watch for any boar that might wander along. It was a perfect plan. Since wild pigs have no predators from the sky, they rarely look up when moving through the forest.

As morning progressed into another lethargic tropical afternoon, Pilli soon found an agreeable niche and promptly fell asleep while his friend Arno made himself comfortable among the branches of a nearby tree. Lulled by the cool breeze, the pungent aroma of clove flowers, and the incessant song of tropical birds, the youths let the day progress in leisurely island fashion. A wavering pattern of sunlight dappled the forest floor. Insects chittered and buzzed. Perched high above the jungle floor Arno drifted in a hypnotic daze.

Suddenly, his drooping eyes sprung fully open, his attention attracted by a slight discordance in the sound around him. Scanning the forest, Arno's keen young eyes spotted stealthy movement in a tall stand of bamboo. Some of those stately stalks were twitching their bright-green heads in a manner that had nothing to do with the prevailing breeze. He shifted his weight, feeling the rough tree bark abrade his right leg. Ever so slowly, he reached behind his neck to flick away a large insect. Then, with the infinite patience of an accomplished hunter, he waited.

As Arno watched, the wavering bamboo stalks indicated purposeful movement slowly advancing his way. It had to be a wild boar, and a big one. No other animal on the island could move through such thick bamboo. The excitement mounted. Like all island boys, Arno often talked about killing a wild boar. In reality, few remained on the island, and those were wily old creatures well versed in avoiding people. The chances of discovering and killing one were extremely rare.

Glancing down, he saw Pilli sleeping close to where the boar would exit the bush. Arno fervently prayed his friend would not start snoring, a dubious talent for which he was renowned. Should Pilli make the slightest sound, that boar, which represented a potentially wonderful dinner for the whole family and praise from the village for Arno's prowess as a hunter, would quickly vanish.

Arno's concentration sharpened at the thought of what bringing back such a prize would mean for his future. Killing a large wild pig would make him the village hero. It would also make him a champion in the eyes of Rosa, whose attention Arno dearly coveted. Rosa was the most beautiful girl Arno had ever seen. For years, he had dreamed of marrying her, although for the moment just getting her attention would be an important step forward.

From his elevated position, Arno saw that if the boar continued its current route, it would be exposed and vulnerable while crossing an open space between two large stands of bamboo. When it emerged, Arno knew the hog would pause to sniff the air and listen for signs of danger. Then he must strike.

Carefully selecting his lucky arrow, Arno touched the head to his brow and mouthed the traditional hunter's prayer, silently seeking support from the spirits of his ancestors.

By leaning around the tree, Arno could draw his bow and make the shot. It would be difficult at that angle, but he felt confident of a clean release. Then, of course, they would dress the boar and carry it back to the village, where he could tease his friends and play the mighty hunter in front of Rosa. Arno could almost taste the best pieces of roasted meat that would be his by right, either to enjoy or share.

With fantasies of a glowing future in mind, Arno waited, barely breathing, for what seemed like ages. Afraid to open his mouth, lest the boar hear the heartbeat thundering in his chest, his entire being was passionately focused on a slight opening where the bamboo stopped and the clearing began.

First, a small green shoot twitched, then a large snout came into view, questing between the bushes; cautiously sniffing the air for signs of danger, the wild pig's head slowly emerged. Arno held his breath. This was no ordinary boar. It was enormous. There, only a few meters away, stood the great-grandmother of all wild hogs, just waiting for the kiss of his arrow.

After what seemed an eternity, the gigantic beast cautiously nosed its way into the clearing, then stopped. Arno could not believe his luck. There in the open stood an immense sow; within seconds several small piglets came scampering out of the foliage to join their mother. This was a fabulous treasure, straight from his wildest dreams of wealth and riches.

His mouth suddenly became as dry as a desert. If he killed the sow, those piglets would be easy to capture. Taken home to be raised by his family, they represented enormous wealth. It might even be enough for him to ask for Rosa's hand in marriage.

After all, two of those piglets would set them up nicely with a house and fishing canoe. Another two small pigs should satisfy even her greedy old father. The remainder would go to his own family, winning him prestige in their eyes and in the eyes of the community. The whole island would talk about this day for years to come. Arno would be famous. Fathers would hold him up as a shining example for their sons to emulate.

Tingling with excitement, he slowly drew the bow to its fullest extension. One of the arrow's feathers touched his cheek. Adrenaline coursed through his body. His heart quickened as he carefully aimed one finger width behind the pigs left shoulder. An arrow striking deeply there would pierce the boar's mighty heart, instantly dropping her where she stood.

After another small prayer for luck, he breathed Rosa's name and released the long, iron-tipped arrow. The bowstring twanged. Arno's spirits surged as he watched the arrow he had worked so hard to make fly straight and true, directly toward its intended target. That is, it flew straight and true until a tree branch, suddenly shifting in the breeze, deflected it.

As Arno watched in slow-motion horror, his deadly arrow wobbled away on a new trajectory, directly toward his sleeping companion. There was no time to call out or even blink. With a dull wet-sounding thump, the arrow imbedded itself deep in Pilli's side.

Startled, the wild pig squealed before bolting back into the thicket, followed by her piglets. Within seconds Pilli's shriek of mortal agony echoed through the forest. Arno's moment of triumph had become a deadly disaster.

CHAPTER 27

With Razor Blades and a Prayer

Arno dropped his bow and arrows then half slid, half fell to the ground, ignoring the clove tree's coarse bark as it tore at his hands and feet. All he could hear were Pilli's shrieks of mortal agony. All he saw was thick red blood oozing from around the arrow wound.

Half blinded by tears, Arno scrambled crab-like to his friend's side. Words of apology tumbled from his lips. Seeing what he feared most, his mouth suddenly went dry; the meter-long arrow was deeply embedded in the side of his friend's belly. Everyone knew belly wounds ended in a slow, painful death.

Panic set in. Through streaming tears, Arno begged Pilli not to die. Then with fumbling hands he reached to pull the arrow out. No sooner had he touched it than Pilli's agonized scream stopped him. Sitting back on his haunches, Arno wiped the tears from his eyes and tried to think. There was only one hope. They must go back down the steep volcano to the village where Baba Eki, "The Needleman," would know what to do. Baba Eki always knew what to do. Struggling to his feet, he called on God and all his ancestors for help, then explained the plan to Pilli.

With Pilli leaning heavily against him, they began the long, difficult descent. As they stumbled along, the blood-stained arrow shaft came loose from its head. Neither of the boys noticed it fall to the ground. Nor did they remark the distance they slowly covered. Both were lost in their thoughts and fears. For Pilli, it was constant agonizing pain and fear of dying. For Arno, the repeated image of his arrow's flight and the sickening wet thunk as it drove deep into Pilli's side.

Twice during that seemingly endless journey, Pilli lost consciousness. Without warning, there would be a whimper as his knees turned to rubber. Both times, Arno carefully lowered Pilli to the ground, certain his lifelong friend had died. Only the occasional whimper of pain and Pilli's rapidly fluttering eyelids indicated he was still alive.

Arno pleaded with his friend not to die, promising him his best fishing line and favorite bush knife, if only he would live. He also prayed. Fervent entreaties filled with promises never again to drink *sopi* and to go to church every Sunday if God would spare his friend's life. Each time, as Pilli slowly returned to consciousness, Arno gently helped him to stand. As they slowly made their way down the mountain, Arno did his best to distract Pilli from his misery by telling stories about the good times they had shared. He even tried to sing a song, until Pilli told him to shut up, commenting between clinched teeth that one painful experience was more than enough. When Pilli faltered, Arno coaxed him onward, one step at a time. Anything to bring them another stride closer to the village and Baba Eki.

It took four interminable hours for the boys to negotiate their way down that tortuous mountain path to an outlying area of the village where neighbors soon answered their frantic calls. Friends and family rushed to their aid. On seeing her son covered in blood, Pilli's mother cried out and began tearing at her hair. Children raced away in search of "The Needleman." After a stretcher was quickly fashioned, four strong men solemnly carried Pilli to Baba Eki's house.

Exhausted from the effort and stress, Arno fell to the ground under a clove tree. Pulling his knees up against his chest, he wrapped both arms around them, letting his head come to rest in the cradle they formed. He was parched and needed rest, but most of all he needed to know Pilli would live. He had never felt so helpless and alone in his life.

A hand touched Arno's arm. At first, he wanted to shrug it off, but then he opened his eyes and saw it was Rosa. He tried to smile but couldn't. Kneeling beside him, Rosa held a gourd of lime-flavored water to his lips, then without a word took him in her arms. Holding him tightly. Rocking him like a baby. Somewhere deep inside a dam broke. Trembling from grief, Arno's tears soon drenched her shoulder.

As news of the disaster spread throughout their village, a barely conscious Pilli arrived at Baba Eki's house. There they gently laid him on a rough-hewn wooden table sheltered under a grass-thatched roof. The village clinic. While Ma Lala began to boil water, someone tolled the meetinghouse bell. Others banged out the news on bamboo jungle drums. Within minutes the entire island knew there was an emergency.

Baba Eki was tending his garden when the turmoil began. Excited children, calling his name, soon followed the initial shouting. When the meetinghouse bell began sounding a slow, somber rhythm, he knew something was very wrong. Resting his shovel against a tree, he wiped his hands. With a worried expression on his naturally cheerful face, Baba Eki settled the wide-brimmed straw hat firmly on his head, then stepped out along the path to his house.

For almost thirty years, Baba Eki had done his best to care for the villagers. He was always there to bandage their wounds with scraps of cloth and help as best he could by employing traditional medications when they were sick. Having cut out so many fishhooks, sewed up so many cuts, and set so many broken bones, he no longer kept count. Yet, when he saw Pilli lying on the table with the stub of an arrow protruding from his belly, he knew this was different.

Looking down at the injured boy, one thing was certain: Pilli's future teetered on an unseen knife edge. This case would test Baba Eki's paltry medical skills to their limits. Like it or not, the boy's life, a life he had helped bring into this world, was in his hands. Baba Eki slowly shook his head. He had none of the supplies, training, or even equipment needed to treat such a wound.

Slashing away the boy's blood-soaked shirt, Baba Eki laid bare Pilli's stomach, exposing the dreadful wound. Bending close he sniffed. If the intestines were pierced, without antibiotics and special sutures, of which he had none, the boy would die. There was the sharp metallic sent of blood but no smell of feces to indicate the boy's intestines were punctured. Looking closer, he could see the arrow had entered at a sharp angle. As his examination progressed, Baba Eki felt a glimmer of hope. But even if he successfully removed the arrow, the pall of deadly infection would still remain. With no medications, no surgical supplies, and no painkillers, he faced a major surgical intervention, one with little hope of success.

For Baba Eki, doing nothing was not an option. If he did not intervene, the boy would die. If he tried and failed, the result would be the same. Nevertheless, if he was very careful and extremely lucky, there was a small chance Pilli might live.

So it was that while their meetinghouse bell called the village to pray for Pilli's life, Baba Eki prepared himself and the few paltry tools at his disposal for major surgery.

Those tools consisted of five old-style double-sided razor blades, a pair of scissors, and some bandages made from rags. To close the wound, he had a sewing needle and cotton thread. He knew the stiches would pose a problem later, yet that was all he had. Fortunately, he also had a good supply of *sopi*: a powerful concoction the islanders distill from palm wine. Some say it is almost pure alcohol; others call it efficient radiator cleaner. I call it unadulterated rotgut. Being almost pure alcohol, *sopi* makes an amazingly effective disinfectant.

While Pilli's father plied his son with liberal doses of *sopi* as a painkiller, Baba Eki used it to sterilize his hands, scissors, and razor blades. By the time they were ready to begin, night had fallen. Without a word, people brought every coconut-oil lamp and homemade candle in the village to the small health post, so that Baba Eki would have light to work by. Against a backdrop of hymns from the small village church, Baba Eki sent up a prayer of his own, then began an operation that lasted for five stress-filled hours.

It soon became clear he could not remove the arrow by cutting around it and then pulling it out. The sharp barb would surely rip an intestine, condemning the boy to a slow, lingering death from infection. The only hope was slowly working the sharp arrowhead along the layer between muscle and intestines, then removing it from the back. Using two tablespoons, carefully sterilized with *sopi* and fire, to surround the arrow's lethal head, centimeter by centimeter Baba Eki carefully negotiated a way past the boy's intestines by gently opening a path with one of his razor blades, then guiding the arrowhead toward a point where it would be safe to push it through.

The tension would have been unbearable were he not so intent on the work at hand. He was not even aware of Ma Lila wiping the sweat from his brow or Ma Rosa, the island midwife, passing him tools or sponging away blood as it pooled around the wound. Hours of intense concentration faded into the past unnoticed. Fortunately, Pilli spent most of that time passed out from the pain and liberal doses of *sopi*.

It was well past midnight when Baba Eki finally eased the arrow between two muscles and gently pushed it out through the boy's side. Holding the bloody arrowhead in the dim lamplight, he breathed a sigh of relief. The boy's intestines appeared undamaged. So after carefully closing the wound with a common sewing needle and thread, they left Pilli under the watchful eye of Arno, who had remained by his side throughout the operation. All that night prayers and hymns filled the air as the community gathered in their small meetinghouse-cum-church, beseeching God to spare Pilli's life.

The next few days were nerve-racking. Several times Pilli ran a high fever. Each time the fever abated after only a few hours. Thankfully, there were no signs of virulent deep-seated infection. It was on the twelfth day that Baba Eki finally admitted there was hope. A week later, it was all they could do to keep Pilli in bed.

Until this day, Pilli has a nasty scar, replete with stitch marks that would have most doctors unceremoniously booted from the profession. Nevertheless, he is alive and still best friends with the man who accidently shot him. Arno finally married the girl of his dreams. He and Rosa now have three lovely children, one of which they named Pilli.

We had yet to hear the arrow story when we presented Baba Eki his first health worker kit, containing antibiotics, painkillers, minor surgical implements, and other important tools for community health care. What I did see were tears in a proud man's eyes as he unpacked that black ballistic nylon bag and carefully examined each item. When he came to the book, *Where There Is No Doctor* in Bahasa, he clutched it to his heart. Looking up he said, "I have needed something like this for thirty-five years. Thank you."

Sometime back, I read where a famous philosopher once said, "The things we do for ourselves will die with us; the things we do for others are our chance at immortality"—or some such gibberish. In any case, I like to think he was right.

CHAPTER 28

Another Island, Another World

It is hard for us to imagine the difficulties faced by a traditional midwife in isolated surroundings. Poorly trained, with only the most basic equipment, she struggles to care for the women of her village. Often, because of her basic health care knowledge, a midwife is also the informal village nurse.

You want to know what I think? No one will ever understand the needs and priorities of a remote community better than the inhabitants of that community. It always amazes me when some big aid agency sends Doctor Sniffle P. Muggins, PhD, et al. to waste a few trees writing another sociological report on the requirements of some rural village located out in the back of beyond. Think about it for a minute. For ages, those people have survived, raised families, and even found time for a bit of fun, in conditions where left to his own devices Doctor Muggins would not last a week.

The problems are clear, and every year millions of children under the age of five and women giving birth die from easily preventable causes. Basic training, medical implements, and drugs can save most women who die giving birth. So if we want to start reducing fatalities, we need to get basic supplies and equipment, along with practical training, to the ones who care for those babies and their mothers.

Most of the places we go depend on traditional midwives, a dedicated group with more practical experience than you could ever imagine. When we asked what they needed most to do the job, every one of them said training and supplies. So now you know where the idea for our traditional midwife kits came from. People like Dr. Aida, Dr. Celso, and Dr. Dan, who are constantly out in the bushes treating cases and solving problems, estimate that those midwife and health worker kits have reduced maternal and infant mortality by as much as 40 percent. Even more in some places. Not a bad day's work for a 130-year-old boat crewed by a few lost souls trying their best to be helpful. And, when you figure we do it on almost nonexistent budgets, well, not bad at all.

A few days' sail from Baba Eki's island is another unspoiled little slice of paradise whose inhabitants were cast adrift by the budget cuts of 1978. Since then, life on their island has continued much as it would have hundreds of years before.

Until *Vega* arrived, many of the inhabitants were only vaguely aware an outside world existed. Although the elders told stories of great ships that belched fire from deep in their bellies, to young islanders those tales seemed like mystical legends. The few who set out in their canoes to search for that illusive outside world never returned.

Standing alone in the doorway of a bamboo-and-thatch house, the light from an ancient oil lamp cast Lela in silhouette against its deep-orange glow. Never intended to burn coconut oil, the lamp sputtered and smoked no matter how she adjusted its homemade wick. The chimney glass had broken long ago, causing it to smoke even worse. She hated that lamp, yet it was all she had.

The clatter of a shovel laboring against stony volcanic soil disturbed the night. By the light of a waning moon, she sensed the man's presence, a darker shadow against the night dolefully digging a small shallow grave. A faint sob told her he was crying. Taking a deep breath, Lela turned, looking back into the dimly lit house. A woman lay on the only bed. A bed covered in blood. The man's suffering was far from over.

Close by, she could hear the rippling sound of surf and a soft breeze rustling palm leaves; her island was once again peaceful. That silence was welcome. It stood in stark contrast to the agonized screams of a woman tormented by a difficult childbirth. A woman who, sweating, panting, and gasping, had bravely fought against the pain to bring forth her baby, trusting Lela's skill as the island midwife to bring them both safely through the ordeal.

It had been a long, hard delivery. Even so, the baby died in Lela's arms before taking its first breath. Now her main concern was saving the mother, who was bleeding badly. She hung her head. A strand of loose hair fell across her eyes. There was nothing more Lela could do. Her birthing kit consisted of a sharp knife and a piece of string made from coconut fiber. Exactly the same tools her great-great-grandmother had used.

Turning away from the door, Lela brushed the errant strand of hair from her face and stepped back into the single-room house. Sitting awkwardly on a rough-hewn wooden stool by the bed, she gently took the woman's hand in hers, feeling a slight pressure as her childhood friend tried to squeeze. She was fighting back. That was always a good sign. If only the bleeding would stop, she might live.

Rhythmically patting the woman's hand, Lela allowed her mind to drift. This was not the first nor would it be the last time she sat like this watching a friend struggle for her life. Unable to do more than provide encouragement, Lela felt helpless. A bowl of fresh water sat beside the bed. Lela dipped the corner of a rag and began wiping the woman's forehead.

For as long as anyone could remember, Lela's family had provided the island "bidan." A tradition passed along from mother to firstborn daughter for countless generations. Fortunately for Lela, her older sister had neither the interest nor ability to take on the task. She still remembered the day her mother asked if Lela would like to become a midwife.

Lela was proud of her position in the community. She had worked hard at her mother's side, learning all she could about the art of bringing new life into this world. Yet, deep in her heart, she knew there was much she did not know. The mysterious ways doctors had of saving lives was knowledge denied to her. Lela bowed her head, taking several deep breaths in silence while splaying the fingers of her free hand across her brow.

Drops of water from an old cast-iron kettle hissed as they hit the fire, bringing her back to the present. She crushed a selection of medicinal herbs into a chipped enamel mug, then poured boiling water over them. Stirring the infusion with a twig, she sat back, blowing gently into the mug to help the mixture cool.

Minutes later, the woman stirred ever so slightly. Lela reached out, pushing back a loose strand of hair from her friend's forehead. Supporting the girl's head with one hand, Lela held the still warm mug of medicine to her patient's lips. With luck, those herbs would help stop the bleeding. A faint smile from the exhausted woman was her reward.

Ponderously getting to her feet, for Lela was not a small woman, she removed the bundle of rags resting between the woman's legs. They were soaked with blood, yet it seemed there was much less now than when she last checked. Either the bleeding was slowing, or the woman would soon be dead. Stepping once again to the door, she immersed the blood-stained rags in a wooden bucket filled with cold water. She would wash them out in the morning. After all, cloth was a rare commodity on the island.

Faintly from the village meetinghouse, she heard her neighbors singing hymns. At times like these, the village gathered in support, imploring heaven to spare one of their own. Lela silently added a prayer of her own.

For Lela, change came in the form of a small sailing ship that silently arrived one morning and anchored close to her village. The appearance of a vessel from the outside, the first many of the islanders had ever seen, frightened several people so badly they hid in the forest. Some of the men took up their hunting bows and arrows or fishing spears, determined to defend their homes and families. The longer the boat sat there peacefully riding at its anchor, the more intrigued the islanders became.

Clearly, something had to be done. As the day wore on, five people were seen moving around on that strange vessel, including several women. At last it was decided the island headman, along with a delegation of notables, should investigate. After all, the elders always claimed most people from the outside were friendly. It was also decided that perhaps a few invigorating cups of *sopi* were in order before undertaking such a dubious mission.

While the village leaders were busy fortifying themselves with *sopi*, several children took matters into their own hands. Having drifted back from their hiding places in the forest, they were soon speculating on what treasures such a strange vessel might hold. When someone was seen out on the mystery vessel's deck, the children called out greetings and waved. When people on the boat waved back in a friendly manner, the more adventurous youngsters promptly dove into the water—fully intent on exploring something new and exciting. Worried parents calling them back were promptly ignored.

While the children were swimming out, someone lowered the ship's dinghy. By the time they arrived it was tied alongside. Children being children, they launched themselves over the side and into the dinghy like playful little otters. A woman on the boat welcomed them in their own language, and soon the air was filled with excited squeals and a thousand questions. Then, wonder of wonders, the woman gave each of them a piece of hard candy, something none of them had seen before.

By then the more than slightly inebriated village notables found themselves being heckled by the older women, who laughingly teased their bravery. With no other choice, and seeing the children seemed to be enjoying themselves immensely, a canoe was launched and a tipsy delegation of island grandees set out to greet the newly arrived visitors. The meeting went extremely well, and it was soon agreed that since they were tired from days at sea the boat's crew would come ashore early the following morning.

The next morning, when the sun was about two hands above the horizon, four of the ship's crew boarded their small boat and came ashore. Among them was an Indonesian doctor. No real doctor had ever visited the island. On hearing this, Lela timidly introduced herself as the island midwife and nurse, fully expecting a full medical doctor to look down on her and her uneducated ways. Yet the friendly lady doctor had smiled with gentle brown eyes and taken her hand.

Lela was truly shocked when the doctor not only offered to hold a clinic on the island but also insisted that Lela assist her. Within minutes, the two women became deeply engrossed in various technical aspects of their profession. Three hours later, dazed from the wealth of information her simple questions had brought forth, Lela still had no idea how a pulse oximeter worked, or even what one was, but at least now she felt ignorant in much greater detail than ever before.

For the next two days, Lela eagerly absorbed new medical techniques and knowledge from the doctor. Those were exciting times. Every morning she sat on the beach anxiously waiting for the doctor to come ashore. Every night she sat up late reviewing in her mind's eye each precious new gem of knowledge.

Far from treating her as uneducated—Lela could read and was extremely proud of the fact—the doctor spent long hours every day freely sharing her knowledge and skills. Yet, as the doctor frequently pointed out, skill and knowledge alone were not enough. To be a fully effective midwife and nurse, Lela required the proper drugs and equipment. She also needed to understand their use.

For Lela, living on a small, remote island far out in the Banda Sea, the prospect of finding those drugs and equipment seemed a depressingly impossible task. Yet without them, women and babies would continue to die. The more she learned, the more frustrated she became. Lela could be saving lives using simple techniques, but those techniques required materials she could never dream of having.

Then came the most magnificent day in Lela's life, a day that changed the lives of every person on her island. Stepping gingerly ashore, the doctor reached back into the boat and tried to lift out a heavy black bag. From where she stood, Lela could see a slightly smaller bag sitting beside it.

Looking around, the doctor called for Lela to come help carry the bags, something she was happy to do. Then again, was that not what children are for? Using her authority, she soon had two boys scampering down the beach toward her house, a black ballistic nylon bag balanced on the head of each. As they ran along, they played with a football someone on the ship had given them.

Beside Lela's house stands a raised bamboo platform, carpeted with a mat woven from palm fronds. It is a place where she, her family, and her friends frequently sit to enjoy the cool shade and gentle breeze, the palm-leaf roof being more for the shadow it casts than protection from rain.

Lifting one of the bags from the sand where the boys had left them, the doctor placed it on the platform. She then motioned for Lela to do the same with the other bag. Lifting her bag, she noticed it was small yet quite heavy. Lela marveled at the two stoutly made black ballistic nylon bags with their heavy plastic zippers and various snap pockets. More than a little envious, she wished for even a small bag like that.

For the next few minutes, the two women sat together comfortably sipping herbal tea, enjoying the cool breeze and each other's company. The black bags rested innocently between them. Noting the bags were tightly packed, Lela wondered what they contained. She was so curious she could hardly restrain herself, yet her inherent dignity prevailed. The doctor's face wore an enigmatic smile. As they talked, the conversation naturally drifted to medical matters.

Pulling the smaller bag closer to herself, the doctor unsnapped one of the side pockets. Reaching in, she extracted a medium-sized paperback book. At first, Lela thought it was in English, a language she did not understand.

Then she noticed the title was in Bahasa. As she read that title, her heart leaped; the book was *A Guide for Rural Midwives*.

As the doctor passed that precious book to Lela, she explained some of its contents. Everything Lela had always wanted to know was contained between those covers. Caressing the book, Lela clasped it to her ample breast. Then the doctor opened the opposite end of the smaller bag, easily extracting another book. In silence, yet with a little smile she could not hide, she passed this new book to Lela.

The second book made Lela's heart beat even faster; emotions overwhelmed her, unbidden tears came to her eyes. The title of that book was *Where There Is No Doctor*. Opening a page at random, she saw this was no deeply complicated medical tome but a simply worded book intended for people like her. And, it was in her language.

Lela's breath caught in her throat. Without thinking, she leaned across the bags to hug the doctor tightly, all the time thanking and blessing her profusely. Overwhelmed by their private thoughts and emotions, time ceased to exist for the university-trained medical doctor and traditional island midwife.

Finally breaking the spell, the doctor encouraged Lela to open the two bags and explore their contents. With trembling hands, Lela unzipped the larger bag. It was packed tightly with bandages and drugs. Piece by piece, as the two women emptied the bag, the doctor carefully explained each item and its proper use. Lela was stunned. All she could do was nod her head, gaping in awe as each new item emerged from that magnificent treasure trove.

Turning to the second, smaller bag, the doctor slid open the zipper. Lying on top of the contents was a carefully folded black nylon shoulder bag. The doctor quickly explained how that was to become Lela's "carry-out bag." Grinning like a little girl, Lela simply could not resist getting to her feet and strutting up and down a few times carrying the new bag on her shoulder.

The second bag seemed to be packed with small boxes. One by one, the women extracted each box, carefully opening it to reveal the medical equipment contained within. Blood pressure cuff, Doppler fetal heartbeat monitor, stethoscope, surgical implements, a natal resuscitator, suction device, syringes, and sutures—even two stainless-steel kidney dishes.

One at a time, these treasures emerged. Like little children with new toys, as they removed each from its box to assemble it, the doctor explained its use. There was even a small solar panel to recharge the batteries that some of the equipment required.

When the doctor opened a small blue box, Lela's mouth fell open. It contained a stainless-steel nurse's watch. Lela had never seen a watch before, much less even dreamed of owning one. It was the only watch on the island. Holding it in her hand, Lela fumbled with the clasp until the doctor showed her its secrets, explaining the watch was an important tool for timing contractions. Thirty exciting minutes later, Lela had more or less mastered the mystery of clocks.

As they worked, the doctor warned Lela that the next few days would be intense. There was much to learn and little time to teach. In her awed state, and in between surreptitious glances at her new watch, Lela could do little more than nod her head—often forgetting to keep her mouth closed.

The next few days were indeed strenuous. They were also magical. Lela discovered the mysteries of blood pressure, how to prepare and give injections, how to clear a new baby's breathing passage and how to use the natal resuscitator, even how to sterilize her surgical implements to avoid infection. At first, the fetal heartbeat monitor mystified her, until a sudden inspiration brought understanding.

It was a pleasant surprise when the doctor suggested using *sopi* as a readily available antiseptic. Just when Lela thought her head was about to explode, they began with the drugs and their proper use. Lela was relieved to discover the drugs in her bag corresponded precisely to the ones mentioned in her new books. When a book suggested a drug, she knew it was there for her to use. More than once, the doctor warned that she should not waste those drugs, admonishing her to use them only when she was certain they were needed.

All too soon, it was time for the doctor to leave. As she explained, the old sailing ship she arrived on would be visiting other islands to train and equip more midwives like Lela, but with luck, they would return the following year to resupply Lela's kit, provide her with more training, and help with other village projects. Lela had been so intent on learning she had scarcely noticed what others from the ship were doing. Later, she discovered they were also busy.

The next morning, as silently as it had arrived, the old ship pulled up its anchor and sailed away. The whole village gathered on the beach to wave them goodbye.

At sunset that evening, Lela visited a small grave beside the house of her childhood friend. Some years ago, the woman had almost died in childbirth. Her baby had not survived. Kneeling beside the small grave, Lela placed her precious new books on each side of the small mound. Deep in prayer, she gave thanks for what she had learned over the past few days. Now she had the skills and equipment to save babies like this one. As a single tear ran down her cheek, she swore that never again would a baby die like this one had, or a mother bleed to death.

CHAPTER 29

The Sighting of Komba

Outward bound on our delivery route one morning, we were sailing along just a few miles north of Kawula Island when I spotted a strange-looking cloud almost due north of us. Nature is not notorious for symmetrically shaped clouds, yet there on the horizon a perfectly round cloud ascended into the sky. Being the curious type and bored to thumb-twiddling distraction, I watched it for a while then lost interest until a few minutes later I spotted another spherical cloud from roughly the same position.

Since those were practically the only clouds in the sky that morning, I began watching that sector more closely. Within minutes, a similar cloud appeared. If there is one thing Meggi and I dearly love, it is a mysterious place in need of exploration.

Clouds do not simply form themselves at ground level and rapidly rise up into the sky unaided. So, carefully taking a bearing on those mystery clouds with the hand compass, I went below to consult our chart. Sure enough, about nine miles from our position, on precisely the bearing I had just taken, the map indicated a small island by the name of Komba. A notation alongside its name read, "Volcano—erupting."

Hmm, thinks I, those mystery clouds are coming from an active volcano. After calling Meggi and Jo to share the discovery, we sat together on the cabin roof watching as roughly every twelve minutes another globular cloud made its way into the morning sky.

We soon decided to visit that little island, if for no other reason than to watch it pop it's top every few minutes. We would have done it then and there were we not short on fuel, as usual, and with a volunteer crewmember hopping from foot to foot worried he would miss his flight from Dili to Singapore in a few days' time.

Why people insist on booking their flights so far in advance is a mystery to me. We do warn them *Vega* is a sailing boat and not the Lisbon Packet. I never give exact arrival dates, simply because we never know what the wind or seas will send us.

For the moment we could only dream of watching an active volcano thunder and roar. With a glance between us, Meggi and I decided to visit Komba. A promise we kept several months later on the way back to Jakarta.

With Komba Island yet unvisited and several days in our past, *Vega* was once again running along at five knots under her main square sail, outer jib, and mizzen staysail. The weather was idyllic. A gentle following breeze wafted us over calm seas. Considering all the excitement we could have been facing, everything seemed to be working perfectly. To me that was a warning signal I have learned the hard way not to ignore. When everything seems to be going along just fine, I worry.

If there is one thing I have learned about boats and the ocean, it's that as soon as you think everything is the way it should be, something is going wrong that you haven't noticed yet, and will, most likely, not become apparent until around three in the morning. Or just at the end of your night watch. Whichever comes first.

How I see it, the only logical way to deal with the ocean is by employing a healthy dose of paranoia. It also helps if you have a strong streak of cowardice in your general makeup. Both of those are useful traits that tend to make you think twice before setting out when the weather forecasts a dodgy day. The armchair macho types who want to battle the elements scare me witless. Which is easy enough to do.

As a general observer of life, I am totally convinced paranoia is a major survival trait, one that allowed our far-distant ancestors to make it down from the trees and remain alive long enough to spread out and prosper.

You try existing in an environment ripe with stealthy, fast-moving teeth and sharp claws that just love the taste of raw human flesh and see what happens to your stress levels. The result of all this is that I am rather proud of being more than a little paranoid. You see, after so many years at sea, I do not believe the ocean is out to get me. I know for a fact it is. Never forget that old sailor's proverb, "Anything that can go wrong at sea will go wrong, and at the worst possible moment."

There must be a reason why in every language Nature is female. I can just imagine two of my ancient ancestors fresh from the trees huddling in what little shelter they could find and looking around apprehensively when one whispered to the other:

"Hey Og, I been thinking about this nature stuff. Must be a woman nature, because for sure she's a real Mother." At which Og nodded knowingly, then went back to watching the dark lurking shadows around their small island of humanity. "Yeah mate, I just wish someone would hurry up and discover that fire stuff. Old Zog says we have to invent gods first so one of us can slip round and nick it from them."

Those people had it tough. Little wonder it took thousands of years for them to start living in caves. After all, bigger and stronger things than our quivering ancestors already had long-term rights on all the better caves. "Hey, I have it!" says Og. "Let's go live in that cave up there." "Right mate," says another sloping brow, "and who's going to evict the saber-toothed tiger that currently holds the lease?"

Meggi says I worry too much. But I doubt if you *can* worry too much at sea. I even worry about the things I am forgetting to worry about. Then again, an old mentor of mine once said, "It's never the emergency you prepare for that happens," which is not much help because the ones you do not prepare for are always bigger than the ones you do prepare for. If I followed that line of thinking any further, I would sell the boat and buy a cactus farm out in the desert somewhere.

Fast-forward enough to make a Hollywood special effects man dizzy, and you have the likes of me sitting my midnight-until-three trick at the wheel of an old wooden sailboat on its way across the Banda Sea, busy deliberating on what is about to break now that everything is going so smoothly.

CHAPTER 30

Dolphin Trivia and Our Lazy Cat

I have no idea where it came from, but the great river of cool monsoon wind pouring across *Vega*'s stern quarter to thrust against her taught red sails seemed in a hurry to get somewhere. *Vega* danced along her route. Broad reaching across the sea, as if running on rails she trailed an arrow-straight wake. The only thing missing were a few seagulls wheeling around the masthead, keening in time to the rhythmic creak of lines running through wooden blocks.

Scourge, the ship's cat, had herself wrapped around the compass binnacle peacefully snoozing away in one of those impossible positions guaranteed to give any conscientious chiropractor nightmares or make contortionists the world over envious. Her front legs faced one way while her aft legs, being contorted 180 degrees, reposed in an entirely different direction. Her paws occasionally twitched, as in her dreams she subdued yet another vicious flying fish or perhaps stalked a giant yellow bag of cat biscuits through some dense pier-side jungle. You can never be certain with cats.

With the wind and waves coming from her stern quarter, *Vega* bowled along at an exhilarating pace. As each wave reached amidships, a torrent of blue water poured over the rail, bursting into brilliant white foam that sloshed around the deck before draining away through the relieving ports, just in time for the next watery deluge. The rigging whistled a merry tune, accompanied by the creak of blocks and the working of lines. The whole rhythmically changing pitch as the boat rolled to each new swell.

Cracking on at a consistent nine knots, our little ship raced along with a bone in her teeth, contented skipper at the helm, and only her basic working canvas on display. Their reddish-tan bark tint etched sharply against the deep blue of our surroundings. A random scattering of fleecy white clouds accented the stark cobalt-blue dome overhead. What a great day for sailing.

Earlier in my watch, dawn had transformed a sea of wrathful malice into a scene of majestic beauty, a stately progression of breathtaking waves mutating with the dawn from sinister hissing gray to the grandeur of a gloriously beautiful day on the open ocean. Try to imagine slight trepidation blended with unfettered awe, the whole so magnificent, so vast, that words become impotent, incapable of capturing such a powerful emotional essence that few will ever experience firsthand.

Above me an enormous sky, the deepest blue imaginable at its zenith, slowly, imperceptibly fading as it approaches the horizon. You hear about big skies, well, take my word for it, the concept has no real meaning until you witness a day like that. The Grand Canyon and Sahara Desert paled in comparison.

If only I could take you there, share the sights, the sounds, the motion, moments when *majestic, grandiose, stately*—all those high-sounding words—become dry, empty attempts to package what I witness firsthand. One thing for certain, when it comes to the ocean, no matter how big a plasma screen television you have, it will never rival the real thing, or even come close. The only times I experienced such awe-inspiring endless horizons were deep in the open desert, and at sea. Places where you realize how small you are, and how immense the rest of the world is.

Standing on the foredeck with the heave of the swell and tilt of the deck, the gliding rush of a well-found sailing ship thundering along on a welter of foam, never fails to start my blood to pumping faster. Those are the times when your senses become razor sharp, fleeting moments that last forever in your memory. Times when you really live.

Having the watch, I decided to pass my time catching up on my ropework. Touching up whippings and making a few new working lines are menial tasks for a sailor, but enjoyable all the same. I had the tools arrayed around where I sat. Electrical tape, waxed string, gas burner, small Swedish fid, and of course my seaman's knife, honed to a razor-sharp edge.

I was pulling tight the whipping on a working line when a flicker of light gray followed by a slight splash drew my attention. Looking that way, I saw a dolphin gracefully roll on the swell, then race toward our bow. As always,

I yelled down the hatch to say we had dolphins around. Everyone enjoys watching those highly intelligent creatures frolic around the boat.

Dolphins often play around the bow. But do you know why they do it? When I first learned this titbit of dolphin lore I was amazed and more than a little skeptical. Now, after years of close observation, I know it for a fact.

Next time a group of dolphins comes to play around your boat, watch them closely. Notice how they pass close to the bow, then swim off on a specific course. No matter which side of the hull they run down, they always, without fail, turn away on the same heading. Their objective is to tease your boat into chasing them in that direction.

The dolphins who do this are designated guards, whose job it is to protect the main pod, warn of approaching danger, kill sharks, and amuse passing sailors. If you look in the opposite direction to the one they want you to take, you will invariably find the main pod either happily feeding or traveling along in formation.

The way a dolphin sees it, they are imitating a tasty morsel passing close in front of a mouth full of danger at speeds that make them appear an easy catch. In reality, they are swimming ridiculously slow, for a dolphin that is. With a flick of the tail, they can accelerate to speeds few other ocean dwellers can match.

Think of it as the dolphin way of swimming up to the school bully to thumb its nose while blurting out a rude raspberry, then running like mad to avoid a swat. The fact they can most likely swim five times faster than your boat makes it even more fun. No wonder they always look so smug and happy when they play that game.

I was not the only member of our motley crew enjoying that lovely morning. Returning to my place at the helm, I discovered Scourge luxuriating in the early morning sun, adapting the gentle rolling motion to her esoteric feline requirements. As the boat rolled to port, she would roll with it, waving all four paws in the air until she landed with a flop on her other side, squirming to rub her back against the deck. Then as the boat rolled back to starboard, she repeated the exercise. Watching her playful antics, I remembered the first time I saw her. It was in Singapore, where we were doing some work on the boat. I was in the midst of a complicated long splice that day when Meggi came bouncing down the pier beaming from ear to ear. She looked happier than the mouse in a cheese factory. Quickly climbing on board, Meggi rushed up to me babbling, "Look what I found! Look what I found!"

Holding up her cupped hands, she spread them slightly. There between her palms I saw a small ball of fur highlighted by two tiny black eyes peering timidly up at me. It was a diminutive cat. Reaching out a single finger, I caressed the kitten's head and was rewarded by a lick from its miniature pink tongue.

Meggi had been out rummaging around the boatyard when she came upon the night watchman's shed. Inside, carefully arranged along one wall, she discovered seven sets of feline dinnerware. Each with its own water and food bowl. Clearly, the night guard spent a lot of time with his cat, who had recently brought off a litter of kittens. Meggi had gone back that afternoon to ask the guard if she could have one of his kittens for our boat. With his consent, she proceeded to choose one.

This little bundle of fur, with two tiny sparkling eyes and a bright pink nose, emerged the lucky winner. In the end, Meggi picked the smallest of the litter, rationalizing that the runt needed all the help it could get in life. The way I see it, if we were Chinese, we would have named her "One Lucky Cat" or "Lucky" for short. Then again, "Two Lucky Cat" might be a better play on words.

That cat now lives a life of luxury, with scratches on demand, autoreplenishing water and food bowls, and a self-cleaning litter box. In any case, that was the day we signed on another full-time member of *Vega*'s crew. I must admit, she takes her duties seriously. Scourge is always ready for a good scratching, to play or snuggle up beside whoever has the watch. She even caught a rat, once.

I finished the eye splice with a taper, then applied a Cornish whipping to the other end. Amazing how daydreaming makes a job go faster. Burning off the ends, I tossed the newly made working line onto the small pile growing at my feet. Remembering how the starboard main cap shroud deadeye needed a new lanyard, I selected a larger piece of line and began working a Mathew Walker knot into it.

Off our bow, the dull gray shadow of land slowly crept over the horizon. Resisting the impulse to yell, "Laaaaaaand Hooooo, Haarrrrrrd on the Starrrrrborrrd Boooow"—like I said, it was one of those days straight out of the golden age of sail—I went down and checked the chart; 90 percent certain I was seeing the mountains of East Timor. In the crisp, clean air, they looked so close, yet I knew it would be half a day or more before we arrived. With any luck, it would be anchors down in Dili harbor by sunset.

CHAPTER 31

A Successful Failure

Dr. Aida Gonzales briskly closed her lecture notes. In front of her sat six women who for the past few hours had diligently assimilated her every word as only people who depend on their memory rather than the written word can. She knew that years from now any one of those women would easily recall her lecture almost verbatim.

This was their final session, ending three intensive months of training during which these women had gone from being traditional rural birthing assistants to possessing all the skills and knowledge of clinically trained midwives. The change was nothing short of spectacular. It was also a moment Aida had dreamed of for years.

Leaving her notebook on the crudely made wooden lectern, Dr. Aida stepped out to mingle with her students. Her lecture hall was a small windowless room at the back of Dili's free Bario Pite Clinic, where her students sat on an odd assortment of cast-offs ranging from an old office swivel chair missing one wheel to bright pink plastic lawn chairs. One particular woman, whose expansive bottom seemed to swallow the birthing stool she perched on, caused Aida to smile. It was easy to imagine her standing up and taking the stool with her.

As usual, after class they gathered in the center of the room to discuss the day's topics, the most important being their impending graduation. Looking around the room, Aida felt proud of these women and what they would go on to accomplish for their remote villages. She had not felt such pride since the day she graduated medical school.

No one would ever reproach Dr. Aida for being tall, although some might effortlessly accuse her of being highly intelligent and attractive. Even her detractors admitted that what Aida lacked in centimeters she easily made up for in kilowatts of energy.

With her dark eyes framed by intensely black hair, Aida is a naturally cheerful person, yet woe to anyone who crosses her when she is in what her friends call "Doctor Mode," those highly intense moments when she is in perfect control or when, arms crossed and foot tapping, lips pursed to a pencil-thin line, her eyes flash like black diamonds, moments when the hospital staff and her smarter interns suddenly discover other places they urgently need to be.

Stepping out of her dimly lit little lecture room, she was greeted by bright tropical sunshine. Although swelling with pride in what she had accomplished, a depressing fact overshadowed her triumph. She had trained this first group of students well. Returning to their villages, they would be ready to save lives. Yet in one respect, she had seriously failed them.

The problem was not one of knowledge; it was equipment and supplies. Tomorrow she would be sending these dedicated women home to their villages full of knowledge but with empty hands. Without equipment and drugs to work with, they would be like factory-trained mechanics without tools or spare parts.

Failure was not a concept that Dr. Aida accepted easily, but throwing herself into the office chair, she knew that it was staring her in the face and laughing. One of her interns chose that moment to open the door, fully intent on asking a question about one of their patients. After a single look at Dr. Aida's scowling face, he quietly closed the door and beat a hasty retreat.

In the highly energetic Dr. Aida, we discovered a wealth of vital information and a dedicated partner to work with in East Timor. Aida was born in East Timor and speaks the local language fluently, an advantage that allows her to understand the rural Timorese mentality far better than any expatriate aid worker ever will. When we first met her, Aida was wrapping up the initial year of a well-thought-out program to train rural traditional midwives at the free Bario Pite Clinic in Dili.

The concept for her program came the day she noticed that rural women, being a very conservative lot, did not trust the few official midwives provided for their area by the government. They preferred to put their trust in the local traditional midwife, who had most likely delivered them into this world and perhaps their parents as well.

Her concept is simple and effective. The community chooses a woman they trust to be their midwife. Aida then trains that woman and sends her back to the community as a fully qualified midwife. The training aspect of her program worked perfectly. Even so, she still faced a major dilemma: where to find the supplies and equipment these newly trained midwives needed to properly do their job?

Training is important, but to be truly effective a midwife needs certain pieces of equipment and other medical supplies. Those supplies had to come from outside East Timor. Inside East Timor, shops offering proper midwife supplies are almost nonexistent, or prohibitively expensive.

While Dr. Aida explained her problem, Meggi and I looked at each other, quickly exchanging thoughts through those mysterious perceptual channels two people develop after twenty years of not strangling each other. With a small mental nod of the head, I knew we both agreed. Here was a woman we could and should help. In return, we would benefit from her extensive experience with isolated rural communities to design the midwife and health worker kits we were contemplating.

We long ago learned never to tell people living under conditions where you or I could not survive what they need. We ask what is required to realize a community's goals and objectives, then do our best to provide what's needed. You see, there are times when an inexpensive handful of fish hooks or a kilo of nails is worth more than gold.

Meggi and I are not out to build an empire or change the world. All we want to do, in our own small way, is help others in a manner that makes a meaningful contribution, by delivering training, tools, educational, and medical supplies directly into the hands of those who need them to make a difference.

With enthusiastic sparks of creativity flying every direction, a very exciting morning followed. By the end of that first meeting, we had made a new friend and outlined the contents of fully comprehensive midwife and health worker kits.

Promises for next year are great, but what Aida needed urgently were supplies to equip the midwives she was currently training. Fortunately, we had most of what was required for a few basic kits on board *Vega*. Those first kits were far from complete but enough to start with. As far as Aida was concerned, they appeared like manna from heaven.

As we talked and planned, Aida often became so animated I thought she might vibrate off her chair. Even though it would be a year before we could return with complete sets, and we could make no concrete promises, at least we had a target to aim for. To me, this new development represented more items to gather from our supporters—as if the lists we already had were not enough to effectively keep us off the streets and out of the bars.

I readily admit the thought of finding all the things needed for those kits seemed impossible. And, considering the other islands we assist, the numbers were truly daunting. We would need at least one-hundred-and-twenty-two complete midwife and health worker kits. Each of which required a wide selection of supplies, equipment, and ballistic nylon bag.

We were no longer looking for a few items at a time but hundreds, even thousands, of them. Stethoscopes, blood pressure cuffs, umbilical clamps, antibiotics, sutures, 125 waterproof bags, and 90,000 paracetamol tablets come to mind.

Since Meggi and I had already decided everything going into those kits had to be new and in date—if we were going to do this, we wanted to do it right—each kit easily represented several thousand dollars. How would we ever locate all those items and then find funding to purchase them? Fortunately, I underestimated the willingness of our supporters and our own ability to blatantly mooch, beg, and grovel for such a worthy cause.

I also forgot the huge disparity in cost between countries for exactly the same drug. For example, in the United States the average price of amoxicillin—a penicillin antibiotic used against a variety of bacterial infections—is seventeen dollars for twenty-one capsules. In Indonesia a seventeen-dollar donation from one of our supporters buys almost six times that amount. Same company. Same dosage. It's enough to have your favorite saint scratching his head or to make a Cyclops cross-eyed.

Creating those first kits was often frustrating enough to depress the Good Fairy. Well, you try spending an entire day in that gigantic snarl they call traffic in Jakarta, only to return home empty-handed, and see what that does for your outlook on life. Mind you, things we expected to be difficult often proved the easiest. Once we discovered a few tricks.

In Europe and North America professional stethoscopes sell for several hundred dollars each, and quality blood pressure cuffs are not far behind.

Multiply those numbers by over a hundred and they become frightening for a small "mom and pop" charity with microscopic budgets. The good news is both of the top brands are made in China. So a few hours digging on the internet rooted out the manufacturer, who offered the exact same stethoscope and blood pressure cuff, as a set, for a tenth of the price—with shipping included.

In Jakarta we met the owner of a pharmaceutical wholesale company who took us under his wing, offering what he had in stock at cost. When the money ran out, he donated important antibiotics and drugs to control postpartum bleeding from his own account. A thousand blessings on him and our other supporters who made it all possible. But, even so, when it came time to sail, many essential items remained outstanding and our pockets were so empty even the lint balls had grown bored and decamped.

I know from experience, Fate has a sick sense of humor, yet occasionally she can also be helpful. We were taking in our mooring lines to leave Jakarta when a young couple came trundling down the pier lugging a large, awkward box between them and calling on us to wait. They arrived at the boat red-faced, gasping, and panting. Swiping a shirt sleeve across his forehead the fellow said, "This is for you, but it only arrived this morning."

The contents of that box should have come in a brass-bound pirate-style treasure chest. With a grin that grew wider by the moment, I mentally ticked outstanding things off our list while Meggi squeaked and squealed with delight as she rummaged the contents. Two-hundred thermometers were only the beginning. After that, I almost forgave Fate for the two days of blustery wind and constant rain that followed.

Although we did our best, those first midwife and health worker kits were far from complete. Yet not only was Dr. Aida overjoyed, so were all the other midwives and village health workers we assist. Where we saw the missing items as another failure, they saw what we delivered as a major improvement in their ability to save lives.

The new and resupply/upgrade sets for our second year were much closer to being complete, and since the third year, we have been resupplying and upgrading 122 fully comprehensive kits, each to a standard none of us would have believed possible that sunny tropical morning when we first sat with Doctor Aida planning them out.

The effect those sets are having is what excites me the most. They have improved thousands of people's lives. In some areas we support, maternal and natal mortality rates have fallen by over 40 percent. Postpartum infections are now, mostly, a thing of the past. As Meggi often says, "We cannot save the world, but we can make a few small parts of it a little bit better."

CHAPTER 32

Matius Goes to School

Waving away the small swarm of flies with his broad-brimmed hat, Matius sat in the shade on a large flat rock and watched his ponies graze. He did not begrudge them those few moments of rest after such a long, hard climb, even though it might mean reaching his village after sundown. Matius loved those mountains. Their majestic natural beauty never failed to captivate him.

With an unconscious motion born from years of habit, Matius jammed the hat back in place, pulling its wide brim low over his eyes. Taking out the soft leather tobacco pouch his wife had made for him, he began rolling a cigarette. While his fingers moved more or less on autopilot, he gazed out over the valley. A few miles farther on, and roughly one thousand feet below where he sat, a little village nestled on the precipitous shoulder of this scenic valley. Squinting against the glare of the sun, he could just make out the red tiled roof of his house.

This is a harsh land, his father had often told him, but fertile enough for those willing to accept its caprices and work its rich soil. For half of every year the land lays desiccated, thirsting for rain that never comes, while the remainder of the year brings torrential rains. When the rains do come, that dry riverbed snaking along the valley floor becomes an impassable raging torrent, completely isolating his half of the valley from any contact with the outside world. Then the hills surrounding this dry brown landscape turn a luxurious green so deep and rich it almost glows. But for now, the air smelled of sun-baked dust. There would be no rain for months to come.

Shoving the newly rolled cigarette between his lips, he scratched a strike-anywhere match on the stone where he sat and lit up. He could still remember the first time his father brought him along this path, one of the few connecting his village to the outside world. Matius had been about ten years old. Just old enough to help lead their string of tough little mountain ponies from the village through this high pass to the town of Ermera, where an elderly Portuguese merchant purchased the coffee beans his family harvested.

Slowly exhaling a cloud of smoke, Matius studied his string of horses. His ponies might not be big, but they were sturdy creatures and sure-footed as mountain goats. He knew from long experience they could easily carry two fifty-kilo bags of coffee beans all day long without tiring.

Lali came over to where he sat, resting her soft muzzle on his shoulder. Her warm breath was like a velvety caress. Matius found her strong smell of horse both familiar and comforting. She had decided it was time for them to push on. Matius agreed. He had no wish to be on the trail after dark when the path would all but disappear and the temperature plummet. Slowly getting to his feet, he dusted himself off.

Matius picked up Lali's reins, then smoothly swung into the new saddle he had made during last year's rainy season. He was rather pleased with it. Adjusting his hat, he nudged Lali toward the trail, then whistled to the lead packhorse. In a few more hours, they would be home.

The old people claimed there were once roads through these mountains wide enough for carts, rather than narrow trails like the one he was following. According to them, on one occasion an automobile actually came to the village.

If they ever existed, those roads were long gone, most likely washed away by the torrential yearly rains. Everyone knew the only practical way to travel in these mountains is by horse or on foot. Of course, Matius also knew you had to be careful believing old people; they claimed just about everything was better back then. The way he saw it, of course everything is better when you are young. Almost anything would beat being old and worn out. Remembering what his grandfather had once said, Matius chuckled to himself. "The problem with old age is there is no future in it."

When Matius was young, there had been a school down in the valley with a real teacher. A pretty woman from Dili who patiently taught him to read, write, and do sums. These days, he grudging admitted those times spent scratching his head were well worth the effort. In his village, he was one of only three who had these skills. Thanks to his abilities, he was now considered a village elder. A man to be respected. Those same talents had also earned him the post of volunteer teacher at the new school.

Collecting his string of ponies, he urged Lila forward onto the well-worn path, a path she had walked many times before. Settling into his saddle, Matius felt proud as he looked to where the new school building stood. That small structure took the village three years to build, using local materials and volunteer labor. Even the tables and benches for the students to sit at were village made. The objective was simple, to provide their children with an education, or at least the start of one. An opportunity most villagers never had.

Lured by the dream of a brighter future for their children, they now had a school building. What they did not have were the things that only money could buy. Things like exercise books, pencils, pens, or even chalk for the blackboard.

The village was poor. Most families existed on less than one American dollar a day, so money to buy school supplies was hard to come by. Currently, Matius taught the children by repetition. Letters and numbers they learned outside on the playground, where his students would squat in small groups scratching in the dirt with sharp sticks. Matius knew that was not the best system for learning, but it was all he could think of.

He clearly remembered the first day they opened the new school. The whole village turned out dressed in their finest clothes for that long-awaited event. Oh, how they cheered to see their children entering "the school." It was a very special occasion, when every member of the community felt proud of what they had accomplished.

It did not take long for him to realize how challenging it was being the head master and only teacher for a school with thirty students ranging in age from seven to fourteen. Removing his hat, Matius swiped a shirt sleeve across his brow. As much as he wished not to admit it, in his heart Matius knew the school was failing. The village did all they could with their meager resources, and he always did his best, but it was simply not enough.

CHAPTER 33

A Change of Heart

I spent the greater part of my time in school either bored to distraction or plotting another escape. Mind you, I am sure my teachers were happiest when those plans succeeded. Looking back, I clearly see how the turbines of boredom powered my enforced scholastic servitude. There I sat, daydreaming, squirming, and scratching, as those mighty turbines hummed away in the background, *tidihum-drum-hum-drum.*

Personally, school was a form of purgatory, so it never ceases to amaze me how excited children in remote villages become about attending classes. Maybe something in all that fresh mountain air makes them a little strange. Whatever it is, they actually look forward to confinement in a stuffy classroom, repeating the same stuff over and over. I say repeating, because pencils, pens, and paper are hard to come by for most of those schools. Even chalk is a commodity employed with the greatest of care. The reason for that is poverty.

When you are supporting a large family on the equal of one U.S. dollar a day—or less—there is precious little left over to purchase school supplies for the youngsters, much less for the school. In most cases, it is all those families can do to feed themselves and keep the older children in what passes for clothes. Mind you, that clothing is often a hand-me-down collection of holes held together by wishful thinking.

Imagine a farming family so poor they lack the basic tools to work their farm, or even seeds for planting. Picture a school with one volunteer teacher and thirty students—no chalk, no pencils, no exercise books, and few if any textbooks. On the other hand, imagine a community health post that has no medication at all, not even aspirin or bandages.

These are places so poor midwives deliver babies by candlelight, equipped with only a sharp knife and a piece of coconut string. Every year hundreds, maybe even thousands, of children die from easily cured illnesses, while the number of women lost during childbirth is appalling. Even the smallest infection can be life threatening when there are no drugs available to treat it. The majority of villages do not have a first-aid kit, much less an official health post.

It may seem incredible to you, but for most of the people we assist, those are the sad realities of their existence. Even the most basic education is seen as a way to escape that grinding poverty, and in a way it is. When we give a child the tools to learn, we help provide them with a brighter future. Their little faces glow with happiness, and I wonder, will one of them grow up to change the world?

You may be asking yourself, what happened to make me forget all the torture and torment my teachers inflicted on me? The answer is simple. I saw the light and became a devout supporter of education for others. This sudden about-face did not stem from a latent streak of sadism on my part. It grew from an experience Meggi and I shared in East Timor several years ago while visiting a remote village high up in the mountains. It required several hours of arduous travel to reach the place; the return journey took even longer.

Dawn's first light painted the mountaintops with a golden-hued brush as the bluish mist of night began to lift, revealing a stark landscape of rugged lunar-like mountains raising above a carpet of thick tropical jungle. Stretching and yawning, I drained my morning mug of coffee to the dregs while running an eye over our little expedition. A group of youngsters lounged around the compound, laughing and joking with each other. Having arrived during the night, they would be the porters for our mission. Rubbing the final vestiges of sleep from my eyes, I could not help but envy their boundless energy.

This was not some televised adventure in a can, or even a wild dream; we were about to set out along a narrow, often precipitous track into the high mountain jungles. Our objective: the delivery of educational, medical, and farming supplies to a remote village accessible only by horse or on foot.

Clapping my hands to get everyone's attention, I gestured toward the mound of boxes and bags we would be transporting, and the adventure began. Amid laughter and good-natured banter, the children divided their cargo of school bags and other supplies into easily carried bundles. There was none of the surliness you would expect from modern city kids when faced with arduous physical effort, only happy young people cheerfully doing something to help improve their own future and the community.

The first stage of our journey followed a rural dirt road before veering off across an open field. Although not very wide, that well-used trail led toward an isolated stand of trees. There we discovered the beginning of another path branching off into the mountains, a trail that soon became more rugged as the real ascent began alongside a swift-flowing jungle river.

Gracefully balancing packages on their heads, the children formed a line snaking off along a footpath that was soon engulfed by verdant tropical jungle. The heavier boxes were carried suspended from bamboo shafts resting on the shoulders of stronger boys. They cushioned the load by wrapping each end in large dry teak tree leaves.

Our little caravan soon entered a tunnel of lush green foliage where, over the ages, vines and trees had grown together, surrounding the trail more effectively than any man-made fence. Making our way through the stark contrast provided by this wondrous landscape was hot work, the still air oppressive, almost claustrophobic, under that dense forest of interwoven greenery, yet the children never faltered.

Always pushing onward, they took turns inventing stanzas to a well-known song. Occasionally a literary gem emerged, and the others would chant it back with great gusto while laughing uproariously. To my astonishment, this uproar had not the slightest effect on the birds, who maintained a constant din of squawks and squeals. Some had melodious voices, while others reminded me of wooden cart axles in need of a proper greasing.

Dodging around massive boulders as big as buses or plunging through tunnels of dense jungle, at first I failed to notice the subtle aroma of flowers. Spotting a large clump of brightly colored blossoms, I stopped to give them a sniff. It was then I noticed that smell was everywhere, surrounding us not with the mildewing scent you would expect from a tropical rain forest but with the all-pervading fragrance of jungle blooms. It was not long before Meggi adorned her hair with a halo of exquisite tropical blossoms.

Meggi was in her glory, scurrying from one exotic flower to the next or excitedly poking and prodding any local wildlife that appeared along our path moving slower than her. When she discovered a stand of ferns inhabited by tiny tree frogs, none larger that the nail on your smallest finger, I thought we would never get her away. I think I spent half the day looking behind us to make sure she was still somewhere in sight. By the end of the morning, I am certain the local birds were all adding to their vocabulary or making space on their branches in expectation of some new type of parrot whose call was, "Lookatthis! Lookatthis!"

Every so often, without any rhyme or reason, our entire safari, for that is how I came to think of our little caravan, stopped. Then it was everyone into the river for a well-earned swim.

Cold from its rapid decent, the crystal-clear river formed picturesque waterfalls with deep pools at their base. These refreshing oases quickly filled with happy children all laughing, splashing, and chasing each other. It was as if the steep climb loaded with their precious cargo had not even begun to reduce their energy, although I did note several who started out carrying packages in their arms had now cleverly employed local vines to create ad hoc backpacks.

Those youngsters were full of life and the energy of youth. I wish I could have said the same for myself. A life at sea prepares you for many things, but mountain climbing is not one of them. By the time we reached those welcome rest stops, I was gasping and wheezing like a leaky steam engine and wondering how much further we had to climb.

What with frolicking in the cool water, then drying off in the sun on one of the large smooth boulders that are such a dominant feature of the landscape, each of those well-earned breaks lasted between fifteen and twenty minutes. Moments that cooled us off while washing away the sticky layer of dust mixed with perspiration accumulated along the trail. Those halts also made the grueling uphill grind easier to endure.

Overall, a three-and-a-half-hour expedition through the thick forests of East Timor, which by the way was only the walking time, stretched into a daylong journey that finally culminated at our destination just as the sun decided to put on an explosive display representing every hue of yellow through orange to vibrant deep red imaginable.

As if sunset were a cue from the director of nature's nocturnal orchestra, thousands of insects began chanting their symphony of the wild, an all-pervading riot of sound exotic to our ears. What I knew to be the insect version of, "I have a great big tonker," or "Come on baby how about it," in most cases sounded like the wildest combination of computer-generated *plings* and *bloings* imaginable.

One little insect, although it might have been a spider as big as your hand, broadcast a constant *blee-bloop, blee-bloop, blee-bloop* that sounded like a French police car with its siren going. Others successfully imitated every electronic alarm made by man. Absolute proof that nature is copying man in her latest evolutionary efforts.

I swear there was even a creature that sounded exactly like my mobile phone ringing. Those sounds were so pure they made computer-generated versions seem hollow, a barren parody of nature's perfection, which of course they are. Besides, most of the time when my phone rings it is either someone trying to sell me something I would never dream of buying or an SMS from the cell phone company offering another wonderful opportunity to part with my money.

Not to be outdone for ingenuity, one insect did a lovely job imitating a very loud water drop falling into a still pond, which is the only way I can describe the perfectly clear *plink, poling ki, plink* that rang out every few seconds. When you think about all the time and energy insects spend advertising their sexual prowess, it almost makes we humans appear reticent.

By the time we arrived at the village, I was gasping, panting, and ready for the knacker's yard, while the students who diligently lugged all those boxes and bags up the trail seemed as fresh as when we started out. Getting old is no fun at all, although it definitely beats the alternative.

Hobbling on aching legs to the first available stool, I plonked down with a sigh of relief heard all the way to the next village. A gibbous moon was on the rise, several dogs barked energetically, and somewhere a cat yowled as I began to slide into delectable exhausted oblivion. Of course, no sooner did I sit down than the welcoming reception began. Stumbling to my feet, I forced my face to smile and bravely shoved out a paw. The climb may have ended, but that day's activities were far from over.

While we industriously labored up the mountain, those devious folk had spent the day idly relaxing. They were well rested and ready to celebrate. All I could do, coherently, was ponder where the next uninhabited bed might be—that and pray for a handful of paracetamol.

Somehow, I survived the speeches, had my mitt mangled by half the village, and avoided falling face first into my pudding, although I do not remember Meggi dragging me off to bed. Without her, I would most likely have spent the night under a table somewhere.

CHAPTER 34

Transforming a Dream

Early the next morning, after a lifesaving cup of coffee, several paracetamol tablets, and a few delicious homemade buns, the volunteer teacher and several community notables proudly took us to visit their village school, a modest one-room building constructed from bamboo with a thatched roof and dirt floor. The village children diligently trailed along behind carrying the various boxes and bags of educational supplies. The entire community turned out to join our progression through the village. By the time we reached the schoolhouse, I doubt if even the village idiot was missing.

Having a school is something special for that village. Every family in the community donated labor and materials to make it possible. The school is equipped with handmade wooden tables and benches for the children and a plywood panel painted black for the chalkboard. Although most of us would not use the place for a goat shed, the community is justifiably proud of their accomplishment.

Inside, the classroom was dark and stuffy yet brightly illuminated by the exuberance of thirty happy children specially dressed in homemade school uniforms and fidgeting on their seats. I doubt any two of those skirts or shorts were the same shade of blue, and even though clean, the shirts were far from white. I did not see a single pencil, notebook, or piece of loose paper.

Senhor Matius, the volunteer teacher, took us to the front of his class to proudly show us "The Desk," a rickety wooden construction that resembled the kitchen table from an abandoned farmhouse. Under "The Desk" was a wooden box. Inside, he solemnly informed us, were the school's educational supplies.

I was not expecting much, but the contents were appalling. At first, I thought there was nothing there, other than an old piece of newspaper used for the lining. That was before Matius rummaged around and brought out a small stub of white chalk, two half pencils, and a dried-up ballpoint pen, which he proudly displayed before informing us the carefully folded news-paper provided practice at spotting letters and numbers from the alphabet. The sad part is Matius's school is not an exception. Little wonder he beamed from ear to ear when he saw the school supplies his students had diligently lugged up the mountain.

Here were people so poor that basic meals are a luxury, trying their best to provide an education for their children, gladly sacrificing what little they have so their kids might aspire to a better life. Mind you, having a strong family ethic helps. After all, if little Muggins grows up to be a doctor, the community wins better medical care and old grandpa will be looked after in style.

After Matius brought the students to attention and they sang a little song about ABCs and 123s, we brought in the boxes of school supplies. Pushing several tables together in front of the class provided a platform to exhibit the contents of each box as they emerged.

While Meggi unpacked the boxes, I carefully positioned each item as if on display in a shop window. Soon the tables were covered. Meanwhile, Matius, who could not restrain himself, was picking up things to ooh and aah over. I thought he was going to have an apoplexy when we started pull-ing out boxes of white chalk—that is, until several boxes of colored chalk appeared, sending him into fits of ecstasy. Once we revealed all the school supplies and shuffled our feet through the obligatory speeches, it was time for the Kits-4-Kids bags.

After lugging the Kits-4-Kids bags into the classroom, one by one we removed them from their protective plastic bags and stacked those backpacks on the floor by Matius's desk. When the children saw those lovely new backpacks, the room suddenly fell silent. Many of them had never seen a backpack before. None had even dreamed of ever owning one.

Selecting one at random, Matius opened it. Removing the contents, he explained each item to his students before laying it out on his desk. When he told his pupils that those bags were for them, his message took a moment to register. When it did, pandemonium broke out. It took several minutes for Matius to restore a semblance of order.

Starting at the back of the class, one at a time Matius called students up to the desk, where Meggi shook each by the hand, then carefully selected a suitable bag to hand over. Backpack in hand, the lucky youngster went outside where I had my shop set up.

Standing them up against a wall, I photographed four students at a time, each prominently holding their new backpack. Those pictures were so the kids who donated those bags could see exactly where their backpacks went. One little boy became so excited he widdled his pants, much to the delight of the others. The room rapidly filled with squeals and whoops of delight as small stuffed animals and other toys were discovered among the school supplies. Mind you, most of those children had never owned or even seen a real toy.

One boy hit the jackpot. Opening his bag, he discovered a full-size official FIFA football. Bubbling over with excitement, every boy in the room converged on him, dancing and waving their arms in the air. In their village, there were no real footballs. They played with a bundle of large leaves held together with vines or string. We intended that football for the school. In order not to leave it behind, Meggi had put it in the boy's bag and then forgotten it was there. At that point, we could not possibly take it back without breaking the lad's heart.

Having always taken a backpack for granted, I was surprised to see that most of the kids had no idea how to use one. The majority thought it was meant to be worn in front, where they could see it, rather than on their back. Once Meggi demonstrated how a backpack works, it was comical watching those who mastered the art industriously passing along that esoteric skill to their friends.

Memories can be funny things, yet I still cherish one from that day that stands out from the rest. In the back of the class was a young boy about ten years old. You could tell he was excited by the way he spent the whole time bouncing from foot to foot, waiting his turn. When the teacher finally did call his name, he ran to the front of the class.

As Meggi reached out to hand him a bag, he did not even slow down. Going full speed, he grabbed his backpack and ran out the door. Puffs of dust exploded from his bare feet as he accelerated across the schoolyard. The last we saw of him, the lad was legging it into the forest, the new school bag tightly clutched to his chest. If you ask me, that boy was not going to hang about, risking the chance we might ask him to give it back.

Once the final Kits-4-Kids bag found a proud new owner, Matius released the students. In a rush for the door, they noisily erupted into the open like a cheap takeaway curry. The boys raced away in the direction of the village football pitch, yelling and calling out to each other, while the girls gathered in small groups under the shade of a large tree. Squeals of delight hailed each newly discovered treasure. After the last student departed, Matius closed the door, latching it with a piece of string, then led Meggi and I to where the traditional village midwife lived. It was time to deliver a midwife kit.

Living at sea level on a small boat where there is little room for long walks, I was totally unprepared for a full day hiking up mountainsides. Do you remember those old horror films where stiff-legged zombies come lurching toward the camera? Well, I could have played that part to perfection when early the following morning we set off down the mountain. Every muscle in my body screamed in protest.

The Kits-4-Kids bags were an idea we toyed with for years until one day a friendly teacher asked what the kids at his academy could do to help children in the poor schools we visit. Somehow, Kits-4-Kids slipped into our conversation. What would he think of having each of his pupils provide a backpack stuffed with the basics a primary school student needs for their studies?

Like all good schemes, Kits-4-Kids is simplicity itself. In a flash, his eyes began to sparkle and I knew we had a new program. I could easily visualize kids who never had a pencil to call their own opening a new backpack full of pencils, pens, exercise books, ruler, protractor, and all the other things a kid needs for school. Mind you, the backpack alone would become a family treasure.

With a little polishing, Kits-4-Kids soon became a reality, the beauty being that the whole concept fits perfectly with our motto of "directly from the hand of someone who wants to help into the hand of someone who needs help in the form of the tools and supplies needed to do their job." However, this time it was being applied to schoolchildren.

A few months later, we returned to Singapore where a big surprise awaited us. Kits-4-Kids was a huge success that grew from several very simple concepts. Unwittingly, we distilled the entire aid concept into a simple "one on one" exercise. By stripping away all the big agencies and other peripheral paraphernalia, the entire exercise became a personal interaction between two kids. A practical, hands-on lesson in social responsibility with some interesting, often amusing, results.

From a child's point of view, they could interact directly with other kids, without intrusive intermediaries. The result was they stuffed their bags not only with the items on our list but also with dolls, stuffed animals, toys, hair clasps, and many other small things that children find important. Things adults would never think of.

To make the process more intimate, each child wrote a short note explaining who they are, where they live, and the like, which went into their Kits-4-Kids bag. Not to be outdone, some include a photograph of themselves. One even added a picture of his pet goldfish, which caused Meggi some consternation as she tried to explain the idea of a pet fish.

These heart-to-heart gifts add a highly valued personal touch for kids who spend their days in tattered T-shirts and ragged shorts that are often held together by wishful thinking. Life is hard where these bags go. Unenviable places, where even the most basic necessities are few.

When the day for loading arrived, over 350 primary students from the German European School in Singapore delivered their Kits-4-Kids bags to *Vega*. Their visit to the boat was our way of saying thank you. It was also an adventure for them and a chance to see how their Kits-4-Kids bags would be delivered. We wanted them to follow the entire process, from preparing their bags to handing them over to the kids who receive them.

Those visits were a huge success, with the final group helping me fight off a "pirate," who after a lot of "Har-har-haring" and cardboard sword fighting was pushed off the bowsprit and into the water. Seeing as how we had no plank to make him walk, that was the best we could do.

The pirate was our friend the chief engineer on a super yacht parked beside *Vega* who offered to dress up with a black patch over one eye—along with all the piratical accoutrements he could think of—then pretend to attack the boat. He and I would have a sword fight and he would fall off the bowsprit with lots of "Aggggghs" and "I'm been kilt maties." Since the idea sounded like lots of fun and a kid's dream come true, I agreed at once.

In the excitement, he and I both forgot one small detail. Why would a pirate bring one sword for himself and another for me? At the last minute, as he came stomping his way down the pier, I informed the kids we were under attack by that black dog of a pirate scoundrel Captain Parrot-finch. By bringing two swords, the wicked captain was invoking the infamous "pirate's challenge." We would fight to the end. The winner would take over the ship.

Well, the fight was soon on as he and I called each other scurvy dogs, with lots of *yo-ho-hos* and shiver me scuppers. All good authentic Hollywood pirate stuff, you see. But we had forgotten the kids. They didn't hesitate a second before quickly jumping right in and laughing as they tackled the poor guy from all sides so I could have a stab at him. Right blood-thirsty little band of imps they were.

One at a time primary school kids are not much to deal with for a fully grown man. But you try moving about with ten or so hanging on wherever they can find a grip and see what happens. Not only did he almost lose his pants—imagine six kids dangling on your belt—he also had the devil of a time getting to the bow. By then the kids were well and truly into the spirit of things. I even had a few traitorous little monsters hanging off me.

What with one thing and another, mostly me trying to sword fight with one hand while holding my pants up with the other, it took us a while to win through to the bowsprit. With all the *har-har-haring* and trying to shake off a load of kids, we must have made quite a sight. The girls were the worst, mind you. If you ask me, they watch too many Keira Knightley movies.

It took a while, but we made it out onto the bowsprit, where I could finally do him to his just reward with a cardboard-bending stab. Crying, "You've killed me matie," the pirate clutched his chest in typical Hollywoodian mortal agony and plummeted from the bowsprit into the water with an enormous splash.

The kids all jeered as he swam away shaking his fist, swearing he would be back with everyone from the dogcatcher to the pizza delivery boy. Meanwhile our lot were verbally giving as good as they got. Amazing how creatively insulting an innocent-looking seven-year-old can be—from a safe distance.

With the last backpacks safely stowed away, we had over four hundred Kits-4-Kids bags on board. Although Meggi was having fits finding places to put them for the voyage, we both recognized Kits-4-Kids as a wonderful idea that would make quite a few very poor children extremely happy.

CHAPTER 35

The Great Fuel Drama

"Scruples, what scruples?" I responded to Meggi's rather pointed question. "If we fail to find another 650 liters of fuel, it's going to be pretty tough between here and the Banda Islands. And if you think I'm sailing this boat into the anchorage at Nila, you're madder than a shop full of hatters."

You see, fuel is always one of our biggest worries, especially during deliveries. After all, what good is a boat fully loaded with the finest educational and medical supplies if we cannot get to the places where they are needed? Every year, I spend a lot of time scheming new and exciting ways to keep the fuel tanks topped up. Amazingly, some of those schemes actually work.

Arriving in Dili after a long slog against strong currents and the Southeast Monsoon, our fuel tanks resembled the Sahara Desert on a dry day. Our good friend Juan Carlos promptly chipped in two hundred liters, and thanks to other generous friends we amassed a total of four hundred liters over two weeks. Although sincerely appreciated, even with good wind, that was well short of what we needed for the next stage of our voyage.

Being close to the equator, we frequently experience long periods of calm. So, even though we prefer sailing, motoring is often our only option—that is, if we want to arrive before the next coronation but one. Good winds are a wished for, but seldom conceded, blessing. One I never count on. So, after closely inspecting the central bank account, which meant shifting through all our pockets, and a careful search behind the sofa cushions, revealed our sad financial state, I found myself called on for yet another devious scheme.

You know, the type of idea where a little light bulb goes *bling* and suddenly everything seems simple? Well, I needed one of those bright flashes, and soon. Otherwise, *Vega* might become a permanent fixture in Dili harbor, without much in the way of lights.

I envy those gifted individuals who easily invent solutions to sticky problems at the snap of their fingers. Me? I need to meditate on such quandaries, often at great length, while fervently hoping someone else will come up with a workable solution. I say workable, as some of the wild schemes what I euphemistically call a brain has come up with in the past would astound you.

There I was, diligently scratching various parts of my anatomy, distractedly watching the cat, with no doubt small puffs of steam emerging from my ears. Well, you try inventing an alternative to purchasing fuel and see how far you get. Mind you, watching the cat can be an inspiring pastime.

While most cats are famous for grace and agility, our ship's cat is a bit if a klutz. More than once, I have seen her leap at something and miss. It seems she cannot understand that when the boat moves, the place she is aiming for does also. It really is amusing to see her dive for the hatch entrance, then about halfway from launch to arrival the landing zone changes. And splat goes the cat—again. It never seems to hurt her, if you ignore the damage to her dignity. Which for a cat is an item of major importance. Her delicate manner of leaping in and out of portholes long ago earned her the sobriquet "Feather Foot."

Returning to my fuel conundrum, I shortly considered distilling the contents of her litter box. The result might be explosive enough, but the high acid content would undoubtedly eat away our fuel injectors in no time. So I quickly rejected that idea.

About then Joanne strolled by with a steaming bowel of instant noodles in her hand. In one of those blindly obvious flashes of inspiration, I found a solution. A stroke of genius that might not provide all the fuel we needed, but at least part of it.

I would have kissed that crazy Singaporean if it were not for her famous right hook and left jab. Those Singaporean girls can be tough under their innocent-looking exterior. It must be all that racing around the megamalls lugging heavy shopping bags that keeps them in trim.

Just before leaving Jakarta, a friend gave us nine cases of instant noodles. Shrimp flavored, if I remember correctly. Those noodles contain a whole alphabet soup of chemicals for flavoring and never a real shrimp in the whole factory, unless it snuck in among the contents of some worker's lunch pail. I think Jo was the only one who ever ate the things, more than once. The fact is, Indonesians dote on the stuff. In certain strata of society, instant noodles are considered posh.

With all the small Indonesian cargo boats in port, I should be able to trade a few boxes of noodles for jerry cans of fuel, considering the owners of those boats are notoriously tight-fisted creatures who make Scrooge look like a giddy philanthropist. That means the crew usually survive on rice and what fish they can catch over the side. For them, a few cases of instant noodles would be a treat fit for the holidays.

All I had to do is a row over to the first cargo boat and convince the crew to trade some of the owner's fuel for an upgrade on their dinner vouchers. Easy enough to do in Indonesia, where the average person tends to be rather practical and, I might add, casual about such things. That is, if you speak the language, which I do not.

Over the years, I have traveled through some remarkably out-of-the-way places. Settings where the local language is more akin to a throat disease than comprehensible communications. And, before you start doubting me, you try ordering lunch from a phrase book in Polish and see how far you get.

Those experiences taught me the value of hand gestures, facial expressions, and in general acting like the stereotypical foreign prat locals generally find amusing. Eventually they figure out what I want, if for no other reason than to avoid sore stomach muscles from laughing so hard.

Language or no language, if I wanted to trade noodles for fuel, I had best jump in the dinghy and get on with it. So, while visions of fuel pouring into our tanks danced in my head, I hopped in the dinghy and set out for the nearest cargo boat with a case of shrimp-flavored instant noodles proudly on display.

Three boats later, vibrating like an old jigsaw from enough coffee to float a barge, I stumbled on a sailor who spoke trader English. Bless the lad. He was exactly what I needed to get the deal going. Thirty minutes later, I had a practical solution.

Salvation came in the form of an old Indonesian cargo boat with a broken engine that was slowly rotting away in a corner of the port. Practically abandoned by the owner, the crew had not seen their salary in months, nor received any money for provisions. Reduced to begging from other ships, they were more than ready to trade the whole boat for anything they could eat, smoke, or drink.

I have seen it all over the world. A ship breaks down and the owners simply act as if it no longer exists, at least as far as salaries and provisions are concerned. The crew find themselves stranded without a coin to their name, scrounging along in a strange place, surviving as best they can on the generosity of seamen from other ships. In those cases, sailors take care of each other. After all, one day it might be you marooned on an empty belly and trying to survive.

The crew from that old boat were ecstatic at the thought of trading fuel for noodles. After all, it was not their fuel but it was their stomachs—and they were currently rather disgruntled with the owner.

We agreed I would bring our empty fuel cans, and some noodles of course, at about nine that evening when the local maritime police usually went out to eat and watch football on TV. They insisted I use a roundabout route, approaching from the side farthest away from the cop shop. Since the outboard motor might attract unwanted attention, I should row. None of that posed a problem.

Now you know how a moonless night in Dili found me slipping away from the side of *Vega* and quietly rowing a stealthy approach to that crippled cargo boat. The dinghy was loaded with several cases of instant noodles, half a bottle of cheap whiskey no one on *Vega* knew what to do with, and every empty diesel container we owned.

Gliding up alongside the broken ship, I whispered a call. The English-speaking sailor answered, having come along to ensure everything went according to plan. But first things first. So I passed up several boxes of noodles and the half-empty whiskey bottle. Treasures in hand, the entire crew beat a rapid retreat to the steering house, where they set about boiling water to create an instant noodle feast. All I could do for the next half hour was watch them gobble down those foul things and politely decline joining them.

Soon after downing the compulsory 440-volt coffee, without sugar, mind you, we finally got down to the business of filling fuel cans. I had thirteen of them in the dinghy. Well stuffed they could hold almost three hundred liters. The question was, how many would they fill in trade? I need not have worried.

It is amazing what a full belly, followed by a tot of whiskey and a post-prandial smoke, does for one's attitude. Knowing Indonesian sailors just love the things, I also brought along a carton of clove cigarettes someone gave us. That went over a treat. After such a fest, generosity seemed to be the order of the day. I just passed up jerry cans and they kept filling them. Half an hour later they lowered the last container of diesel into my dinghy. After promising to return the following night with even more goodies, I untied the painter and set out for home, grinning wider than Ali Babba after a good day chasing caravans.

CHAPTER 36

A Rocky Row Home

Ever notice how just when you think everything is progressing splendidly something always goes wrong? There I was, rowing away to propel myself, the dinghy, and about three hundred kilos of fuel through the water and, funny how you remember these things, softly singing the refrain from that old Beatles song "Yellow Submarine" to myself.

We all live, *stroke and glide*, in a yellow submarine, *stroke and glide*. I rowed over water as calm as a lake, content in the knowledge of another devious scheme well hatched, until suddenly the boat lurched to a stop, before slowly tilting to one side. My paddle powered fuel barge was hard aground.

In my distracted exuberance, I misjudged the reef passage. Of course, with so much inertia behind it, the dinghy slid well up onto the shallows, leaving half her bottom and the embarrassed expression on my face exposed. And, just to keep things interesting, the tide was rapidly falling. Ah yes, blessed and many are the wonders of a life on the salty main.

Surrounded by stygian darkness without a glimmer of moonlight to help, stepping out of a small boat onto a reef can be quite the adventure for an overly active imagination populated with everything from sea urchins to stonefish and stingrays. The water being too shallow for sharks was the only consolation in that equation.

Easing one foot over the side, I gingerly explored the bottom. My toes found firm sand, not the jagged coral I feared. Carefully studying the situation, I realized that with a bit of luck, accompanied by energetic cursing, grunting, and groaning, I might be able to shove the little monster into deep water again. Well, I always was an optimist.

At least that seemed like a noble scheme, until after several minutes of intense effort it dawned on me the dinghy is deeper aft than forward. That meant the more I tried to push it back the more the keel dug into the sand; imitating a very efficient anchor. I needed to pivot the boat around so its bow faced in the opposite direction.

I grunted. I groaned. I cursed profusely in several different languages. I even begged and pleaded with any gods currently infesting the neighborhood until at last, a dull crepitation trumpeted my failure to move the blasted thing a single centimeter. It was time for plan B. Remove some of the jerry cans, swing the boat around and then set it afloat again. Once back in its proper element, I could reload the dinghy and row home. I wound up taking out all but two jerry cans before finally getting the little brute turned around.

Then came the fun part. Salvaging my errant jerry cans. While I grunted, groaned and cursed the dinghy back into its natural environment, my cargo of diesel fuel decided to go sightseeing. Gathering it together again made herding cats look easy. Then of course, I still faced the multifarious pleasures of hauling it back into the boat.

Although easy to chuckle at in retrospect, I was not laughing at the time. Those moments stand out as glimpses of me splashing about chasing fuel cans and in general having a memorable time of it. Of course, some instances are more vividly etched in my memory than others. Things like the jerry can that floated well up on the reef, causing me major grief to retrieve.

The dinghy painter is a long one. It needs to be for tying off on *Vega*, trees on beaches, and the like. In this case, try as I would, the painter was always about thirty centimeters too short for me to reach that blasted fuel can.

With the current now happily running out to sea, if I released the painter our dinghy would quickly escape, leaving me to swim home. On the other hand, if I grounded it enough to recover the jerry can, I might not get it off again without taking the other fuel cans out. The bottom being sand, there was not even a piece of coral to tie the painter on while perpetrating the great jerry can rescue.

Picture me, dancing around on one foot, trying to reach the damn thing with my other foot, while bending over at the waist like some aquatic yoga practitioner to hold the dinghy painter at full stretch. Mind you, I did manage to get a toe on it—once. Gently cajoling it closer, until my foot slipped on the fuel soaked plastic. Helpless, I watched it wallowed away, coming to rest just out of reach.

As if that were not enough, I lost my balance, spun around, and landed with a splash. Believe me, I blessed that jerry can with so many foul insults it is a wonder the maritime cops didn't turn out to investigate the ruckus.

I have no idea how long I desperately tried everything I could think of, to no avail. In the end, I simply give up. Tacitly accepting the loss of twenty-two precious liters of fuel. Muscling the dinghy toward open water, I scrambled on board, banging my knee on an oarlock along the way.

Of course, after my hasty unloading and reloading, the fuel cans were stowed chaotically, leaving precious little space for me to perch, much less row. Then just to keep things interesting on my first stroke, the portside oar hit something floating in the water.

Of course, it was the errant diesel container peacefully adrift beside the boat, yet still just out of reach. Trust me. I rowed some impressive circles that night before finally hauling it on board. In the end, I was glad to have it back, but the thing left my rowing position all the worse for its presence.

The row back to *Vega* seemed to take forever. I like rowing, as long as I have room to shift the oars in long clean strokes. The kind that put your whole body into the effort. That's the perfect ticket to rowing for miles without risking a heart attack. The short choppy strokes I was getting that night would barely move an inflatable rubber duck across the bathtub, much less a loaded dinghy. Still, I beavered away, expending an enormous amount of effort for very little result.

I was ready for the knacker's by the time *Vega*'s welcome side appeared. At least I had three hundred liters of fuel to show for the night's effort. And people wonder why I look funny when they suggest life on *Vega* must be a wonderful time blissfully relaxing, cold drink in hand, as we sail the tropics on gentle breezes.

In case you're curious, I made another clandestine trading voyage the following night, successfully winning an additional three hundred liters of diesel in exchange for four more boxes of instant noodles, three cans of corned beef, two bottles of imitation chili sauce, and half a bottle of Captain Morgan rum. Granted, the rum was a major sacrifice, but we needed fuel more.

What we gained was not a surfeit of diesel. Nevertheless, with care and a favorable wind, we arrived safely in the Banda Islands. Mind you, on the final day of that voyage, I was chewing my nails, what with our fuel indicator pegged on zero and the wind turning sour.

CHAPTER 37

Of Charts and Counter Jumpers

Most of the stops along our route are so remote that the last proper ocean-ographic survey was back in the Dutch colonial days. So it comes as no surprise the charts we buy are nothing more than upgraded copies of originals from the mid-1800s. I had one chart where the latest printing date was 2012; it said, "Based on an original survey from 1824."

In those days, when ships sighted an unknown island, they sent a boat crew ashore with a sextant and clock to record its position. Some made unenthusiastic efforts to take soundings in places that might provide good anchorage. Even when an official survey vessel made the rounds, they often managed to avoid the smaller isles.

In most cases, ships stopping at one of those islands would simply heave to offshore and send in a boat to fetch someone with local knowledge of the reefs and water depths. Then, ease their way into whatever anchorage presented itself. We do that frequently in places like Nila where the reefs and channels are so convoluted they would have Guru Chunkachundra chewing his beard by the time we get our anchors down.

One trick that appears repeatedly in the older Admiralty Sailing Instructions is, "Hang an anchor to a depth of x fathoms under the bow and approach with care until the anchor touches, then release your cable until an appropriate scope is reached." A disclaimer inevitably follows, such as, "This anchorage is not safe in all sea conditions or rough weather and should only be used in favorable conditions."

We try to have the latest up-to-date paper and electronic charts on board, for what little good they do us. After all, having the latest charts is just good seamanship. Although modern electronics are very useful tools (as long as they work), the thing about paper charts is when the power fails they still work just fine. On the other hand, those charts are a major expense.

Imagine the cost of a single paper chart these days. A counter jumper at the chart shop looks you in the eye and with a perfectly straight face asks fifty dollars for a piece of paper the size of an old Jimmy Hendrix poster. And if you ask why government-produced charts—paid for with tax dollars, mind you—are so expensive, he just shrugs and goes back to reading Facebook messages on his iPad.

Oh, and did I mention they usually find some insidious way to add an exorbitant amount of tax to the already astronomical cost? Take out the ship's stamp and papers, then remind the jerk you have a right to buy stores and navigational materials tax free, and do you know what happens? They look at you funny and go back to uploading selfies on Instagram. Sure, you have the right, but most chart shops cannot be bothered. Huff, huff!

If you ask me, it all hinges on the fact commercial vessels are required by law to have up-to-date paper charts on board at all times. So, as with any mandatory monopoly, it became a rigged market.

The computerized charts are even worse. I should mention there are two types of electronic charts, the ones used by commercial vessels and those "For Pleasure Use Only." The second are for chart plotters on yachts. They come with fancy names like Gold or Max, and I trust them almost as far as I would a politician or a used car salesman. The real electronic charts have about ten times the detail, and price.

I once asked the cost for a set of commercial-grade electronic charts for Southeast Asia. Without batting an eye, the man quoted me almost two thousand dollars. Oh, and the program to run them was another two grand. The compendium of certified charts for the entire world comes on a single DVD. The program to run them resides on a single CD disk. Little wonder there is such a thriving black market in chart copies and the programs to run them.

Yet even the most accurate, up-to-date charts are often misleading. Especially in areas not frequented by commercial shipping. Those expensive sea charts often show islands miles from where they really are.

And the yacht-grade charts are even worse. One island was so far off that our electronic charts showed us nicely anchored on top of a volcano, doing a modern-day imitation of Noah's Ark. Our position was displayed within meters, on a different island two miles away. In one case, the island of Banda Neira, which happens to be the densely populated capital of the Banda archipelago, did not even appear.

In the old days, sailors had few illusions about how accurate their charts were. They knew the things were often missing minor details like whole continents, much less small islands and reefs. Positions shown could be off by miles. As a result, the old boys went through life keeping a sharp lookout and constantly fearing the worst.

If you ask me, those seaman-like habits are even more important today than they were back then. The number of people I meet, on boats loaded with fancy electronics, who have not the slightest idea how to navigate, is appalling. And if you ask them about reading a weather map, they look your way as if you just confessed to having a communicable social disease.

In practical terms, those discrepancies in charted position can be dangerous when trying to negotiate a narrow entrance between jagged coral reefs to reach an island only one and a half miles wide and two miles long. Some of those channels are only fifty meters wide. So with that in mind, you do the math and then calculate what my blood pressure and heart rate must be like by the time we get the anchors down and set. It's a wonder I haven't chewed all ten fingernails down to my elbows by now.

CHAPTER 38

Goat Tracks and Leaky Roofs

By now you must think most of our deliveries are to remote, often isolated, little islands. And many of them are. But we also spend a lot of time in East Timor. As the poorest country in Southeast Asia, East Timor has villages so remote that for half of every year they are *completely* isolated. Some have not seen an outside face in ages, which is perfectly understandable when you see the state of what they euphemistically call roads.

The rugged scenery is spectacular, and some of those pristine hidden valleys are enough to trigger anyone's log cabin fantasies. If you want a little slice of paradise, complete with private waterfall and mini lake, have a look in the mountains of East Timor. Where else in the world will you find a valley officially called Mondo Perdido? That means "Lost World," in case you're interested.

Each year, over a period of six to seven days, we visit small villages in Ermera District. The Bakhita Center kindly provides us with a base of operations, good food, transportation, and access to their extensive local knowledge. Being an established grassroots community project, they help ensure our supplies reach the poorest, most deserving places. Mind you, getting to those villages can be interesting.

Lete-Foho is a remote mountain-top community in East Timor that dates back to early Portuguese times, when the rich surrounding valleys were home to extensive plantations of coffee and other cash crops. These days the dilapidated buildings and run-down appearance make it difficult to imagine how those remote mountain vales ever provided enough to feed East Timor, with a healthy amount left over for export. Once a net exporter of agricultural products, East Timor must now import most of the food it needs—and pretty well everything else, for that matter.

After a long, nerve-racking—if not downright frightening—six-hour drive up into the mountains, arriving at Lete-Foho is like emerging from the jungle into civilization. The first thing you notice is a huge church overlooking the town. A basilica so big it borders on being a cathedral is made even more incongruous by the unique style of its steeple. Try to imagine a normal church spire, then replace the upper part with two huge—as in over twenty meters high—hands positioned in the classic palms together position for prayer. Those hands alone must have cost the town a year of beer money.

We arrived on market day, when people from all the outlying areas congregate to share the latest gossip, buy basic provisions, and sell what their farms produced since last market day. Wherever I looked, there was something new and exciting to see. The whole town square fills with portable market stalls tendering everything from solar panels to knitting needles. Women stroll around offering baskets full of farm produce that they carry balanced on their heads. Like the hamper of sweat potatoes Meggi purchased, after some serious haggling.

Those sweat potatoes, including the woven basket, cost her less than half what they would in Dili. Even so, the old woman she bought them from wore a wraparound grin as she wandered off into the crowd with Meggi's carefully counted dollar bills safely stashed in her bodice.

Since most farmers live quite far from town, they often arrive the day before in order to begin trading and socializing early the next morning. No one wants to miss a minute of this important community event.

Outside of the town, roads are almost nonexistent. Travel is by footpaths and trails. For the people living in those mountains, horses are still the most practical mode of transportation. Squat, shaggy beasts with intelligent-looking faces, those tough little ponies are extremely sure-footed and capable of maintaining a steady pace either uphill or down for days at a time. Their clear eyes mirror the stoic nature of their owners.

There are no fancy leather saddles here. The local saddles are hand made from bent tree branches wrapped with what appears to be a broad leaf, which once dried must be extremely robust. The brightly colored saddle blankets are hand woven, and the bridles are made from braded grass. On market days, special equestrian parking lots are set aside by driving stakes into the ground in a clear grassy area. Tethered to these stakes on long ropes made of woven grass, the horses are free to graze while their owners wander the market or imbibe vast quantities of locally distilled rotgut.

The farmers all wear a variation on the infamous American cowboy hat, almost like a gentleman's panama from the 1920s or 1930s, bent to resemble a Stetson. The uniform continues with the standard-issue blue jean overall, complete with bib and suspenders, worn over a checkered woolen shirt. A striking similarity between the high-mountain farmers of East Timor and those I saw as a small boy in the Blue Ridge Mountains of North Carolina. The same weather-worn nut-brown faces and wide callused hands. The only thing missing were black 1950s vintage pickup trucks loaded with vegetables, or tobacco more often than not.

After finding a shady place to sit and light up a smoke, I studied the market more carefully. Clearly, people were buying and selling, but I saw another level as well. Young men with their hats perched at a rakish angle paraded clockwise around the square, admiring girls dressed in their finest apparel who aimlessly strolled in the opposite direction, trying their best to act nonchalant. Obviously, what I saw was an ageless traditional dance. Looking around, I wondered how many older couples there that day had once done exactly the same thing, until their eyes met across a crowded market square.

Children, who inhabit a world of their own, raced around in small groups. Effortlessly dodging between market stalls and the legs of adults, squealing and laughing as they went.

As I watched an ad hoc football match began on an open space beside the square. Apparently the game consisted of five teams with two different sets of goals. And, I swear, some youngsters considered any one of those four goals ripe for attack. I also noted the ease with which players from one team would suddenly lose interest and switch to another side. Everyone seemed to be having fun, even the goalies, who frequently found themselves defending against two balls at the same time. Occasionally, for no apparent reason, one budding young football star would run around in circles waving his arms in the air while screaming unintelligible gibberish.

Having stretched our legs and admired the market, it was time for our deliveries to begin. Piling back into the Bakita Toyota Hilux, we headed for the local primary school, a place we had heard much about yet never visited.

Just a short distance from the church, our driver stopped beside a goat track that meandered off downhill at a precarious angle before disappearing behind several small buildings. After a lot of backing and filling, he headed down that path. The track pitched forward at such an angle we all pressed our hands against the seat in front or dashboard. Thirty meters farther along that dastardly rut was a sharp hairpin turn where the road once again plummeted at an angle steep enough to make mountain goats leery, then twisted abruptly to the left.

By the time we reached our destination, I was in the midst of a deeply moving religious experience, righteously petrified and with my knees knocking, while praising the fact I was still alive. That demonic track, some might cynically call a road, disgorged us in front of what appeared to be a series of half-abandoned colonial buildings. I soon discovered they make up the Pico Ramalau Primary School.

At a guess, after being constructed in the mid-1800s, no one had bothered to maintain those buildings in any meaningful manner for at least 150 years. The roof had long ago collapsed on the building they called the "Old School." It did not take much to envision Noah scratching his head and counting fingers during navigation classes there. That said, the grounds were spotlessly clean, with a carefully tended row of flowers in front of each classroom.

Lete-Foho primary school has five working classrooms for 138 students. Of those five schoolrooms, only two are even close to what most of us would consider suitable. The rest exist in various states of disrepair. Two working classrooms were so unbelievable none of us even noticed them until it was time to leave, when Meggi and I managed a brief peek inside. After a quick glance around, it was apparent why the teachers preferred not to show them.

The school had grown over the years into a row of disparate buildings starting with the Old School and ending with two woven-bamboo-walled huts, each sporting a thatched roof. Both of those traditional shelters stand about one and a half meters above ground level on thick wooden pilings. What we thought were farm buildings bordering on school property each contained neat rows of locally made desks and benches with a homemade chalkboard on one wall.

Beams of bright sunlight streamed in through holes in the corrugated tin roof belonging to the first building along from the Old School. Considering the duration and intensity of the rainy season, that started me wondering. What about the children who often walk for kilometers to reach the school when it rains. It then occurred to me that including a small, well-made rain slicker in every Kits-4-Kids bag might be a good idea. At least they schedule the long school holidays during the worst of the monsoon rains.

When we entered that building, I thought they were either showing us the school storeroom or a graveyard for ancient furniture rather than a working classroom. Piles of old desks occupied one corner and abandoned wooden beams lay along another wall. Shattered in several places, great gaping holes rendered the floor a blend of broken cement and dirt. What with the perforated roof, it was easy to visualize that classroom as a muddy bog during the Northeast Monsoon.

Behind an ancient desk adorned with scattered papers and several fresh flowers a teacher stood. Although she was taping the blackboard with a well-worn stick, there was nothing written on it. The reason for this soon became apparent. There was not a single stick of chalk in the entire school.

After a short tour of the other classrooms, diligently ignoring the two rustic constructions at the end of the row, we returned to the first building since it best portrayed the general condition of Pico Ramalau Primary School. There we requisitioned several tables and began laying out the supplies and teaching aids we had for them.

As the boxes were opened and supplies began to appear, I saw one teacher's mouth drop open shortly before both hands flew up to cover her mouth in that universal expression of shocked surprise apparently built into the female gene. In this case, bulging eyes and a little gasp of astonishment accompanied her gesture.

While I prepared a display of educational supplies in front of the building, Meggi busied herself with another project. Since oral hygiene is an important part of community health that is all too often overlooked in favor of more obvious medical needs, some years ago we began including oral hygiene teaching posters in the supply pack for every school and a new toothbrush in every Kits-4-Kids bag.

As Meggi showed teachers the various posters and printed materials concerning dental care and prepared her pile of Kits-4-Kids bags, teachers herded the children into a line in front of her. One by one, as the students approached, Meggi gave each of them a Kits-4-Kids backpack. Judging from the laughter and squeals of delight, there were some happy youngsters around where she had set up shop.

While Meggi passed out school bags, I busied myself arranging a cornucopia of carefully selected educational supplies and teaching aids, all specifically designed for primary schools. It did not take long before the teachers congregated around where I worked. Excitedly shuffling their feet like small children awaiting a free ice cream cone, they politely queued up to get their hands on the materials we brought.

Getting pictures of items arriving where the need is greatest is an important part of what we do. Those visual images are one way to share the experience of being there delivering the tools teachers or health workers so desperately need to do their job. Through our pictures, the people who donate those supplies clearly see exactly where and to whom their donation goes. The person who donates a case of red pencils can see those pencils displayed along with the teachers or students who receive them.

Once the photography was finished, the scrum began. Teachers jostled up to the tables, grabbing boxes of chalk and pencils or pens. It was all I could do to keep a straight face when the head teacher blew her whistle, like a football referee. Another long blast and briskly shouted instructions soon brought order. Like naughty children caught with their hands in the cookie jar, under the stern regard of the principal, recently confiscated items magically returned to the table.

As we were shaking hands and getting ready to leave, I decided to have a final look at the first classroom with its display of ancient furniture and rotting roof beams. Sticking my head in the door, I stopped. Sitting hunched over the desk in that empty schoolroom was the teacher. With a handful of fingers splayed across her brow and a full box of chalk in the other hand, she was crying. I doubt she even notice when I snapped a picture then silently withdrew.

With another wish list tucked away in Meggi's backpack and our mission to Lete-Foho successfully completed, it was time to leave. The road back to our base of operations was not going to improve or become shorter, and we wanted to arrive back at the Bakhita Center before dark. So, surrounded by happy waving children, our vehicle struggled up the hill. Grinding its way in four-wheel drive back onto a more civilized road. Someone heaved a sigh of relief when we arrived at the main track. It was me.

CHAPTER 39

Back to the Mountains

High in the mountains of East Timor, it gets chilly at night, especially if you're accustomed to life in the tropics, where it rarely becomes cool enough for more than shorts and a T-shirt. While we loaded Kits-4-Kids bags onto the back of an old Toyota Hilux, for the first time in years I was in a place so cold that each breath created a brief suggestion of dense fog in the early morning air.

That day our mission would take us to the subsistence-farming village of Lou-mo, a remote village we have been supporting for several years with school and medical supplies, the odd piece of farm equipment, and seeds.

The school at Lou-mo is typical of many we see along our route. The building was constructed using local materials and volunteer community labor, as were the wooden desks and benches. Mothers carefully hand sew the children's school uniforms, which are only worn on special occasions. They even find a piece of plywood somewhere that, once painted black, becomes the teacher's chalkboard. Volunteers from the village take time off from farming to act as teachers. Up until that point, the community educational system works pretty well, at least for the basics.

The village is ready and willing to provide the best they can for their children, but they have no money to spend on school supplies or teaching aids. Most of their economy depends on barter in one form or another. Cash is a rare commodity, usually reserved for such important things as farm inputs or tools.

Getting to Lou-mo is a bone-rattling all-day adventure. Most of it on some of the worst roads I have ever seen. Actually, I have seen worse tracks in both Africa and Afghanistan, but no one had the nerve to call them roads. Our four-wheel drive vehicle often slows to a crawl as the driver picks his way across or down the center of a river or up the side of a steep embankment. The village is located twelve kilometers from the Bakhita Center, but as our friend Eddie is fond of saying, we could get there faster and save a lot of fuel by walking.

After hours of rattling around inside that truck, I would happily have gotten out to walk. The problem is transporting Kits-4-Kids bags, one large school resupply kit, and various packets of seeds and tools. The back of Eddie's Hilux was packed with boxes and bags full of useful items on their way to a new home.

The same day we arrived at Bakhita, word went out to Lou-mo and the other villages that we would soon be delivering another load of supplies. So I was not astonished when we arrived at the top of a hill and found a full-blown reception committee lined up and waiting. Not surprising when you consider our visit is one of the biggest community events of the year, not only for the school but also the village in general. Since they heard our 4x4 grinding its way up the mountain long before we arrived, the welcoming committee had loads of time to position themselves in advance.

Once the Hilux rumbled to a stop, I stumbled out of the cab and into the center of a small riot. Laughing cheering children, several noisy chickens, a rather smelly goat, and every one of the local dignitaries were there, along with anyone else who could find an excuse to attend.

I was still staggering around trying to get my well-shaken wits back in order when that merry band of well-wishers descended on us in force.

Usually I do not mind the inanities, much. It's the mangling of my mitt that puts me off. Some of those farmers do not know their own strength. Little wonder politicians have such long, thin hands. And here I always thought it was from stretching their fingers to reach a few more pies.

While the local authorities diligently buttonholed me, the rest of our team began offloading Kits-4-Kids bags and the other things we brought. Once decanted from the Hilux, those supplies made an impressive pile.

We dealt with the village supplies first. Handing over bags of seeds, farm tools, and the like took us all of half an hour. Most of that due to the thank-you speeches and receiving a new wish list for next year's delivery.

Before we could hand over school supplies and Kits-4-Kids bags, there were more ceremonies to endure. We smiled through another speech from the mayor and the school song. At least I assume it was the school song. It could have been the latest top-forty hit in Tetun or even an ode to their favorite tree for all I know. Another speech from the teacher and a small handful of wildflowers for Meggi soon followed. Then some kid jumped up to recite a poem about how we should be made saints or some such gibberish. Mind you, those formalities are more important to the village's pride and dignity than they are to us.

When the formalities concluded, we went to work. First came the school. You would be amazed at all the things a school needs to function properly, everything from chalk to report cards and footballs. Over the years, we have pretty well standardized our school packs into those that use white board markers and those using chalk.

Oddly, that distinction tells us more than just how a teacher writes on the board. It also gives us a good idea of how well off that school is. Poor rural schools tend to use chalk, whereas the schools in larger communities, the ones with "official" teachers, tend to have whiteboards.

Once we opened each box and displayed its contents for everyone to see, we took a few photographs so that the people who donated those supplies could see where their donations went. That done, the teacher repacked it all and we moved on to the next box.

Mind you, every village dignitary with a viable excuse was hovering around, all wearing ear-to-ear grins like drunks loose at night in a distillery. School supplies are fine, but the real cheers, from both adults and kids alike, came when we brought out the sports equipment. Nothing seems to stir interest like a new regulation football, or a two-team set of T-shirts, shorts, and sports socks.

Badminton is a game that always failed miserably to enthrall me, yet those villages seem to love it. That and volleyball. Having a real net for either game is a major status symbol; having a net for both is tantamount to a town charter or seeing their village marked on the map.

All of that takes time. So it was well into lunch break before we could get down to the business of passing out Kits-4-Kids bags. A backpack stuffed with all a student needs for a year at school is a fortune beyond most of these children's wildest dreams. The backpack alone rapidly becomes a family treasure, often passed from one child to the next for years to come. To make a very rough comparison, just imagine someone giving you a new

17-inch MacBook Pro and you will have about 35 percent of the elation Kits-4-Kids bags bring children in one of those remote schools.

As we brought the Kits-4-Kids bags into their classroom, every child there was imagining what it would be like to own such a luxurious status symbol. The students were so thrilled they forgot about lunch. You could feel the excitement building. Wistful longing mixed with hopeful anticipation glistened in those bright young eyes.

When Meggi went to the front of the class and picked up the first backpack, a hush fell over the room, one that soon spread to those standing in the doorway and schoolyard. Every eye was on the bag in Meggi's hand. Every child in that room held their breath. Then the teacher called out the first student's name. A young girl sitting in the first row came forward to stand before Meggi. Her eyes were in constant motion between the bag in Meggi's hand and a pink Barbie bag still on the pile.

Through Eddie, Meggi explained to the students that these bags were from primary school students in Singapore, along with a lot of other stuff about friendship and the like. While they prattled on, I watched the children's faces, so I missed most of what she said. What I did see was Meggi put the backpack in her hand back on the pile and pick up the Barbie bag. When she took that bright-pink bag from the pile, the little girl, so excited she was shaking, almost had her eyes bulge out of her head.

When Meggi explained that each of the students was to receive a bag, pandemonium broke out, not only in the classroom but among adults in the schoolyard as well. All those well-behaved youngsters suddenly went wild. It was all the teacher could do to calm them down long enough for Meggi to pass out the bags.

Throughout this explosion of exuberance, the little girl's eyes never left that pink backpack. When at last some semblance of calm returned to the classroom, Meggi started passing out bags. The first was a tacky pink Barbie backpack that went to a little girl who accepted it reverently. Clutching the bag to her chest, she slowly returned to her seat. As she opened her new treasure and began to sort through its contents, her face wore a stunned joyful expression, mixed with disbelief.

It took half an hour to pass out all the bags and then take a picture of each student with their new backpack. From there we paid a visit to the village midwife-cum-nurse to resupply her midwife and health worker kits.

Between listening to the thanks of various village elders and drinking more coffee than was good for us, by the time we finally finished it was late afternoon. Mind you, they have the best coffee in the world up in those mountains. More about that later.

Piling into Eddie's Toyota, we headed back down the mountain to the Bakhita Center. In our wake, we left many very happy kids, a teacher well equipped for the next year, the midwife/nurse grinning inanely, and a few village projects that could now advance. When we set out, a band of children ran alongside the car for almost a kilometer. Yelling and teasing each other, they took turns coming alongside Meggi's window and calling out, "Thank you Mister, thank you Mister," before peeling off to let the next ones have a go.

Now, when people ask why we do it, I always remember the look on that little girl's face when Meggi handed her a tasteless pink Barbie backpack, or the tears in that Lete-Foho teacher's eyes over a simple box of chalk.

Considering my poor bottom was already battered and bruised when we arrived, the drive back from Lou-mo became pure torture. Going uphill you press back into the seat. Going down is a perpetual state of free fall. Add in the constant jolting from potholes or deep ruts and it's no fun at all. Arriving at the center an hour after sunset sore, hungry, and exhausted, I was almost ready to kiss the ground. Good thing we brought a lot of paracetamol tablets with us.

I keep telling Meggi we are getting too old for this stuff, but every year sees us out doing it again. Hopefully, one day they will improve the roads enough that I can stop arriving at those places feeling like my kidneys have turned to mush.

CHAPTER 40

The Wonders of Coffee

Meggi and I always purchase our yearly coffee supply from the women in Lou-mo village. And for good reason. You see, back before the Second World War, an eccentric Portuguese farmer set up shop on the high plateau above Lou-mo. He then brought in seedlings from somewhere in Ethiopia reputed to be the oldest unadulterated coffee strain in the world, then crossed those with some mysterious Arabica strain. The result was one of the finest coffees imaginable. His plantation was moderately successful, until the war began. When hostilities broke out, he packed up the family, took the first boat back to Portugal, and was never seen again. Over the years his plantation reverted to nature. These days, descendants from those original coffee plants grow wild all over the plateau.

Women and children from Lou-mo go up there at certain times of the year to harvest those plants. Unlike commercial coffee plantations, where beans are stripped from the plant whether green, red, or purple with bright yellow stripes, the women of Lou-mo pick only the ripe red ones, knowing they can return next week as more beans become ripe. Little wonder their coffee is so highly sought after.

Now's probably a good time to talk about just how important coffee is to Meggi and me. On board *Vega* we roast our own coffee, then hand grind it each morning in a seventy-five-year-old cast-iron Spong coffee mill. Meggi and I found that grinder many years ago in Durban, South Africa, and I still say it was one of the best investments we ever made.

We began that tradition after visiting a privately owned coffee farm in Tanzania. Over coffee—what else on a coffee plantation?—the owner explained the intricacies of storing, transporting, roasting, and grinding coffee. His expert enlightenment was an eye-opener. With lovely aromatic cups of coffee in hand, we learned coffee beans could safely be stored for years with only a slight loss in flavor. The trick is to keep them dry in well-ventilated bags.

His second revelation concerned the roasting process. Roasting is how all the hidden flavor is released from coffee. He explained that roasted beans would last quite some time, retaining most of their flavor. Yet, to get the finest aroma and savor, you needed to reroast the beans shortly before grinding them.

He happily rambled on, as experts with a captive audience do, about proteins and peptides and other pollyputdekettleon molecular gibberish he seemed to think important. After the first few minutes, Meggi and I sat there wearing glazed expressions and politely sipped our coffee. The upshot was that beans need a good reroasting within a day or so of use to bring out the best flavor.

Then he explained another key element in the preparation of great coffee. Grinding the beans. If the beans become too hot while grinding, you lose delicate volatile oils responsible for aroma and flavor. Taking us to the kitchen, he introduced a marvel in cast iron. The first wall-mounted, turn-the-crank Spong coffee grinder we had ever seen. That coffee mill, he explained, had been in his family for almost one hundred years and was still going strong. As you can well imagine, Meggi and I fell in love with it.

You may have seen small ornamental coffee grinders in specialty shops. Charming little things made in China, carefully designed to sit on a shelf in the kitchen looking pretty and doing nothing. When you attempt to use them, trying to grind enough coffee for a single cup can drive you nuts. That is, until about the fifth or sixth use, when they inevitably self-destruct. The Spong is about as far from those cheap imitations as chalk from cheese. In fact, Spong is what most of them try to imitate.

So now you know how we started grinding fresh coffee every morning. Over the years, we owned a plethora of coffee grinders, mostly electric. Then one fine day in Durbin two things happened that led us to our very own Spong coffee grinder.

The first incident was due to a fault in the motor of our latest coffee mill, a failure that soon had me casting about in a frantic effort to produce some semblance of ground coffee for our morning caffeine fix. In the end, I dismantled the little monster and mounted the top part of it on an electric drill.

Trust me, that scheme may have amused the neighbors but it did not work as planned. The drill turned too slowly for one thing. We also had the devil's own time keeping the grinder joined to the drill while holding the top on long enough to process a few beans—one of those jobs requiring three hands when you only have two on tap.

They say "desperation is the mother of invention," or should that be "desperation without coffee in the morning is a mother"? In any case, after a lot of effort we managed to produce a sad brown wash that vaguely resembled coffee. And so, suffering from a dismal lack of caffeine, that fateful day began.

Later that morning, Meggi and I set out to purchase some electrical parts and a new coffee grinder. As fate would have it, we happened to pass an antique shop.

Before going any further, it might help if I explain that for Meggi and me antique shops were, and still are, places we exploit as miniature museums without an entrance fee. Places where we can freely nick ideas and get to see how things were done in "the good old days."

Neither one of us had ever spent a penny in an antique shop and had no plan to change that economically healthy habit anytime soon. But that particular shop had a wall-mounted Spong turn-the-crank coffee grinder prominently displayed in the window. After a few moments of wistful dreaming, longing looks, and comments on exactly where in the galley it could be mounted, we wandered off to purchase our electrical parts.

I imagine things would have turned out quite differently had our return route not taken us past the same shop. Of course, we duly stopped before the window for another meditative bit of coffee-grinder reverie. If we had foreseen the fleecing we were in for, both of us would have scampered down the street so fast there would have been a vacuum clap where we had been standing.

You can say one thing for antique dealers. They are an astute lot. Not at all the type to let a potential sale slip through their ring-covered fingers. In an instant, out swished the owner under the pretense of polishing the shop window. More than likely, he was on the way to wipe away the palm and nose prints from our last visit.

The next thing Meggi and I knew, we were being ushered into the shop accompanied by the obligatory flapping of wrists and blatant patronization one expects in such places.

While the owner, now joined by his partner, busied himself with some useless task, I took a casual squint around the place. Funny how I remember reflecting that it was even odds the two of them had sold their hair dressing salon so they could retire to running this quaint little antique shop. Odds on, they lived in a cozy little apartment over the shop, had a poodle named Poopsie, and held a lifetime subscription to *Playgirl* magazine.

Meanwhile Meggi wandered around the place sniffing out interesting items, leaving fingerprints on the brass, poking into dusty corners, and in general doing her best to appear uninterested in coffee grinders.

Before the morning was out, that shop had transmutated into an Afghan bazar stall, complete with a serving of coffee ground in the old Spong grinder. The only things missing as we haggled and bargained were a rug to sit on, a water pipe, and a few camels braying in the background.

As the morning progressed, so did the vicissitudes in our negotiations. I distinctly remember the owner swearing that grinder had come from his sainted old grandmother, having belonged to her mother, who passed it on as a family heirloom on her wedding day. On another occasion, the owner swore his partner would murder him if he let such a valuable treasure slip away for so little money. Hearing that, the other one muttered, "Damn right I would."

When we eventually staggered out of the place, I had the Spong coffee grinder tucked under my arm and Meggi was lugging a kilo of espresso coffee beans she had somehow wrangled into the deal. I found it rather endearing how the owner's partner flounced out of the shop, with a wiggling of hips that should have dislocated several pelvic bones, to find that bag of beans. When he returned, I noticed the bag had a half-torn shop sticker on it. Looking more closely, I could just make out "Reduced for Clearance."

Standing in the doorway waving, the owner's partner seemed on the verge of tears—good actor that one was. The owner, following the age-old ritual, industriously called out that we had robbed the food out of his children's mouths. As if there was any danger of those two producing offspring.

Overall, it had been an interesting, albeit expensive, morning. On the other hand, we were the proud owners of an original Spong turn-the-crank wall-mounted coffee grinder. One of the best investments we ever made.

CHAPTER 41

On the Sea Again

An honor guard of friendly dolphins turned out to see us off as we sailed from Dili one sunny August morning. I should say we set out motoring since the sea was calm as a mirror with not a puff of wind in sight. But you must admit that "setting sail" sounds more romantic, especially with dolphins frolicking in the bow wave.

Considering that short stretch of sea can be quite unpleasant, I planned to avoid the strong west-porting current by hugging the coast, where a countercurrent is often found. My trick is to get out early and scurry as far and as fast as we can before the afternoon breeze starts up—dead against us. If we get far enough along before the wind picks up, I can bear off and sail close-hauled for Kisar, a small island about ninety-five miles east of Dili. Otherwise, once the wind sets in, life becomes very uncomfortable. Being tossed about like ping-pong balls in a washing machine while burning twice as much fuel as normal comes to mind.

The first few miles are always a slog against a current funneling around that headland topped by an enormous statue of Jesus surveying all and sundry. Farther along, the flow gradually loosens its iron grip until somewhere around

Tanjung Liaru, near the old colonial town of Baucau. It was off that scenic cape we had one of those adventures designed to remind you just how fickle the ocean can be. It also gave our bunks, and the cat, a right proper soaking.

The sea is always a bit choppy rounding Tanjung Liaru, where the counterstream running close inshore meets the main current coming from the opposite direction. Of course, the wind usually huffs and puffs at exactly the wrong angle, just to keep things interesting. When that happens, the waves form pyramid-shaped oddities that have the boat dancing up and down, rather than rolling from side to side. Not at all a comfortable experience for us, or for *Vega*.

That cape is always tricky to get around. On the one hand, we must stay close in shore to take advantage of the countercurrent. It's either that or go out and fight the main stream, where more than once I have poured on enough throttle to make six knots and barely gained any headway at all. At the rate our engine guzzles fuel, in times like that even a saint might take up the art of cursing—in several different languages. Nasty place really. One I would gladly avoid if there were an alternative.

It was just another sunny afternoon rounding some bothersome cape until out of nowhere a rogue wave emerged. Growing vertically at an alarming rate, it came roaring straight toward *Vega* like the *Orient Express* on steroids.

With Meggi and Jo on the foredeck preparing to set the fore staysail, I barely had time to turn hard into the wave and scream, "Giant wave, hold fast!" Of course, being female, both of them started asking why, where, what color, and all sorts of irrelevant questions.

By then, I was gawking at a five-meter vertical wall of raging water. And I swear that furious piece of tortured sea was growing in direct proportion to my heart rate and blood pressure. With a thundering roar of foaming sea, the wave slammed into us. *Vega* staggered, then rolled hard onto her starboard side, shedding tons of water from her relieving ports. Water gushed through the skylights and in through every open porthole. With a few indignant bobs and rolls *Vega* brought herself upright again. On the foredeck, Meggi and Jo were unceremoniously dumped squealing and squeaking into the lee scuppers.

Our cat was not so lucky. A cool breeze funneled onto the salon sofa where Scourge was peacefully sleeping under the main skylight, most likely dreaming of a bowl filled with fresh tuna or another flying fish buffet. When the wave hit, half a ton of seawater surged in through the open skylight. The poor cat went ballistic. She must have bounced off every vertical surface in the salon before coming to rest on top of the galley cupboards.

There we were, the skipper looking amazed not to be standing in a puddle that had nothing to do with seawater, two soggy girls on the foredeck, and a well-drenched cat. Lucky for us, there was only one rogue wave out searching for sadistic amusement that day. But one was more than enough. That single wave managed to produce havoc down below.

A ton or more of ocean had poured in through every opening, creating a sodden mess that would take us days to sort out. And, as Sod's law would have it, the only bunk to take a direct dousing belonged to Meggi and me. One of the few disadvantages of having our bunk right under the aft skylight.

For the first few minutes, it was all hands to their panic stations. I switched on the manually operated electric bilge pumps, then looked over the side to ensure the automatic pumps and engine-driven pump were going full bore. Water gushed from both sides at an encouraging rate while *Vega* continued along her route on autopilot as if nothing had happened.

Seeing Scourge in the hatchway doing her drowned rat imitation and howling pathetically, I decided to light up a smoke before diving into the mess below. Meggi came to sit beside me. Since her hands were still wet, I lit a cigarette for her. After sending a cloud of smoke skyward she looked my way and said, "Well, we haven't done that before." After twenty years at sea together, that woman still never ceases to amaze me.

So now you know why we have so many bilge pumps. That and the fact I was once sailing alone on an old boat that sprung a leak in the middle of the Atlantic Ocean. I pumped two tons of water twice a day by hand for almost a month. Try that sometime and I guarantee you too will equip your next boat with every pump you can find.

In the aft cabin, our poor bunk looking more like a swimming pool than a proper bed. The only things missing were goldfish and a bright-yellow rubber ducky. How Meggi managed to get it more or less dry and useable again is still a mystery I rate somewhere between the pyramids and calculus. Yet somehow she did it. Bless her heart.

Fortunately, as a precaution against just such an event, we had our precious cargo of medical and educational supplies inside water-resistant ballistic nylon bags wrapped in copious layers of cling wrap. One thing owning an old wooden boat teaches you is that no matter how hard you try to seal things, outside water will always find a way to become inside water. Assume there are deck leaks and protect everything accordingly is my motto.

CHAPTER 42

The Birth of a Dugout Canoe

Hardly a ripple stirred the placid turquoise water as I strolled along a white sandy beach toward where several men were creating a new dugout canoe. Their axes and adzes rose and fell, creating a melodious rhythm in the key of *thunk*. Their lithe, muscular bodies, clad only in typical island sarongs and improvised turbans, glistened in the early morning sun. Finding a shady palm log bench, I settled in to watch them work.

Seeing locally made canoes pulled up on the beach or afloat in their natural element gives no hint of the huge expenditure of resources and labor that goes into creating one. Yet, for a community dependent on fishing for its main dietary staple, those boats represent more than just wealth. They are important tools for the community's survival. Being naturally curious, I decided to find out what goes into making one. This is what I discovered.

The process starts with chopping down a tree, often so massive two men cannot reach around its trunk. Most of the work is done by the future owner and his family under the direction of a master canoe builder. He in turn relies on generations of knowledge and the experience handed down within his family for centuries.

When the tree is down, a carefully selected piece is removed from the middle. This cutting and segmenting, using only hand axes and a few basic woodworking tools, often requires weeks of intense labor.

When the chosen section is cut out, it is then split in half. But first one end of the log must be squared off. Once that is done, great care and much deliberation goes into selecting the best position for driving in wooden wedges to divide the trunk along its entire length. At this point there is no guarantee the newly cut wood will not suddenly fracture in a way that renders it useless.

Over the following months, the new canoe is laboriously hollowed out with hand adzes, while the outside is carefully shaped with axes. Such work cannot be hurried or the wood will dry out too fast and crack.

After each working day, the new canoe is covered with leaves and branches to shade it from the sun, then left for another week or so to continue drying. The length of time allowed for drying and when to continue work is an important part of the master canoe builder's traditional knowledge. Allowing the wood to dry without splitting is one reason the process moves at such an unhurried pace.

When the rough tree trunk has been fashioned into its basic canoe-like form, the work of transporting it, often as much as a mile or more, from the forest to a place where it can be more easily worked on begins. How the islanders haul that huge mass of wood, using levers, wooden rollers, and rope, would have Rube Goldberg gawking in disbelief.

The journey begins by manhandling the roughly formed log through the bush to a route that leads to the coast. Those tracks are often so narrow that a big canoe is wider than the trail. By itself, that first portion of the journey frequently requires days of backbreaking labor just to reach the path.

Once the nascent canoe has been moved onto the trail, all effort focuses on coercing it over the various humps and bumps and around the many sharp turns until it finally reaches where the master canoe builder has chosen to finish it. Each of those obstructions poses a different set of problems to be carefully overcome. Often, negotiating a particularly difficult obstacle requires days of strenuous effort.

Now you see why fashioning a new canoe can easily take more than a year and employ a large percentage of the island population at various stages. Little wonder launching a new boat is cause for feasting. Mind you, just about anything is justification for a celebration when the most exciting thing to happen for ages was the giant fish uncle Abdul caught last year. So the fact there are three traditional rituals performed during the birth of a canoe should come as no surprise. Each of those services engenders a celebration where copious quantities of food and *sopi* are consumed.

The first, thanking the forest for giving them materials to make a canoe, happens when a tree is cut down and the chosen section removed. The second, most likely thanking any gods patrolling the neighborhood that no one dropped it on their toes, takes place when the roughly shaped canoe is safely transported to the village for finishing. The final ceremony occurs when the new canoe is launched, tested, and approved by all and sundry. Singing, dancing, and massive hangovers aside, those rituals are taken quite seriously since everyone wants the new canoe to be a lucky one.

CHAPTER 43

The Island of Teun

The small island of Teun can be located on most detail charts of Eastern Indonesia twenty-five miles to the east-northeast of Damar Island. Just look for a small ink blotch. If you are lucky, there may even be a name beside it. Like all of these minute islands, Teun is the tip of a semiactive volcano.

On the map, Teun looks to be an almost perfect circle roughly two and a quarter miles in diameter. Its single volcanic crater reaches skyward to a little over two hundred meters above sea level. Teun is an island where water depths go from several hundred to only two or three meters in a boat length. For a vessel like *Vega*, anchoring there in anything other than perfect weather conditions is impossible. The people on this tiny island survive by fishing and what little they can grow in their gardens.

Vega supports Teun mainly with educational and medical supplies, although we also provide vegetable seeds, fishing equipment, basic farming tools, and a host of other useful items that are important for the well-being of a small community. Considering the average sea conditions during the Southeast Monsoon, getting those supplies ashore is usually a challenge.

Arriving off the northwestern coast in the early morning, we heave to in the lee of the island, then announce our arrival by blowing *Vega*'s antique 1940s bronze electric horn. This allows those who are away from the village time to get back before the excitement begins. That done, we launch the dinghy and begin filling it with supplies. Once the dinghy is loaded, one team takes it ashore while I stay aboard slowly steering *Vega* in big circles, taking care to remain well offshore, away from the dense coral reefs surrounding the island.

We select these teams by the ancient tried-and-true system of drawing straws. Being skipper, I am always stuck with holding the straws and staying on board to drive the boat, along with one other poor soul tasked to remain with me in case of an emergency. The rest happily rummage around for their cameras and the like, excited at the prospect of visiting an island where *Vega* is well known, one of the very few boats to stop there during the course of a year.

The landing place is a very slight indentation with about a hundred meters of white sandy beach surrounded by coconut palms. Located just behind the beach is the village of Mesa. Mesa is not the largest village on the island; that would be Layoni, located more to the south on the island's western side. That village even has a modest bay, almost large enough for *Vega*. Were the bay at Layoni not open to the predominately southeastern swell at the time of year when we visit, it would make a perfect anchorage.

Little happens around the island the whole population does not soon know about. With the arrival of a boat, especially *Vega*, half the village turns out to line the beach and help haul our dinghy, supplies and all, to a safe place high and dry. By that time, island drums have the other half of the population moving rapidly toward the beach. In the excitement of the moment, people quickly forget whatever work they have in hand. After all, the work will still be there tomorrow, but the boat will not.

The island telegraph is not something particular to Teun. We have also seen it in use on the islands of Nila and Lesluru. The system is quite basic yet very effective on a small island where everyone knows everyone else.

Short lengths of large-diameter bamboo, with an opening cut down one side, are scattered around the island at strategic points. These bamboo jungle drums hang vertically from convenient trees on a piece of plaited coconut string. Usually, a sturdy piece of wood also hangs beside each "drum" to beat it with.

Every person on the island has a rhythmic *tap-tap* that is his or her address, so if you want to get Pak Jop's attention, you would go to one of these hanging drums and bang out his address a few times or until someone answers. Then you thump out your own code and message. That much I could understand, but when it came to the actual message part I was lost, although my friend assured me that everyone on the island understood the system and it worked just fine for most needs.

Once on shore, our team is greeted by a small mob of happy villagers. While children, carried away with the excitement of the moment, race around screaming and laughing, the village elders insist on feeding us. That of course kicks off an endless stream of herbal teas, fresh coconuts opened for the milk, and various incarnations of banana fritters. Somehow, during all this ceremonial greeting, our hardworking shore team must unload the dinghy and display the latest delivery of supplies. As you can imagine, they have a rough time of it.

Meanwhile somewhere off the coast, *Vega* drifts around, aimlessly wallowing in the swells while those on board heartily wish the shore team would spread a little more canvas. Drifting around on a big open ocean might seem an easy enough task. Most people believe all I need do is take the engine out of gear and grab a book, while the shore party gets on with the work.

The reality is not so simple or comfortable. When you cut power on a boat, it will always drift around until it comes beam on to the wind and seas. With the swell coming on only one side, the boat starts to roll, and roll, and roll. The only solution is to apply a little power and steer in a large circle so that the waves only come at the side for a fraction of each orbit.

While the crew wallow around in the swell, getting greener by the minute, on shore a delighted teacher gets educational supplies and the island's health worker and midwife receive their resupply kits. Of course, there are always a few tools, seeds, and other special items requested the previous year. With those items delivered, the shore party must also gather a new list for next year.

These deliveries take time. It would be impolite, even rude, to rush the welcoming ceremony—complete with herbal tea and a speech or two. By the time that winds down, most of the villagers have arrived on the scene and claimed a patch of sand to perch on. With the whole village in attendance, the show begins.

Mind you, for the islanders *Vega*'s arrival is an annual highlight or at least a major diversion from their daily routine. As we open each large plastic box of items, the contents go on display for villagers to duly ooh and aah over. We then photograph the items alongside their proud new owners, before stuffing them back in the watertight plastic transportation box to make room for the next part of our load. Those large waterproof plastic boxes are so highly valued we could bring them empty and still get a cheer out of the village. In the case of reading glasses, we test each person to find the right strength for them.

All of this takes place on a flat platform covered with woven palm leaf mats. That podium serves as the island health post, school, and community center. The meetinghouse consists of a bamboo stage roughly five meters by six meters with no sidewalls. Suspended between several strong wooden poles, the floor is about one meter above ground level. Made from thatched palm leaves, the roof slopes at a steep angle. Usually, the village elders sit in state on the platform during meetings, while everyone else selects an available piece of sand to roost on.

The surroundings are what you might call tropical idyllic, with palm trees swaying in a gentle breeze and white sand underfoot. Of course, there are no real roads, only sandy paths between widely dispersed houses. They also lack electricity, cell phone coverage, or any other signs of modernity. With few exceptions, the people on these small islands still live exactly the way their great-great-grandparents did.

Each house consists of a raised bamboo platform with woven split-bamboo sidewalls and a steeply inclined roof. Constructed from a combination of woven bamboo and palm thatch, the houses are held together by coconut fiber twine and wooden pegs. Most families have a fence of bamboo poles enclosing their kitchen garden and yard. A stairway consisting of several steps ingeniously fashioned from bamboo leads to a veranda running across the front of the house.

The islanders are wizards when it comes to making complicated things from bamboo. In their deft hands, that stuff becomes anything from houses and water pipes to clothing and musical instruments. One of my favorite traditional musical instruments is a type of trombone consisting of one hollow piece of bamboo that the player blows into much like a trumpet and second, larger-diameter piece that the player slides up and down over the first one to vary the tone.

The entire village is spotlessly clean, with not a single piece of litter to be seen anywhere. Mind you, not having any shops selling junk food or single-portion laundry soap helps a lot. At least the primary source of most current rubbish is absent right from the beginning.

Little wonder we always try to reach Teun early in the morning. By doing so, there is a good chance of the shore team finishing by sundown. Mind you, the place is lovely and the people are ever so friendly. If they had a decent anchorage, we would happily spend a week or more there.

For the crew who stay on board *Vega*, this interval is extremely uncomfortable and boring. Constantly hand steering a large circle makes it impossible to relax and read a book, nor is it possible to leave the steering unattended for more than a minute or two—at best.

With such a small island, even at our slowest speed it only takes about forty-five minutes to emerge from the protected lee of the land into the wind and swell from the open ocean. Being beam on to those seas is not an experience recommended for those with weak stomachs. So, slightly green around the gills, back and forth we go. Taking one- or two-hour shifts, bored to distraction and wishing we could get back to our normal deep-sea routine and a more relaxed workload.

Usually somewhere around sunset, there is an intense burst of activity onshore. Soon after, the dinghy makes its way out between waves, heading back to *Vega*. If you ask me, that lot onshore spent the whole day browsing up their jibs on local delicacies and that highly disreputable local drink called *sopi*, while we honest sailorly types were stuck offshore going in circles. With such a heavy roll on, even making a sandwich means chasing the bread all over our galley counter.

Once the crew is back on board and our dinghy hoisted on the stern davits—and believe me in a rolling sea lifting that dinghy is not a task for the fainthearted—we set sail for the next stop along our route.

CHAPTER 44

The Fine Art of Naviguessing

Over the years, I have watched the ancient art of seamanship slowly follow the dodo bird. Where once sailors were proud of "doing it in a seaman-like manner," these days they pride themselves on having the newest, shiniest, or latest electronic contraptions. Boat gadgets have become like kitchen accessories. It wouldn't surprise me to turn on late-night television some day and hear, "It slices, it splices, and it even tells you where you are. All you need to sail the world for a mere $29.95. Be the envy of your friends. Order yours now by calling. . . ."

People are always asking if I ever get lost at sea. An understandable question, considering we often spend weeks out of sight of land. The truth is, I always know precisely where I am. Mind you, occasionally the rest of the world misplaces itself in a most disconcerting manner. But I always know within centimeters where I am.

The problems occur when I must relate my current position to one on a chart. Once I plot that position, theory says, it will tell me exactly where the land got off to while I was out at sea. You would be amazed how fast a well-known island can drift around if you don't keep an eye on it. I'm surprised it took all those brilliant scientists this long to discover continental drift when any illiterate seaman could have told them about it ages ago.

Navigation is the fine art of knowing not only exactly where you are but also where you are not. Knowing that is often more important than most people imagine. Then there are the metapositions of where you have been, want to be, or wish you were. Hence, the age-old accolade of "naviguesser." An honorific—more or less—traditionally applied to the poor sucker charged with knowing where land is in relation to the ship, and hopefully how to get there.

Over the centuries, various academics attempted to make the art of naviguessing into a science. Since the vast majority got seasick in a rocking chair, their efforts were most likely intended to create another chair at the university they infested or get them on the cover of sensationalist magazines to impress the girls.

Truth be known, navigation is still an art largely reliant on the old MK-1 eyeball and a hefty dose of practical common sense. Maybe the latter is why modern yachties have trouble understanding it, common sense being one of those things that comes without an instruction manual, complete with thirty-two pages of legal disclaimers and safety warnings, important notices, like *Warning: running hard aground at full speed can be hazardous to your wealth.*

Sure, there are scientific underpinnings for navigation that every sailor should be fluent in, and they help a lot. But those rules and techniques are more in the nature of guidelines, designed to be employed with great caution and more than a few judicious grains of salt.

Remember, you need the technical bits down pat, but you must also know how and when to employ those techniques. It also helps to be a bit paranoid. But is it still paranoia if the sea really is out to get you? What with some of the places we go and the navigation equipment I have to work with, it is a miracle I have any fingernails left to chew.

Recently, the proud owner of a factory-fresh condomaran showed me all his electronic toys. I must admit that in his zeal the man left little behind at his local electronics shop. I wouldn't be surprised to learn the chandlery owner retired to Tahiti the very day that check cleared. Talk about bells and whistles, the guy had it all. He even had computer games to stave off boredom.

There were two of just about everything imaginable, from big plotters to radars. He even had two class-B AIS units installed. In his joy of ownership, the man claimed his setup was so good that he and his wife could lead a "normal life inside the boat," watching satellite TV while the electronics, GPS, and autopilot steered and the fully automated AIS/radar combination kept lookout for them.

I just nodded and smiled, trying my best to look interested while not saying very much. Inside I heard the voice of old Captain Irving saying, "Every skipper has his own compass." That while thinking to myself, this man is a danger to himself, his family, and everyone at sea. Suicidal lunatics like him are why I'm awake at three in the morning keeping watch. Well, to be honest, it's people like him along with the fishing boats and the other jolly things that make life at sea so interesting.

A chart plotter coupled to a GPS will indicate a position within several meters. The problem is understanding what those fancy gadgets are telling you. First of all, GPS is very good at telling you exactly and precisely where *it* thinks you are, while chart plotters are only as good as the charts they depend on. And I wouldn't trust most of the charts that come in those plotters to navigate a duck punt.

And here is another lovely thought: Do you have a backup plan to navigate safely when all those fancy electronics crash? If you sail long enough, I can guarantee that one day they will fail. And do not even get me started on the wonders of a lightning strike.

We have four good-quality GPS units on *Vega*. All are from reputable electronics companies. Each claims accuracy to within five meters and is properly set up and calibrated. The interesting part is that not a single one of them ever agrees with any of the others. In fact, only two of them ever manage to give a position that is within five meters of each other—and that rarely.

The other problem I had with that proud condomaran owner's navigational method has to do with watches. Not the kind you wear on your wrist but the kind real sailors keep at sea. Watches are called watches because that means someone is out there *watching* for other boats, fishnets, UFOs, thunderstorms, lost shipping containers, naked girls on rafts, condomarans on autopilot with the owners down below watching television, and all the other things that pop up out there. I am pretty sure watches are called watches because someone is watching, and that does not mean *I Love Lucy* reruns.

The reason you can sleep peacefully when off watch is that you know someone else is *on watch*. I once saw firsthand the result of not keeping a proper lookout when an oil tanker pulled into the port of Dakar with the complete mast and rigging from a forty-five-foot sailboat dangling from their portside anchor. They were not even aware they hit something. And by the way, I have many times observed wooden or plastic fishing boats up close and personal when the radar could not see them at all.

On board *Vega* at sea, there is always someone out on deck keeping watch, twenty-four hours a day, seven days a week. For one thing, it is simply good seamanship. For another, it lets the rest of us sleep knowing a freighter on autopilot with the crew down below watching porno films will not run us over. A proper watch also prevents those uncharted bits of land that can sprout up overnight from crashing into us.

For the watch, on-deck life is mostly a question of fighting boredom, doing small projects as the weather allows, and enjoying the occasional bit of excitement when a pod of dolphins or whales shows up. You would be amazed at the things we see at sea. There was one day we counted seventeen bright-yellow inflatable children's swimming rings, complete with smiling ducky heads, as they drifted by. Or the time off Surabaya when we passed through a whole armada of colorful balloons. Add that to schools of tuna, the comical antics of flying fish, or the odd whale jumping, and watches can be almost interesting. In any case, most deck watches are only slightly more exciting than counting your toes or exploring a nasal cavity.

On watch, you look for things that do not belong, shapes that are unusual or movement that a wave would never make. Those visual clues automatically attract your attention. When the watch spotted a small dark shadow bobbing up and down one morning about two miles away from our route, at first it was only mildly thought provoking. A passing point of interest to observe while waiting for the clock to ticktock its way toward the change of watch.

As *Vega* drew closer, the binoculars came out to diligently inspect such an enigmatic object. It soon became apparent this was not another log in the water but an unoccupied dugout canoe. Such thrilling news soon had most of the crew up on deck. This was real excitement, a high point for the day, and no one wanted to miss it. While I diligently altered course toward the mystery boat, one of the lads shot up the ratlines for a better view. None of us was prepared for what he reported from that lofty perch.

CHAPTER 45

The Castaways

Most of the small islands we visit have no regular communication with the outside world, only the occasional interisland ferry or when they mount a major expedition to the next island in one of their own small boats.

As sailors, we often look at most of those local craft and wonder how anyone would ever dream of going to sea in one, much less attempt a voyage far from land. To give you an idea, the "new" boat on Nila has a small single-cylinder diesel engine left behind by the Japanese after World War II. Mind you, originally the "new" boat's engine had no motor mounts holding it down. When it was running, someone had to stand on top of the cooling water header to keep it from coming adrift.

Last year we brought a set of motor mounts and some long coach bolts so they could mount it properly. For the island youngsters, who were traditionally stuck with the job of human engine bracket, those parts were a life-changing revelation in the art of modern engineering.

The fact is those boats are not only important tools for the islanders, they are also dangerous. Island-built dugout canoes are not deep-sea boats, nor are they what one would call dependable. Most have no motor. They depend on a small sail for reaching or running and Armstrong-powered paddles to make headway against the prevailing monsoon. For most of the year, the area is subject to strong wind and fierce currents. The monsoon wind averages fifteen to twenty knots, and the west-porting current often runs at one or two knots.

Most of us tend to view these people as happy natives, almost like fish when it comes to living and working around water. Some of that image is well earned. I have seen those strong young lads dancing around their canoes with the equilibrium of a cat. They can paddle all day without breaking a sweat and know every fluke of the wind and current around their island. But that is no protection against disaster.

Every year, due to various misfortunes, the wind and current sweep fishing canoes or small local ferryboats out to sea. In most cases, the lost boat reappears after a few days with the exhausted fishermen still on board, their safe return cause for an island-wide celebration. Over the next few weeks, the tales of fighting the wind and current and their every strategy of sail and paddle entertain the entire village. In other cases, neither boat nor crew is ever seen again. On an island where everyone is related, such a loss is equal to a national tragedy.

"Skipper, there are people in that thing and they look dead."

Every sailor whose IQ is higher than a radish fears shipwreck more than a visit from the mother-in-law or a tax audit. The thought of being adrift at sea without food or water and precious little chance of rescue is the stuff of a seafarer's nightmares. For that very reason, since the day after Zog discovered wood floats, seamen have always gone to each other's assistance without hesitation or question.

Having taken over the helm, I reduced power and spun the wheel, altering our course to come alongside the now clearly visible canoe from upwind. While the boat lost speed, we prepared fenders on the downwind side and several lines to tie off the little vessel.

During the approach, our man up the mast continued his running commentary until we could easily see two people lying in the bottom of a waterlogged canoe. As we watched, one of them weakly raised a hand and tried to wave. Halfway through that gesture, his arm collapsed back into the boat.

As *Vega* drew closer, we saw two emaciated young men in an island-style canoe containing some fishing gear and two paddles, one of them broken. There was also a large white sack, apparently full. Neither of the boys moved as we hove to alongside, making their canoe fast to *Vega*'s starboard cathead with their own bowline.

While one of our crewmembers ran below to get a water bottle, another gingerly stepped into the canoe. Kneeling beside the first boy, he probed for a pulse. What he felt was weak, but there. His report of "This one's alive" caused a long exhalation of breath none of us realized we were holding. It did not take long to discover that the boy who tried to wave was also still breathing. Someone passed a water bottle to our man in the canoe, who administered a few small sips of water to both boys. I shall never forget the moan distinctly heard from one of them as life-giving liquid dribbled between his cracked lips.

With both boys effectively incapacitated, bringing them on board *Vega* was not an easy task. In the end, we rigged a whip and bowline from the main yard. One at a time, we struggled getting each of them onto our boat. Once on board *Vega* we carried each boy to the shade of a small awning rigged between the masts. A few moments later, we hoisted the white sack on board.

None of us had experience dealing with extreme dehydration, which seemed to be the most urgent problem. I did know from my time strolling across the Sahara Desert that the worst thing we could do was let them drink their fill all at once. At best, that would make them sick; at worst, their systems might experience a fatal convulsive shock.

Since the very name "rehydration salts" seemed to say it all, we made up another water bottle with two packets of Oralite mixed in. While part of the crew did their best to slowly rehydrate our newly rescued castaways, we tied their boat off our stern. A canoe is a valuable thing in those islands, so we would tow it behind *Vega* until we reached the next landfall. Getting us back up to a speed where the little boat would not tow under, I once again established our intended route. That done, I hit the autopilot button and went forward to see what was happening.

Both of the boys were dressed in ragged shorts and old T-shirts. A quick hunt through their pockets turned up a small folding knife, two seashells, and one well-used harmonica. The knife was old. Its blade sharpened so many times that only half of the original metal remained. That search also turned up a small leather pouch containing several tiny stones, each with a hole in it. Although interesting, none of those items indicated where the boys came from or why they were so far out at sea.

The white bag proved to be full of sundried cloves. The canoe itself offered even less information. Although an islander can recognize every canoe on their island and knows exactly who made it and who uses it, we did not have the luxury of such information. Our only hope of solving the mystery lay in the two crumpled heaps lying on top of the cabin roof under an awning. We took turns dribbling water between their lips a few precious drops at a time, and sponging off their salt sores with fresh water.

It is not easy getting water into someone who has essentially passed out. Unless you do it a few drops at a time, there is a very real risk of drowning the person you want to save. We noticed that dribbling a few drops right as their breathing reached its peak of inhalation seemed to work the best. I am sure a paramedic would have made a better job of it, but we did the best we could. Everything I found in our first-aid books assumed the person is awake and so was of little help.

As the day wore on, our fore-deck clinic improved. Sport mattresses and pillows made an appearance. Careful sponging removed most of the deeply encrusted salt that covered both boys. By early afternoon, we had gotten slightly over a liter of fresh water with rehydration salts into each of them. Both were breathing easier and occasionally moved a bit. Since Meggi had made one of her famous chicken soups—lovingly known as Jewish penicillin—the day before, we began dribbling some of that into our rapidly improving patients.

CHAPTER 46

The Castaways' Tale

Trying to staff an ad hoc clinic and sail *Vega* with a crew of four was not an easy proposition, yet no one complained when we set up a new schedule dividing our time between ship watches and nursing duties. All through the night, we hovered over those two young men, trying our best to rehydrate them and feed them at the same time. It was not until about four the next morning that they both drifted into real sleep rather than a semicoma. The difference was clear in their breathing, and the way they moved to make themselves more comfortable. About then we began to nurture hope for their recovery. For the next twelve hours, they both slept soundly. Although we continued the soup treatment from time to time, it seemed best to simply let them rest and recover. Fortunately, the wind remained light and sea calm.

When one of the boys regained consciousness, we soon discovered his formal name was one of those unpronounceable alphabet-soup titles the islanders love, and that most people called him Mandi. His friend, Indi, took another three hours to find his way back into the land of the living. When he awoke, the first thing Indi said to his friend translates to, "This is the last time I am helping you get a wife."

Finally, we could learn how they came to be so far out to sea and so near death. The whole crew gathered around as Mandi tried his best to narrate their great adventure. Mind you, it was a production based on hand gestures and a pocket-sized Bahasa dictionary. Between the language barrier and Mandi constantly eating anything that failed to eat him first, it was a long tale and, as we soon realized, a love story.

The yarn our castaways told involved a beautiful island girl called Yanni, her greedy old father, and two devoted friends who set out together on a perilous adventure so that one of them could win the woman of his dreams. The two boys we now had on board *Vega* were the result of that adventure.

It seems the girl's father was not against the idea of having Mandi for a son-in-law, providing he met the bride price of three pigs—one of which had to be a sow—a new canoe for three men, and most difficult of all, twelve pieces of cloth and two new cooking pots. That in addition to what Mandi and Yanni would need to set up their own house.

Somehow, the boys managed to get the pigs by building and setting traps in the forest. Then they diligently labored for almost eight months making a new dugout canoe. Through a stroke of luck, it even had a blue plastic sail that they found on the beach after a storm. The whole village agreed the canoe was a good one. The real problems were the twelve pieces of cloth and, of course, the metal cooking pots.

There are no shops on their island selling cloth or pots, and the boys had no money to buy those things even if there had been. Indi claimed this was the old man's way of being tricky. Their only hope was a bigger island with more people who might have shops selling cloth and pots. Even so, they would still need something to exchange for such valuable items.

Everyone knew the Japanese once sent a geologist to the island exploring for gold. The old people said he found some, but it was too difficult to get at, and in any case, there was not enough to make it worthwhile. But surely there would be enough for twelve pieces of cloth. Based on an old tale that if you look hard enough sometimes you can find small pieces of gold, the boys spent weeks searching in the various streams and outfalls.

Eventually, the discovery of a few tiny nuggets rewarded their effort. Unfortunately, that treasure proved to be iron pyrite, commonly called fool's gold. After all their work, Indi and Mandi were heartbroken. Then it occurred to them that they could gather cloves from the wild trees high up on the volcano and trade those.

This was something they knew how to do, even if finding trees that were unclaimed would be a tough task. It took time and a lot of effort, but at last they managed to gather a full sack containing over fifty kilograms of prime cloves. Then their real problems began.

Both boys had grown up on the water and were at home in canoes. What they lacked was experience and knowledge of navigation between the islands. Since few people from their village had ever journeyed to other islands, interisland navigation was an art few had learned. Those who had made such a perilous voyage jealously guarded their knowledge. All the two boys knew was that the next island was "about two days' journey 'that way'—with the right wind," although no one seemed to know when or what the right wind was.

In that part of the Banda Sea, wind and currents are seasonal. They depend on which monsoon is active at the time and how strong it is. Then there are the months between monsoons when the current slacks to almost nothing and the wind can die for days at a time. All this was knowledge the boys were only vaguely aware of as they sat on the beach dreaming of the great voyage they were going to make. In fact, having only ever experienced the inshore currents around their island, they were barely aware of the powerful offshore flow that can reach two and a half knots.

Another problem they faced was knowing how far away the next island really was. The old people, at least the ones who would talk about it, claimed it was two days away with a good wind and pointed toward the west. No one seemed to know how far away two days' sailing was. To find out, the boys decided to make a test with their canoe, an old half-rotten dugout that once belonged to Indi's uncle.

They sailed around the island as fast as they could from just before sunrise until just after sunset and then tried to imagine four times that distance. Accordingly, they calculated the next island must be slightly more than a day's sail past the horizon.

Both boys knew that asking their fathers for permission for such a perilous voyage was hopeless. So adopting the same option as millions of young people before them, they made their plans and gathered their provisions in secret. When the time came, they would tell everyone they were going up the volcano for a few days to hunt wild boar. With luck, they would be back, treasures in hand, before anyone remarked on their absence.

They judged full moon the best time for such a voyage. That way if they came to the island at night they would spot it. Both boys were aware that in the immensity of the ocean, on a moonless night it would be easy to pass by a small island without ever seeing it. As the moon grew fatter, their excitement mounted until at last the chosen day for their departure arrived.

Expecting the voyage to last two days, they loaded their canoe with water and provisions for three, then rigged the boat with an old mast and canvas sail. After a small ceremony to ensure the journey would be safe, they set out at sunset. They planned to keep the morning sun at their backs and the afternoon sun in their faces during the day. At night their navigation would depend on stars they knew always came up and set in the same place as the sun.

Although logical enough, they later discovered that on the ocean all directions look the same at midday. During those times, they soon discovered keeping the boat on the same angle to the prevailing waves worked well enough.

Throughout the first night and well into the next day the boys took turns steering by bracing a paddle against the side of the boat as their canoe raced across the ocean, propelled by its ancient sail. It was an exciting time when the island of their dreams always seemed to be just over the next horizon. They passed the time by discussing their victorious return home and the fame they would win from such an adventurous voyage. On the second night, they kept a careful lookout, expecting to see their destination rise above the horizon at any moment.

Up until then the wind and sea had been kind to them, but around midnight their luck changed. A dark cloud appeared on the horizon, blocking out the stars as it progressed in their direction. It was a typical one-cloud tropical thunderstorm, where the wind blows for a while and rain pours down like a waterfall until eventually the storm wonders off to molest someone else. For most well-found boats, such a blow poses no danger at all. But for an ancient canoe with a half-rotten sail, such a storm can be deadly.

One of the first gusts to hit them almost capsized the canoe before blowing out their sail. While one boy used his cupped hands to bail water from the canoe, the other struggled to keep them running in front of the wind and waves. Without the sail, that was a difficult task requiring constant vigilance. Although the squall only lasted a few minutes, the destruction it left behind was extensive.

Once the thunderstorm passed, they bailed out their boat and took stock of the damage. Not only had they lost the sail, waves lapping over the side soaked most of their food in salt water. Two of the precious coconuts they used as freshwater containers also fell victim. Although these things represented major setbacks, they consoled themselves. The big island would soon come in sight, ending the first part of their voyage.

Sure enough, halfway through the next morning they spotted an island looming low on the horizon, almost directly in front of them. Rowing with that consistent rhythm islanders can maintain for days, the boys headed in that direction, confident their difficulties would soon be over.

As the day progressed, the island came steadily closer, yet it also appeared to move from west to east at a disconcerting rate. The current was sweeping them past their objective faster than they could approach it. Realizing this, and with only a few miles separating them from their destination, the boys rowed harder, driving their canoe through the water faster. Maintaining a slight angle to help offset the current, by the end of the first hour they could easily make out houses on the shore and even people walking along the beach. It would be a close race but apparently they were winning.

Gathering their energy for one final effort, they chanted an ancient war song. Rhythmically digging their paddles deep into the water, their youthful energy propelled the heavy canoe even faster. With their goal now clearly in sight, they goaded each other to even greater displays of force. Mandi began chanting, "Yan-ni, Yan-ni," with every stroke of his paddle, directing every ounce of his strength into rowing. The canoe surged forward. Then, halfway through one of those powerful strokes, disaster struck. With a rending crack, Mandi's wooden oar shattered.

CHAPTER 47

Without a Paddle

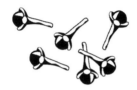

Faced with disaster, Indi never missed a stroke. He paddled with all the force his young body could muster while Mandi kneeled to continue paddling with one hand on each side of the canoe, using the power from his arms and back to propel them toward the beach, a place of safety they could see so clearly. Despite their best efforts, the heavy old canoe soon lost its forward momentum while the current close to shore grew even stronger.

With energy born of desperation, they struggled as the fierce current swept them parallel to the beach. They yelled and waved their arms to attract attention, but no one on shore noticed them.

Alternately praying and cursing, both boys paddled frantically. They were so close, the smell of the forest and spicy smoke from cooking fires drifted across the water to where they vainly fought an unrelenting current. By late afternoon, having drifted past the island, disappointment and exhaustion overtook them. Just after sunset, they both fell into a deeply troubled sleep.

The following morning, they awoke to clear skies without the slightest sign of land. Taking stock of their meagre provisions, they found two coconuts filled with fresh water, some dried fish, and a piece of cake only slightly spoiled by salt water.

With thirst tormenting them, both boys wished nothing more than to grab one of those coconuts and drain it to the last drop. Instead, they settled on a system of rationing, limiting themselves to a few small sips at a time.

Breakfast that morning consisted of half a small dried fish between the two of them and one sip of fresh water each. That single mouthful of stale water was the finest drink either of them had ever tasted. They spent the rest of the morning huddled under a scrap that remained from their sail.

Neither boy was under any illusions. Their situation was grave, the possibility of rescue or reaching another island poor. The fact is, although they knew of other islands and even continents somewhere out there, they had not the slightest idea where those lands might be or how far away.

Four days later, they were nearing the end. The fresh water was gone, and although they had watched several tropical thunderstorms pass close by, not a drop of rain fell on their canoe. Drifting in and out of consciousness, both boys lay in the bottom of their boat awaiting death. When the shadow of *Vega* fell across them, Indi was certain it was just another hallucination; even so, he tried to wave.

We picked the boys up roughly seventy miles downwind from the nearest landfall. As it turned out, they came from an island where we stop to deliver medical and educational supplies every year. After a bit of confusion, it turned out they knew about us. We had one delivery stop to make before we took them home.

Over the days that followed, their story slowly emerged. As it did, Meggi and I decided to play Cupid; in exchange for their bag of cloves, we provided the cloth and cooking pots so that Mandi could marry Yanni. We also gave both boys a heavy stainless-steel bush knife with a sharpening stone and well-made leather scabbard. Other crewmembers chipped in T-shirts and a few short pants to improve their wardrobe. Someone even found them each a pair of rubber sandals. These treasures they stowed in two brightly colored backpacks we had left over from Kits-4-Kids.

A week later, we anchored off their island. The first thing we noticed was the somber atmosphere, no happy groups of people formed on the beach, and only one canoe came out to greet us. The people in that boat looked miserable, until Mandi and Indi appeared on deck jabbering away in the local dialect.

Both of the boys were dressed in their finest new clothes, with the new bush knives dangling from a piece of rope tied around their waist. Mandi had even found a pair of gaudy plastic sunglasses he proudly wore at every opportunity.

Suddenly it was huge smiles and laughing all round. There was yelling back and forth to the shore, where the happiness quickly spread like oil on water. The village had been in deep mourning for two of their young men presumed lost at sea. It turned out the boys were not as sneaky as they thought. A fisherman spotted their sail the evening they left. Naturally, the villagers assumed the wind and current had carried them away. The day we arrived they were preparing for a memorial service in the village church.

One of the first to arrive in the second batch of canoes was a very attractive young woman. Jumping onto *Vega*, she ran to Mandi and threw herself into his arms. Well, to be precise, she threw her arms around his neck and wrapped her legs tightly around his waist. She was crying and laughing at the same time, while Mandi staggered around the deck, trying not to fall over. One of our friends provided a rough translation of her first words to Mandi: "You great idiot, if you ever do something like that again I will unmarry you the same day and make you sleep with the pigs."

At last count, Mandi and Yanni have two lovely children. They named their firstborn, a pretty little girl, Vega. Indi also married his childhood sweetheart. Several years ago, he asked us to bring him a selection of vegetable seeds. Having vowed never to set foot on a boat again, he is now the island's most successful farmer.

CHAPTER 48

The Great Sewing Machine Drama

Getting to the remote islands where *Vega's* supplies make such an impact can be a grueling task. Yet, knowing there is a difficult mission to accomplish and success depends on us, Meggi and I often manage alone for months at a time.

Our reward is a powerful sense of personal accomplishment, coupled with the knowledge that our hard work is saving lives and helping improve the future for forgotten people who dream of simple things like better tools to farm or fish with, better schools for their children, or better care from the local health post. Unhampered by political or religious agendas, *Vega* is a catalyst for action, impartially assisting local communities to achieve their own vision of how to develop.

But often small things can make a big difference. For instance, when Dr. Ruth discovered most islanders were suffering from vitamin deficiency due to limited diet, we began providing vegetable seeds specially adapted for their soil and environment.

A young Indonesian doctor who pitched up on the pier one day in Jakarta saying, "I want to go sailing with you," Dr. Ruth quickly became a welcome addition to *Vega's* crew. When I asked why she wanted to go with us, her answer was simple. "I want an adventure and the chance to help people on the remote islands you visit." She never did learn to tie a proper knot, but that woman is amazing with people. And she loves to teach.

It is almost impossible for people living in big cities, where just about anything is available at the swipe of a card, to imagine how important a treadle-powered sewing machine can be on an island without electricity and no shops to buy things in. For a community that once boasted two of those machines, having both of them broken amounted to a major catastrophe.

On our latest wish list from the island of Nila, right at the top and underlined twice, Baba Eki wrote "Foot Sewing Machine." Having seen the tragic state both of their existing sewing machines were in, I could understand the importance of his request. I spent quite some time that year with my trusty can of WD-40 and a few small hand tools doing my best to resuscitate at least one of those machines by stealing parts from the other.

To begin with, both machines needed a serious cleaning. When I opened them up, it appeared as if someone had coated the delicate internal workings with glue. A bit of forensic detective work soon discovered that palm oil was the local sewing machine lubricant of choice. Hand-pressed palm oil is not only too thick for fine machinery, but it also dries out rather rapidly, leaving behind a thick, sticky residue.

It took me hours to clean that muck out of the gears, and then came the tedious task of removing it from the bearings and bushings. Even then, and after liberal applications of WD-40, both machines refused to function as advertised.

Water seeping in through a leak in the roof had damaged one of them, creating serious rust on the gears and other moving parts. Once I removed the palm oil paste and thick layers of rust, it still refused to function. Well, you try playing at sewing machine mechanic with a bunch of matronly old biddies hovering over your shoulder giving advice in a language you do not understand and see how far you get.

No matter what I did, the clearances between just about every part in that machine were too sloppy for it to work. Either the needle missed the bobbin, crashed into the footplate holding the bobbin in place, or both. And no amount of adjustment seemed to make a difference.

The other sewing machine was in much better shape, but a small metal ring that holds the bobbin in place was broken. I know it was beyond the ability of superglue to repair, because I tried that.

Mind you, I never professed myself a sewing machine repairman, but there I was, scratching my head and pondering why all my fingers had suddenly turned into thumbs. Where normally I would watch someone else do the job while nodding in a knowing manner and making helpful sounds when they seemed appropriate, Meggi had to go touting me as a general whiz with machinery, fully competent to fix just about anything. Teach me to show away for the girls, that will.

I guess it was really my own fault for trying so hard to impress her with my manly mechanical skills. Even today, she has still not realized that half the stuff I "fix" somehow manages to repair itself after a good cleanup. Most of the time I haven't the slightest idea what I did to make it work again. Maybe all those leftover screws, nuts, washers, and other assorted bits were getting in the way. Machines can be funny like that.

To be honest, sewing machines make me nervous. There are all those finely machined parts, complete with little gears and oscillating bits, just begging for a chance to drive me nuts. Imagine, if you take the thing apart and put just one gear back a single tooth off from where it should be, the whingie-ma-ding will miss the what-ya-macallit every time. The result is a machine that spins around perfectly but refuses to sew a single stitch. And let's not forget the poor slob looking a lot like me tearing at his hair and trying to figure out why the thing refuses to do its duty.

I could not mend one of those machines no matter what I did. It was too far gone to rescue. Maybe someone with a full machine shop and a whole lot more brains than I have could fix it. But there was no way I was going to repair the thing with the few tools and limited knowledge at my disposal. That machine needed to be replaced, no question about it.

The other one was a simple case of being gummed up with palm oil and one small piece well and truly broken. As luck would have it, that was the only piece I could easily see how to take out and put back in again. All I needed was a replacement part. What in Singapore could be remedied with a few phone calls and a stroll to the shopping mall was unfixable on the small island of Nila, where there are no shops at all.

Now the logical solution would be to take the small part from the dead machine and use it to fix the other machine. Logical, like I said, but not politically correct. It seems that several years ago the owner of the one machine said something about the owner of the other machine's sister-in-law's, cousin's, son's table manners, which of course kicked off a feud of epic proportions between those two august matrons of island society. Enough said?

Well, one year and a month later we were back on the island of Nila. And thanks to the efforts of a friend in Jakarta, we had a lovely new, genuine, made-in-China, imitation Singer treadle-powered sewing machine on board. We also had a goodly selection of supplies for it and the other broken machine. Those supplies included several bottles of original Singer sewing machine oil, needles, thread, and a bunch of other bits and bobs Meggi claimed were important for the constructive employment of any sewing machine.

Meggi and I transported that machine on its stand in place of our salon table for over a thousand miles. Having managed its safe passage to Nila, the next trick would be getting it ashore unharmed. Not as straightforward a task as it might seem, considering the sewing machine was bigger than our little dinghy would accept as deck cargo.

In the end, the new machine went ashore on board an island canoe. As precarious a trip as you could ever dream of. By canting the machine and its table at an angle, they managed to make it fit—more or less. It was not what I would call inside the canoe; not exactly. It was more like almost somewhat perhaps on a good day balanced on the sides looking for any excuse to escape its current confinement and go for a swim.

Those young men from Nila have a sense of balance to rival cats. They practically grow up in canoes. Even so, we suggested they lash two canoes together catamaran-style using bamboo poles and rope we would happily provide. Although no one openly scoffed at the idea, they did politely ignore our suggestion as being a waste of time and too complicated by half.

Personally, if I had been Baba Eki transporting Ibu Lila's new sewing machine ashore, I would have used the catamaran system. That woman is always such a jolly old bird, but somehow I have a feeling trying to explain dropping her new sewing machine into the drink might not be the healthiest or most relaxing way to pass an afternoon.

Evidently, the various island youngsters told off to do the job caught on to my logic and agreed with me. For every person rowing, there were at least two supporting the machine. I swear there was even one boy lying flat on his back under it, hanging on to the cast iron base tighter than a limpet does its rock.

We followed along in our dinghy, while Baba Eki rowed around them in a smaller canoe freely imparting his august advice and counsel. Every now and again he must have reminded them what would happen should they drop Ibu Lila's new sewing machine. Hearing that, rowers on board the local door-to-door delivery boat would cringe in unison and paddle more carefully than before.

Once safely ashore, those lads slung the machine between two long poles and manhandled it up the steep path to Baba Eki's house. Once in front of the house, he called Ibu Lila out to have a look at something interesting. Mind you, all of this was an unexpected surprise for her.

And surprised she was. Her mouth flopped open and both palms flew to her cheeks. Ibu Lila opened the machine and closed the machine, repeatedly. She pulled open the drawers then sifted through the various needles and other supplies, all the time squealing like a six-year-old girl in a Barbie doll shop. To say Ibu Lila was a happy camper that day would be a serious understatement.

While Ibu Lila inspected her new sewing machine, Baba Eki diplomatically took us around to where her old machine sat. While he stood guard at the door, I dismantled the parts needed to repair Ibu Rosa's machine.

So it was that after the obligatory dose of herbal tea and a slice or two of Ibu Lila's tasty homemade cake, we set off for the other village and the second part of our mission.

Less than a mile along the coast from where Ibu Lila resides is the small settlement where Ibu Rosa lives. By land, it takes a good half hour of uphill and down to get there. By sea, in our dinghy, it was only a short cruise across a small bay. That is, unless you have Meggi and Jo along, who insist on stopping to ogle every new coral and stone that comes into view. On the other hand, it was still faster than going by land, considering the pair of them would do exactly the same with every new flower, tree, and shrub we passed.

After arriving at Ibu Rosa's house, it only took a moment to have her machine back in service. Although, she insisted on testing it with several different pieces of cloth before giving her final approval. Her husband may be headman of that village, but everyone knows who really runs the shop. You should have heard her giving the daughter-in-law grief while the poor girl tried to thread a needle with trembling hands. We later saved her from at least one drama in life by fitting Ibu Rosa with a pair of reading glasses. Her eyes were so bad that without those glasses she had trouble seeing the sewing machine, much less the needle hole.

CHAPTER 49

The Cat and the Milk Sea

Some of the seas we sail have the largest concentration of healthy phytoplankton on earth. The Banda Sea is notorious for its "Milk Sea," where huge carpets of phosphorescence turn the entire ocean white, or greenish blue when something disturbs them, giving the sea a look like glowing milk. Far from any source of light pollution, the effect is spectacular.

For some bizarre reason, when people think of the sea, they imagine an endless procession of raging storms and huge waves. The truth is, most of the time the sea is rather calm, and I might add boring. Mind you, with the alternatives being what they are, I never complain about boredom at sea. Those periods of calm are when we see some of the most amazing things.

Like the night we were ghosting along on the Banda Sea with a light wind and the water so calm you could see stars by the billions reflected in it. A gentle monsoon breeze filled the sails, easing *Vega* along her route under a blazing interstellar canopy that city lights long ago banished into obscurity for most of us. One of those pure, crystalline evenings when the Milky Way really does look like a pool of spilt milk pouring across the sky, leaving behind a trail of errant orbs perched somewhere just above the light on our masthead.

Well, maties, on a night like that there is precious little to do other than ogle the heavens, read a book, or rummage your mind for something worth deliberating. In the middle of the Banda Sea, spotting another ship, even hull down on the horizon, is a rare event.

I was just settling in with a mug of hot chocolate and a new book—all prepared to enjoy four lovely hours powered by the hum-drum-hum turbines of boredom—when out of the corner of my eye I saw a flash of light.

Eyeing the general direction of that mysterious flash, I waited for it to repeat itself. Several seconds later, the sea along our starboard side erupted in a ghostly flash of greenish white, and when I say the whole sea, I mean the entire shop from boat to horizon suddenly glowed for about ten seconds before settling back into the usual dark water one expects at night. Having seen just about everything you can imagine at sea, especially at night, I can say this was truly exceptional.

Calling down the hatch that there was something strange to see, I went back to staring in the general direction of the original flash. Just about then, a rocket exploded out of the water, leaving a shining trail of ghostly light. A ring of shimmering water spread from where it surfaced. About then the wind began to pick up, and so did our boat speed.

It took me a few seconds to realize that I was seeing a band of dolphins out looking for a bit of amusement and perhaps a midnight snack. I love watching dolphins. Say what you will, they strike me as the happiest creatures at sea. And smart enough not to let on how clever they really are.

This might be a good time to impart a bit of nautical esoterica concerning phosphorescent plant life. I've spent many an enjoyable moment lying with my head protruding over the stern of an old sailing boat as we ghosted along through a sea teeming with tiny luminescent critters. Looking down on that swirling mass of light, I felt like a god overseeing the universe as swirling constellations of every size and type spun away in the wake.

You see, those little critters never phosphoresce when the moon is out. They only turn on the lights when there is no moon. Long ago, I concluded that phytoplankton do this as a defensive mechanism, one that confuses any predators lurking in the area until they lose their appetite and wander off searching for an easier meal.

The logic is simple: since the stars look like tiny spots of light, by imitating stars' luminescence, plankton create a state of mental confusion in which any fish out to eat them begins to believe it has somehow emerged from the water into the air and promptly gets so turned around they forget about dinner and concentrate instead on getting back into the water. About then the plankton switch off the lights and slink away on the nearest available current.

CHAPTER 50

The Original Spice Islands

Reaching across the Southeast Monsoon at a steady seven knots, for the first time in months *Vega* was truly in her element. She loves those long slow swells and enough wind to drive her along under plain working sail. Even though we often meet five- and six-meter waves, the fact they are so far apart means *Vega* rises in a stately manner for several seconds then slowly slides down into the next valley between waves.

Roaring white water cascades over her windward rail, flooding across the deck. Relieving ports open, allowing the water to freely gush from her downwind side on the rise, then thump closed as she rolls back again. Far from shipping routes, reefs, and islands, this is real blue-water sailing at its best, even if some of our volunteer crew members find it a harrowing experience.

That wonderful sojourn at sea was all too soon cut short by our arrival at a small archipelago that inadvertently caused the fall of several ancient South American empires, the conquest of India, and the eventual domination of China by the British. They are the Banda Islands, for thousands of years the world's only source of the most sought-after spices on earth: nutmeg and mace.

Once considered some of the most valuable real estate in the world, Banda enthralled Meggi and me on our first visit with its people, history, and culture. It did not take long to discover a huge contradiction between the legends and traditions our Bandanese friends shared with us and the stories told in European history books.

Almost every official Banda history presents a pre-European portrait of seminaked savages begging for the benefit of European civilization, whereas the history portrayed by modern scholarly works and our Bandanese friends paints an entirely different story.

What is truth and what fiction? Did Europeans intentionally present a distorted image to justify suppressing a rich, vibrant culture, or are the Bandanese, most of whom are now descended from Javanese slaves imported by the Dutch, merely fabricating a fanciful history for themselves?

Our quest soon became one to discover how far back in time we could trace the history and impact of these small islands on global trade, for there can be little doubt that these isles with less land area than most cities had a disproportionate impact on the ancient world, and on the world we live in today.

Yet the export of spices is only part of the story. Far from being a remote outpost, as a terminus for the spice routes these tiny islands played an active role in trade throughout the Indonesian archipelago.

For thousands of years, ships from Arabia, China, and India regularly called at the Banda Islands to trade goods from their own countries for pearls, nutmeg, and cloves. Before the arrival of Europeans, the Banda Islands were the central hub for an extensive seaborne trading network. Locally built vessels ranged far and wide, trading throughout the region. Ceramics, metal, and other goods from China, India, and Arabia were traded onward to New Guinea, Kai, Aru, Timor, and some believe as far as Australia, Malacca, and Madagascar.

Early chroniclers describe how forest products, such as shipbuilding wood, aromatic tree bark, bird feathers, and the staple food sago, were brought from Aru, Kai, and New Guinea in exchange for cloth, rice, metal utensils, and glazed ceramics. Thus, Banda served not only as a spice producer but also as an important transshipment depot.

Some villages specialized in trade with particular regions and in some cases specific islands or even villages. Those communities carefully guarded their navigational secrets and the bits of local language required for their voyages. Such valuable secret knowledge was passed down for generations through the same families.

Some villages sent their trading ships to islands in the eastern regions, such as Seram, Kai, Aru, and New Guinea, while other communities traded with Timor and farther afield. For more than three thousand years, before the European invasion brought that long, rich history to a bloody end, native Banda Islanders actively exploited their knowledge of those trade routes.

That the Bandanese were inveterate traders and seamen is indisputable. The real questions are how far they roamed on those ancient trading voyages and for how long they did it.

So began an intriguing adventure, one that soon encompassed the intricacies of ancient Chinese shipbuilding; a 140-kilometer navigation canal dug at the command of Egyptian pharaohs; the invention of navigation locks; three-thousand-year-old cloves; Ice Age migrations covering half the globe; fifteen-thousand-year-old cave paintings of sailing vessels; adventurous Arab, Chinese, and Indian merchants; and the colonization of Madagascar.

For thousands of years these islands were the world's only source of cloves, nutmeg, and mace, spices so highly valued on the Asian, Middle Eastern, and European markets that Chinese, Indian, Malay, Arabic, and Javanese traders all maintained permanent or semipermanent trading missions on these islands to supply ships from those countries that regularly called.

Some years ago, archaeologists working in the ruins of the ancient Iraqi city of Terqa, on the banks of the Euphrates River, unearthed a sealed ceramic vessel carbon dated at 1750 BC. It contained clove buds that could only have come from the Maluku Islands, thousands of sea miles away. This important find clearly indicates the extent of the spice trade from those small islands over three thousand years before Europeans arrived.

Indeed, the first Europeans to reach the Banda Islands discovered an important international and regional trading center where merchants from India, Arabia, and China exchanged ceramics, metal implements, rice, and cloth for pearls, nutmeg, mace, and cloves.

Spices acquired on these trading ventures often journeyed to China on junk-rigged sailing ships, then onward by camel along the famous Silk and Spice Routes, or to the Persian Gulf on swift-sailing Arab trading dhows. There merchants transferred those spices to caravans destined for the Mediterranean, thus satisfying an ever-growing demand by Middle Eastern and later European nations for Southeast Asian spices.

But there was also a vibrant interisland trade in bird of paradise feathers from the Aru Islands and western New Guinea, along with massoia bark for traditional medicines and salves. Ikat cloth from the Lesser Sundas traded for sago from the Kei Islands, Aru, and Seram. Locally built sail-powered trading vessels called Belang or Orambai ranged far and wide, trading throughout the region.

In his AD 1515 book *Suma Oriental*, the Portuguese apothecary Tomé Pires reported the Bandanese as being part of an Indonesia-wide trading network and the only native Malukuan long-range traders taking cargo to Malacca, although some shipments from Banda were also carried by Javanese traders. Recently discovered cave paintings from East Timor, dated at over fifteen thousand years old, clearly show seaworthy sailing vessels capable of carrying over twenty people and a respectable cargo. Those images display a striking resemblance to the vessels Europeans saw when they first arrived.

A reliable tradition holds that Chinese courtiers in the third century BC were required to carry cloves in their mouths to sweeten their breath when addressing the emperor.

And opposite Luxor in southern Egypt, wall paintings from the tomb of Queen Hatshepsut provide details of the ships and cargo from one of history's first documented spice trading missions. That mission occurred in 1493 BC. (Ironically, Columbus, whose real name was Cristobal Colon, set out in 1492 AD. Although coming to the game almost three thousand years late, he was also searching for the fabled Spice Islands.)

The trade in Far East commodities became so important to the Egyptian economy that they dug a shipping channel from the river Nile to the Red Sea. It took them until the days of Ptolemy II to figure out the system of locks necessary to open that canal to the Red Sea, but they got there in the end.

The Egyptians undertook that colossal engineering project in order to facilitate the flow of spices and other rare commodities. The spice-and-silk trade became so extensive that Pliny feared the annual export of hard currency in the form of gold and silver to import spices from the East would bankrupt the Roman Empire. To quote Pliny, "by the lowest reckoning India, China, and the Arabian states take from our empire over one hundred million sesterces a year (mostly for silk and spices)."

In an effort to break the Arab monopoly on cinnamon, cloves, nutmeg, and mace, in AD 100 the Romans improved the Egyptian canal, then began sending impressive fleets of trading ships as far as India and Thailand. Many of the spices they were searching for originated from the Spice Islands in what is now Indonesia. The Romans were not the first, nor would they be the last Europeans to expend vast fortunes searching for these little islands.

In 1667, the British traded one of these islands to the Dutch for another small island in North America called Manhattan. That trade also included all of New York, Connecticut, New Jersey, and Long Island just to sweeten the deal. At a time when one kilo of nutmeg was valued on par with silver, that deal was not as disproportionate as it seems today.

Controlling the sole source of nutmeg was a monopoly well worth a king's ransom and more. Little wonder the Dutch were so adamant, and brutal, in their efforts to dominate the Banda Islands, then maintain their monopoly, even at the cost of committing genocide. Whereas the Portuguese adhered to the traditional method of trading for spices, often employing resident Chinese, Indian, or Arabic merchants as middlemen, the Dutch had other plans. They wanted nothing less than total domination of the global spice trade.

In 1621, Dutch East India Company (VOC) soldiers and hired Japanese mercenaries, under the command of Governor General Jan Pieterszoon Coen, invaded the islands. In a carefully engineered scheme, they murdered or enslaved up to 90 percent of the original inhabitants. From an estimated indigenous population of 15,000, only about 1,500 survived the carefully orchestrated genocide instigated by Coen.

Old established trading villages sent boats filled with survivors to seek shelter with their trading partners. Many fled to the Kai Islands, where small pockets of original Bandanese society and language still remain.

Where for thousands of years peaceful trade provided the Banda Islanders with a rich market for their spices and a source of goods that allowed them to build their own extensive trading network, suddenly all trade was fiercely controlled by the Dutch. Draconian measures were implemented. Locally owned vessels were forbidden to have sails or venture away from their home island without special permission. Important trade in foodstuff such as sago, which many communities depended on, collapsed.

CHAPTER 51

Pirates, Patrons, and Thieves

If anything indicates the importance these small islands had for their European masters, it is the vast expenditure of treasure and effort they invested in a plethora of fortifications built to enforce and defend their monopoly. Everywhere you look there are watchtowers and ramparts designed with one thing in mind: to keep other greedy European nations from making off with what the current band of interlopers with a royal commission were busy stealing.

That may sound rather crude considering all the time and effort European governments spent convincing their population that the real reason for dominating these islands was to civilize the naked savage inhabitants, not forgetting the other angle so often chanted to the masses: those poor lost souls needed Christianizing, by force of arms if necessary.

The truth was much simpler. The spices grown on these islands were worth their weight in gold, literally. The country that controlled their source could reap a fortune reselling them to other Asian and European nations. Little wonder the nation with the most dynamic merchants wound up colonizing the place.

Those were the halcyon days of Europe's piratical conquests. A time when anyone with a royal letter of marque could fill their pockets by stealing riches beyond their wildest dreams. Those letters usually read a bit like, "I, King Dogfish the Grasper, hereby license my loyal servant Muggins the

Younger and his band of merry men to steal whatever they can get their hands on from anyone far enough away that they can't cause me any trouble, as long as I get my cut." Laugh all you want, but that is exactly what was happening. Of course, if you take a squint around, the same thing is still going on today.

The upshot of all this was that whoever happened to be industriously exploiting some distant land had to diligently defend themselves from others of their ilk, who also wanted to get rich quick on someone else's account. Ah, the glory days of European expansion, when all a lad needed was a stout ship, an eye patch, and a letter of marque to have it almost as good as modern day bankers.

In case you're interested, here is the current definition of *letter of marque*: "a license to fit out an armed vessel and use it in the capture of enemy merchant shipping and to commit acts that would otherwise have constituted piracy."

The capital of the Banda Islands is Neira, an easygoing, friendly little town with a strong colonial flavor. The Portuguese chose this convenient site to establish themselves when they first arrived in the early 1500s and discovered it populated by the aforementioned Chinese, Indian, and Arabic traders who had been installed there for centuries. Not long after that, in 1516, they started building Fort Nassau. The Dutch finished that fort in 1609 but soon decided it was poorly sited. Fort Belgica quickly followed.

In 1611, the Dutch began construction of a new fort. Located atop a small hill overlooking both the northern and southern anchorages, Fort Belgica enjoys a position that was much easier to defend. Both of those old forts make wonderful destinations for an evening stroll through the town.

At one time Neira was famous for its many "perkenier mansions," opulent houses built during the golden age of the Dutch "nutmeg barons," a title that applied to wealthy nutmeg plantation owners. At the height of the nutmeg boom, they squandered immense fortunes importing luxury items in a vain attempt to replicate the lavish lifestyle their wealth would have purchased in Holland. Judging from the number of ancient gin bottles regularly washed ashore in front of the old governor's mansion, they also spent much of their time soused to the gills.

Dutch perkeniers existed like feudal lords, surrounding themselves in arrogant luxury, pampered by a small army of local servants and of course slaves. They were rich. Yet being half a world away from their home country, they could not fully enjoy the benefits of that wealth. Little wonder, between the depressing weather these islands experience for most of the year and enforced isolation so far from home, many Europeans ended their days by committing suicide.

Although shorn of their sumptuous luxuries, many of those once impressive colonial residences, with their stately columns and imported marble floors, still stand. Strolling through those modest provincial palaces, it takes little effort to imagine the frustration those displaced plantation owners experienced. Although wealthy beyond their wildest dreams, they could only retain that wealth through self-imposed exile on these remote eastern islands where it rains every day for most of the year. Of course, for the Dutch, that may have made the place more homelike.

CHAPTER 52

The Banda Islands

Overlooking a sheltered bay formed by the islands of Gunung Api, Banda Neira, and Banda Besar, from high on its hilltop prominence Fort Belgica enjoys a splendid view of both navigable entrances, with Gunung Api's lush tropical green standing proud over all.

This typical five-sided fortification was built to protect Dutch colonialists from invasion by other greedy European powers. It also allowed colonialists to fend off the native islanders, who became irate when the Dutch forcibly kicked out their traditional Chinese, Indian, and Arabic trading partners, then insisted on monopolizing the long-established spice trade.

Approaching Fort Belgica from the town side, a path leads to the curved archway of its main portal. Climbing that walkway, I tried to imagine native warriors charging uphill in a desperate attempt to regain control of their islands. Attacking those high stone walls, from where the thunderous boom of heavy cannon loaded with grape shot and the *pop-pop* of muskets showered down a leaden storm of sudden death, took unwavering courage. The gripping fear as those terrible lead balls ripped into flesh with a dull smacking noise would have tested any man's courage to its limits.

Today, that hill is a pleasant park dotted with flowerbeds and a few scattered shade trees. On one side, local farmers have appropriated modest parcels of land to grow vegetables. Gardening plots are at a premium on Banda Neira, so any space where vegetables can grow soon becomes someone's vegetable plot.

Just inside Fort Belgica's impressive gray-stone gate is a guardroom where local youngsters studying to be official tour guides collect a modest entrance fee and volunteer to conduct a visit to the fort. The tour they give is quite knowledgeable, even if their stories do become a bit fanciful should the mood strike them.

I prefer wandering through this imaginatively restored historic monument without distraction. Letting my mind drift, searching for the déjà vu impressions I often find in such places. I have always felt something deeply quixotic every time I see one of these old forts, or castles, perched high on a remote hillside. Sadly, that impression rarely survives once inside those massive walls, where the ambiance is typically stark and utilitarian.

From the dimly lit guard chamber, a second stone arch opens to the glaring tropical sunlight of an inner courtyard. Once inside, the pentagonal design of this classic European fortification is easy to discern from the crenulated towers located at each corner. Each tower served as an elevated defensive position and a protected passage for stairways leading to the ramparts.

There is something magical about being inside one of these old five-sided forts. Accustomed to spending our lives in buildings and rooms with four walls, when we confront a building with five sides, something disorienting happens to the way our minds interpret reality. Even consciously trying to count the walls can become a difficult task fraught with frustration.

As with most fortifications from this period, accommodation and storage spaces were constructed under the massive crenellated ramparts between towers. A well stands in the center of the courtyard, giving access to cisterns where an intricate system of drains collects and stores fresh water from Banda's copious rain. Inside the rooms, the ceilings are high-pointed arches designed to support the ramparts above.

The rooms are cool even though the sparse unglazed windows only grudgingly allow a negligible amount of light and even less ventilation to enter. At each of the five corners, almost directly under the towers, a modest suite of rooms existed for the grandees of the fort. Those would have included the commander and his officers or perhaps even the governor and his crew in times of conflict.

Those special lodgings were far from what I would call elegant. In fact, they struck me as cheerless caverns whose only purpose was to provide a safe refuge from an enraged local chamber of commerce.

On a more pragmatic note, even though Meggi and I searched every available nook and cranny, there was no indication the fort had ever sported toilet or bathing facilities. So they must have employed either the "bucket and chuck it" method or found a comfortable place on the wall to practice the venerable "long drop" system. With several hundred men in residence, sneaking around under those great walls at night would have been an undertaking fraught with more than one unpleasant risk. We also failed to discover a kitchen.

Within each tower, the steep half twist of a narrow stairway leads to the wide ramparts above. Emerging from the claustrophobic darkness below into the open air and bright sunshine makes for a very a pleasant change. Crenelated openings in the walls clearly mark positions from which cannon could dominate both anchorages and the hill leading up to the fort.

Today a few corroded old cannons mounted in cement protrude from the walls, while even more lie slowly rusting away from neglect in the high grass that surrounds the fort. If you ask the islanders, they claim there is a plan to "one day" hoist up and mount those old cannons along the walls. We have been going there for years now, and so far "one day" has yet to arrive.

Emerging into the sunlight, Meggi and I explored the southernmost rampart, admiring the spectacular panorama of Banda Besar and Gunung Api. Arriving at the western tower, we ascended even higher. Climbing the narrow ladder that leads to the roof soon became an adventure in itself.

The small square entrance hatch at the top of an iron ladder is so narrow that only after much twisting and several painful contortions did I finally arrive on the roof. At one point, I was sure my knee and backpack were jammed so tightly against the sides that Meggi might have to call for a crane to extricate me. How anyone in full armor, carrying an antique musket and long fighting sword, could have made it up there in a rush is a mystery. Although Meggi kindly reminded me that solders back then were not as tall, nor so well fed, as I am.

If you ask me, it was the vegetable shopping she insisted on stuffing in my backpack. Well, you try wiggling through those narrow openings with a load of cabbage, potatoes, and onions on your back and see how far you get. You would be amazed how bulky a few veggies can be when you find yourself in a tight spot. Good thing I went first. At least that way Meggi missed seeing me flounder onto the roof, then blunder to my feet in an undignified manner.

What it must have been like for a Dutch soldier, standing on those battlements in the 1600s with Gunung Api belching sulfurous smoke and fire as it violently erupted less than a mile away, I can only imagine.

My mind conjured up images of living in remote isolation half a world away from country, friends, and family. A small troop of poorly equipped men, surrounded by thousands of people who would far prefer to see them rotting in hell rather than infesting their islands.

I could almost feel the weight of a heavy metal helmet on my head, hot from the sun beating down on this beautiful tropical bay. And the boredom from weeks and months of watching an eternally empty sea. Long days would pass staring at the same constantly blue or gray horizon, wishing, hoping, praying, yet never sighting one of those rare ships from home. Try to imagine the excitement when after months or even years of monotonous isolation, a sail appeared far out on the horizon.

Frantic signals flashed between those garrisoning the fort high above the village of Lonthor on Banda Besar to where I stood on Banda Neira. Perhaps from my very position the watch saw those signals, then turned to alert his companions that an unknown European vessel was approaching. A throng of excited men swarmed onto the battlements, all intently observing as a slow-moving ship steered for the entrance to the bay.

Much more than the potential joy of seeing a ship from home occupied their minds. Could the approaching ship be full of powerful artillery and heavily armed men intent on invasion? These were hotly contested islands. Several times Portuguese, English, and even Spanish ships attacked with an eye to capturing them for their own merchants to exploit, or at the very least to make off with a shipload of cloves, nutmeg, and mace. Even a successful pirate attack, something the English were not averse to having a go at, might fill a ship with a king's ransom in spices. A jolly morning's work with cannon and sword leading to a cargo so profitable the captain and crew might retire to enjoy a lifetime supply of country houses, pubs, and other sailorly fantasies.

With this in mind, the men of Fort Belgica would have titivated their cannons and double-checked the priming of pistols and muskets and then eased swords in their scabbards. The islands they guarded were a treasure trove whose vast riches stood coveted by every scoundrel on the sea and monarch in Europe.

As the ship slowly approached, apprehension liberally mixed with exhilaration would have been rife. Imagine the joy when the fort commander saw the brightly colored Dutch flag they were praying for. Sailors would look closely to ensure the ship was truly Dutch built, for it could well be a devious enemy flying the Dutch flag.

Flying the enemy's flag was an age-old deception used by many seagoing scoundrels in the hope of approaching closer to an enemy unhindered. Arriving within cannon range uncontested, the attackers would haul down those false colors and hoist their real national flag as they fired the first devastating broadside into an unsuspecting victim. Even a ship clearly built in Holland would be no guarantee. Pirates could easily employ a captured Dutch ship to facilitate a surprise attack.

Meanwhile, excitement spread through the community like wild fire. A ship! A ship has arrived! The whole town turned out, calling and cheering as the vessel glided through the narrow reef-fringed entrance between Gunung Api and Banda Besar. As the critical moment approached, more than one held their breath.

A slow match burned in tubs beside carefully loaded cannon, wafting its special scent along the battlements as gunners tended their pieces, all the time watching for any indication of aggression. Swept up in the turbulence of their times those brave adventurers were alone, far from their home with little hope of assistance should hostilities break out.

The tension during those final moments, as the ship rounded up into the wind in front of the governor's mansion and came to anchor, must have been unbearable. As the anchor splashed down into crystal-clear water, a universal sigh of relief washed over the town. Yet only when the ship began firing a salute to the fort using blank charges would the tension finally ease. The long wait was over at last. They had not been forgotten, or even worse abandoned to their fate, by the mother country.

Excitement ran high. The company vessels that touched here to load pearls and spices also provided luxury items craved by the small Dutch community. For many there would be mail from home, along with everything from cheese to gin and even such items as sewing needles, thread, and shovels stowed in the ship's hold.

Thanks to the highly lucrative spice trade, the affluent Dutch perkeniers could afford to import a cornucopia of luxuries all the way from Holland. Shipowners and captains were more than happy to supply that demand, at exorbitant profit to themselves. The benefits a ship captain might realize on his private-venture trade goods were on a par with what could be earned as his share for successfully transporting a full cargo of nutmeg and mace safely back to Holland.

While the Dutch cavorted with joy at the prospect of gin and cheese from home, descendants from the original inhabitants would not have been happy seeing another European ship arrive. They were the scant few who miraculously survived the genocide. Somber-faced people who remembered when they had not been slaves and their islands were a thriving regional center for trade. Times when their own proud craft carried lucrative cargoes to Malacca and beyond. For them, there was only sadness.

CHAPTER 53

What Is It Like Out There?

I always said one day I would write a book about all the dumb questions people ask me concerning life at sea. Things like, "What do you do at night? Do you put down the anchor and go to sleep?" Or "Where do you do your shopping when you are out there?" Or "Aren't you afraid of the dark at night?" Many of those questions are enough to make you wonder if computers, smartphones, and television really are causing serious brain rot.

I once read about some Swedish kids who did a science fair project subjecting alfalfa seeds to phone microwave emissions while they were sprouting. The seeds that weren't exposed to microwave emissions sprouted nicely and grew normally. The ones exposed to microwaves refused to grow at all. Maybe that explains the problem with today's youth; their seeds never sprout properly.

Most kids who grow up in modern cities have no idea what the real world is like. They believe milk grows on trees in little cartons and meat or chicken comes in plastic packages from a factory somewhere. At least they have the part about meat and chicken almost right. But these days, what was once termed common sense has become so rare we now call it uncommon sense.

One frequently asked question is, "What do you do when the weather is bad and the seas get really rough?" Now that question makes sense, at least to me, and by now, you probably already have an idea of how I respond. What I do in bad weather when the seas are rough enough to make a whale puke is wish with all my heart I could be somewhere else. A log cabin on some pleasant mountainside being first choice, or a date farm in the Sahara. Anyone who says they enjoy being at sea when the weather is acting up is either lying or belongs in a padded room, preferably under restraint, for their own protection.

If you ask me, one of the most fundamental inventions the first sailors made was a foul weather jacket. Of course, the art of producing foul weather gear has progressed dramatically since those early days when Og and Zog sported the first animal-skin ponchos. Maybe one day I should put together a slick glossy coffee-table book full of pictures and illustrations on foul weather gear through the ages and call it *A Leak in Time*.

I base that title on a fact. Every single foul weather jacket made will always start leaking more or less exactly three-quarters of the way through a watch. The precision with which this happens has often had me speculating.

This being the age of highly targeted specialization, I can easily imagine engineers with a long string of letters behind their names slaving away designing insidious leaks into foul weather jackets, some specializing in sleeves, others doing hoods, and of course all of them wanting to reach the pinnacle of their profession—leaks for the back of the neck. Those insidious little infiltrations carefully engineered to send an annoying trickle of cold water down the center of your back, at precisely the moment when it seems you might make it through a watch without getting too wet.

That may not be as dumb as it sounds. After all, there are highly paid engineers who spend their whole lives designing things to break after a very precise amount of time. Some bright lad designs something to do a job properly, then along come those people to ensure it will need replacing precisely when the next model is about to be released, or two days after the warrantee expires.

CHAPTER 54

Pearls of the Banda Islands

Although overshadowed by the demand for spice, for thousands of years the Bandanese have harvested and traded pearls found in the water around their islands. The first pearls would have been discovered by accident during a rustic shellfish buffet. But once their value as a trade item was established, intrepid local divers began harvesting oysters.

Content to purchase what local divers produced, Chinese spice merchants were among the largest consumers until Arab spice traders, seeing the chance to earn a healthy profit, commercialized the harvesting of pearls. The value of Bandanese pearls was such that long before the arrival of Europeans, Arab traders had imported specialized divers from the Red Sea. The locals called those Arab divers *Deba-deba*.

Between 1880 and 1890, with competition for pearls from these islands at its peak, the Baadilla family forged links with local rulers and independent divers to dominate the trade. In order to train local divers, Said Baadilla brought in experienced pearl divers from Portugal and Spain, whose descendants still work as farmers and pearl divers.

Said Baadilla is also credited with the idea of using mother of pearl, the interlining from pearl mollusk, for buttons and a plethora of other decorative products. That innovation, designed to circumvent the Dutch rule against exporting pearls, led to the birth of a global industry and opened a huge market with the English.

By the time global demand for pearls and mother of pearl reached its peak in 1900, Bandanese pearls had become famous for their size, clarity, and delicate color. The mineral-rich waters and wide variety of oysters found between Neira and Lonthor produce a plethora of tantalizing colors, including rare shades of black, silver, yellow, and pink.

In 1958 a Japanese businessman established the world's first commercial pearl farm between Banda Neira and Banda Besar. Although the initial demand was modest, the quality and delicate coloring of those cultured pearls remain in demand today.

Pearls are still cultured between the islands of Neira and Lonthor, and a few local divers continue collecting wild pearls in the traditional manner, often diving to great depths. Although rarely exported, those wild pearls are available to visitors through several reputable sources on Banda Neira. Among those are Abba Rizal, owner of the historic Cilu Bintang Estate, whose family still dives for pearls, and Azwar Baadilla, the great grandson of Said Baadilla.

While I was busy daydreaming, the sun slowly slipped behind Gunung Api, casting the village below in shadow. First one then another of the mosques began their timeless ritual of calling the faithful to prayer. The smell of cooking fires and exotic spices hung in the air. Slowly I turned, strolling over to the ladder that, with some effort and luck, would take me back to twenty-first-century Banda Neira, a sleepy island where motorbikes coexist alongside bicycle-powered rickshaws called bajacks and friendly children call out, "Hello Mister," to every passing stranger.

Taking my leave through the massive entry portal, I noticed another great cannon lying abandoned in the grass beside the wall. I could not help thinking of European occupation in these islands as the poignantly moving account of viciously brutal domination driven by greed. Fortunately, this has not left the islanders in a chronic state of melancholic depression. In fact, despite having suffered so much in their history, they seem to be some of the happiest people I have ever met. Then again, few of the islanders you meet today are direct descendants from the original inhabitants.

CHAPTER 55

A Visit to Waer

Banda Besar, the largest of the Banda Islands, is the home of Fort Lontar (1624) and Fort Concordia (1630). This long thin crescent-shaped chain of mountains about one kilometer to the south of Banda Neira provides the southern anchorage, with superb protection from strong wind and heavy seas.

The name *Banda Besar* means "Big Banda," and it is where the majority of the nutmeg plantations are still located. This island was once the source of fabulous wealth. Since Meggi and I wanted to continue exploring the many historical remains, we decided to combine a trip to historic Banda Besar with our annual delivery of medical and educational supplies for the community of Waer and the island of Hatta.

Waer is a small community located on the southern side of Banda Besar that we have been assisting for the past several years. A historically interesting place, Waer is one of the oldest continuously populated settlements in the archipelago. It first appears on the "Jansonnius Map" from 1620, although the community existed as a base for interisland traders long before being recorded by Europeans. As one of the archipelago's oldest and more remote settlements, Waer has its own special magic.

It was early morning when a roughly built local island boat negotiated its way alongside *Vega*, its peeling pastel-blue paint highlighted by a strip of intense red along the rub strake. At the garishly painted bright-yellow helm, the oldest son of our friend Ishmael stood, proudly steering his small cargo-cum-ferry-boat. The smiling faces of our fellow passengers peeked out from under a sky-blue plastic tarp stretched over the cargo space.

Hearing a light crunch of wood against wood as the two boats joined, Meggi muttered something about "her" paintwork, followed by a most unladylike expression. The scowl she aimed at the boat's cheerful young driver clearly expressed her opinion of his seamanship. It seems no matter how much she fusses with our fenders, those local boats always manage to defeat her, as several deep scratches in *Vega*'s well-cared-for paint attest.

After a bit of fender juggling, we soon had the boat safely tied alongside. With the welcome assistance of Dr. Ruth, we began passing down boxes and bags of supplies destined for the clinic, midwife, and school at Waer and Hatta Island. Since the majority of our fellow travelers were from the town of Waer, they knew of *Vega* and our mission. The cheerful way they pitched in to help and the many thank-yous we received were encouraging.

With our precious stores all loaded and safely protected from saltwater spray by a waterproof plastic tarp, Ishmael's son energetically cranked life into his single-cylinder inboard engine. Meggi and Ruth womaned the bow, carefully fending off his boat from ours as the two slowly separated. With no neutral or reverse gear, maneuvering one of those local boats in a tight space is not easy.

If there is a special sound I associate with those local boats, it is the loud bang and dense, black smoke ring when they first fire, followed by the *pop, pop-pop, pop-pop-pop* of those single-cylinder inboard diesel engines. None of which sport the slightest pretense of an exhaust silencer. I am amazed the drivers are not all deaf. Some of those rough-and-rugged engines can be heard for miles. Yet noisy or not, they are dependable, hardworking little machines that are easily repaired and consume a modest amount of fuel.

The boats themselves are long and narrow, with no decking to speak of. Their only condescension to luxury is a small, hot, noisy aft cabin where lucky passengers can duck in out of the splashing waves, sun, or rain. Primarily designed to house the boat's engine, the inside of those cabins is best described as rustic. A single long wooden bench on each side serves as passenger seating. The open cargo bay is usually better ventilated and more comfortable.

Trying to keep the supplies, and ourselves, as dry as possible during the hour-and-a-half voyage soon became a serious challenge. To reach our destination, the boat must forge its way against the monsoon until it rounds the northern tip of Banda Besar. Of course, the driver wants to go fast in order to make as many trips in a day as possible. That means the ferry constantly bashes into the waves. This slamming throws up thick spray that the wind blows back across the cargo hold with its load of passengers. The boat drivers have either become extremely adept at ducking behind the cabin or inured to being soaked for hours at a time. The unfortunate lads who drive a regular run must be coated with salt and wrinkled as prunes by the end of a rough day.

Lacking their hardened attitude to flying salt water, and having all our boxes and bags of supplies to protect, Meggi and I spend most of the voyage huddled together trying to maintain a pretense of dryness. Ruth, being curious as a kitten, kept sticking her head out from under the tarp for a look-see. Each time, a face full of salt water rewarded her effort. As we thumped and banged our way around Banda Besar, I couldn't help smiling. You won't find an experience like that in the Lonely Planet guide.

You may be wondering why we chose to endure such a long, uncomfortable boat ride rather than take a ferry to the northern landing on Banda Besar, then the short four-kilometer journey to cross the island by road. The reason is simple. Several years before, we tried the short route on motorbikes and swore never again. Try hanging onto the back of a small motorbike slipping and sliding as it struggles to climb a muddy track most goats would shun and see what that does for your blood pressure. That road is in an abysmal state. There are no four-wheel-drive vehicles on the island, and even if they had one, this little boy is not about to risk his life on those crumbling mountain tracks.

A charming little town, Waer straddles a normally placid stream that becomes a raging torrent during the rainy season. An ancient town with a well-preserved fort from the Portuguese days, Waer still has no port. An open stretch of slightly sheltered beach allows small boats to come close enough for passengers to hop over the side and wade ashore. Whatever loads they bring are passed from hand to hand or balanced precariously on someone's head for the trip to dry land.

When the weather is rough, or seas from the south run dangerously high, it becomes impossible to land. During those times, torrential rain renders the tenuous mountain road impassable. For months, Wear is cut off from the outside world. Fortunately for Ruth, Meggi, and me, the seas were relatively calm when our boat grounded on the beach with a grinding crunch.

After hours cooped up under the blue plastic tarpaulin, we looked forward to stretching our legs. Or in my case, discovering where the local dogs hiked their legs. But relief was not to be. There on the beach, our good friend Dr. Celso stood, patiently awaiting our arrival.

Since he was expecting us, Celso had drafted a contingent of local fishermen into service. They stood around shuffling their feet and smoking clove cigarettes, ready and waiting to help offload the supplies we had brought. Having years of experience at it, they made short work of getting everything ashore, and to both Ruth and Celso's relief, all of those supplies arrived dry. One man even offered to carry Meggi or Ruth ashore on his back, an offer he did not bother extending to me.

Our first stop was the Waer community clinic, headed by Dr. Celso. Much to the delight of Waer's gossips, we formed an impromptu parade, soon joined by villagers of all ages that Dr. Celso enlisted to carry boxes and bags destined for the community health post. Once you factor in children running alongside us and older folk coming up to ask what was afoot, there must have been a hundred people in that procession when we eventually arrived at the clinic. On the final stretch, we slowed the pace so Dr. Celso could run ahead and position himself for the official welcome.

A soft-spoken, energetic young man of average height for an Indonesian, Dr. Celso has twinkling brown eyes and black hair that he wears trimmed short. Personally, I find him an amazing person. When the conversation turns to medical problems, those eyes acquire an intensely serious cast and his long delicate hands become animated. Even his normally cheerful voice assumes a different tone. Celso first came to this isolated posting fresh from internship in Jakarta, assigned to Wear as part of his official Ministry of Health national service.

From the very first day, Celso fell in love with the place and its slow, easy way of life, an enormous change from the hustle and bustle of life in the hugely polluted megacity where he was born. When his term of national service ended, Celso volunteered to continue managing the Waer health post. Two years later he met and married a local girl from Banda Naira who had just finished her medical studies in Jakarta. With his years of experience, Celso could have almost any posting available, yet year after year he chooses to stay in Waer. Perhaps his lovely Bandanese wife, Dr. Oki, has something to do with that. In any case, I have rarely met two more content people, even considering the constant frustration caused by a chronic shortage of supplies and equipment.

From his small community clinic, Celso struggles to provide medical services for the southern side of Banda Besar and the nearby island of Hatta. Not at all an easy task since Hatta and southern Banda Besar spend almost half of every year isolated from the outside world. Even though he has a rather nice Ministry of Health water ambulance for emergency cases and mobile clinic visits to the island of Hatta, there is always something wrong with the outboard motor and rarely any money for fuel or oil.

The first time we saw his official health post, it was only from a sense of politeness and wish not to injure his feelings that we managed to call it a clinic. Somewhere Meggi still has several sad photographs from that visit. The roof was falling in, the doors and windows were eaten away by termites, and the whole place desperately needed painting. Of the original eight rooms, only two were serviceable. In one of them the roof leaked so badly Celso had built a tent over the examination table to protect his patients.

He really had almost nothing at all to work with. No drugs. No bandages. Not even a laboratory microscope. The microscope he was using at the time came from a child's introductory biology set. It was all we could do to keep our faces straight when he showed it to us.

Thanks to several of our friends who provided money for materials, and the local community who donated their labor, at least now the roof no longer leaks. The entire building was freshly painted and the doctor's living quarters restored. There have also been other important improvements.

Somewhere in the recently arrived boxes was a professional laboratory microscope, along with a portable ultrasound scanner, multicheck blood analyzer, and several other important pieces of equipment. There was also an extensive stock of expendables and medications. While Celso sent word for the local midwife to come meet with Dr. Ruth and pick up her resupply kit, we began sorting through that year's delivery.

Since we had almost everything he requested the year before, the expression on his face was one of unmitigated delight. A proud man who maintains tight control of his emotions, Dr. Celso has that ingrained dignity one rarely finds these days. Yet, as he sorted through the equipment and supplies we brought, more than once a smile curled his lips and a twinkle lit up those expressive brown eyes. Being a man of few words, his comment was simple: "With this, I can save lives. Thank you."

Coming from Dr. Celso that simple statement was equal to a seven-course knife-and-fork sit-down dinner at the town hall, followed by fireworks, speeches, and a champagne toast. Of course, later we had to stand in front of the clinic while Celso made a blessedly short speech. By then several hundred people were gathered out front, excitedly milling around, gawking, and in general looking happy. Several hawkers roamed the crowd, offering the Indonesian version of popcorn or sausage in a bun.

Just about the time Celso finished his little discourse and I thought we might get off lightly, up pops the town mayor to put his oar in. Being a good politician, he rambled on interminably while I stood there trying to appear pleased. Ruth did her best to look intent, while Meggi shuffled from foot to foot. Once the speakers wound down, the good folks of Waer seemed pretty content. Mind you, they had good reason to be pleased.

Judging by the number that came up later to mangle my paw or pat me on the back, if it had been Election Day I might now be the new lord mayor. Meggi, who usually shuns public appearances like the plague, put on her best face for a deputation from the local ladies sewing circle, while Dr. Ruth wisely managed to slip off looking for a toilet.

Next on our list came Waer's midwife, a dignified elderly woman with a lifetime of experience bringing babes into this world. She learned midwifery from her mother, who learned from her mother, going back so many generations no one knew for sure when her family first took up providing the village with a midwife. Although deeply traditional, she was intensely interested in learning more about her profession.

Several years ago we gave her one of our twenty-two-kilo basic midwife sets, which put a huge smile on her face. Over the ensuing years, we have consistently updated and resupplied that kit. That year we had another resupply, with some serious upgrades, and Dr. Ruth, who instantly took her aside for "Doctor Ruth's Mini Workshop" on how to use the new equipment and medications.

The next thing I knew the two of them were headed into the village, deep in an animated conversation that, for sure, included bottoms, babies, and another cup of tea with biscuits. Four young lads followed behind them. One carried a medium-size box in his arms. Another balanced a large solar panel on his head. The other two boys gamely struggled with a large black nylon bag filled with equipment and supplies.

No woman should be forced to give birth in the dark, and emergency surgery should never be undertaken by candlelight. But the lack of electricity remains a major problem for most remote island health workers and midwives. But thanks to the wonders of modern technology, there are easily implemented solutions.

The lighting sets we brought that year were developed by a friend of ours in Jakarta. The day after Meggi first explained to him the problem he called together the engineering staff at his factory and asked them to develop an inexpensive, compact solar-powered lighting kit for use on remote islands with limited or no electricity. They did a marvelous job. When he brought the first twenty examples to *Vega* as a donation, we thought Christmas had come early that year. They were a huge hit with midwives and health workers.

Consisting of a lightweight, portable control pack with an integral battery and one easily replaceable LED light bulb, and the possibility of adding a second lamp, those solar-charged lighting systems are life changing. The solar panel stays at home to charge the battery pack during the day. When a midwife or health worker is called out at night, they take the battery pack and light with them, safely stowed in their "callout" bag. Each full charge provides eight hours of dependable light.

When we first arrived, more than a few people were lounging about under the giant trees surrounding the clinic on Waer. After another blessedly short speech by Dr. Celso explaining to the assembled host what the supplies we brought meant for the community, he unpacked the boxes and sorted their contents. When he came to the professional binocular laboratory microscope, I thought the man was going to cry.

Opening a box containing pharmaceuticals, he sorted through it until he found what he was looking for. Then taking a dose in his hand, he went to the door and called to someone waiting under the trees to come receive their medicine, along with whatever instructions he felt necessary.

Later Celso explained he had been out of badly needed pharmaceuticals for several months. In fact, things became so bad he was spending his own modest government salary to purchase drugs for his patients at the retail pharmacy on Banda Neira. Knowing we would arrive that day, he sent word to his most needy ambulatory patients to be at the clinic when we arrived.

For the more critical cases, he would personally make a few quick house calls to deliver their medication, while we visited the school. The less urgent patients could wait until he returned from the small island of Hatta. While Celso packed his carryout bag with an assortment of drugs, we turned to our other reason for visiting Waer.

Before continuing to Hatta, Meggi and I had an impressive load of large boxes and bags containing educational supplies, teaching aids, and sports equipment for the village school. Shuffling from foot to foot with excitement, and most likely wishing we would get on with it, several young boys were perched alongside the box containing sports equipment, mesmerized by the new official FIFA footballs and team shirts.

Leaving the clinic and a happy Dr. Celso behind, we set out for the school. Advance rumors of official regulation footballs and team uniforms ensured a surplus of volunteer students, drafted into a little extracurricular activity by their teachers. On our way to the school, a line of children snaked out behind us with boxes or bags balanced on their heads. As our procession of cheerful porters wound their way through Waer village toward the school, it wasn't long before inquisitive kids and interested parents joined the parade. Most tagged along to see what the excitement was about. Others were interested in what we brought for the school. More than one parent mangled my mitt and offered thanks.

Waer's school is government sponsored. That means, being out of sight and out of mind, they are provided with a building, a few teachers paid for by the Ministry of Education, and precisely the degree of material support you might expect a place located far from any major population center to receive. Yet, for the parents of Waer, procuring the very best education possible for their children is serious business. Since the teachers had freely discussed the importance of our past contributions at community meetings, many parents were excited to see this year's donations. They were not disappointed.

The school building had just been refurbished, so it looked almost new under a coat of bright paint and with its recently repaired windows. Once inside, the story changed. Several classrooms had no tables or chairs. Students sat on the floor in organized rows to take their classes.

Even after five years of consistent support from our side, everywhere we looked there was still a dire shortage of basic supplies. We also noted many of the books, posters, and other teaching aids from our previous visits prominently displayed and clearly well used. After the students diligently lined up to sing songs and recite little speeches welcoming us, it didn't take me long to unpack the supplies we had and range them on the floor.

Whenever we make a delivery, we always take photographs that I believe are important. Someone once said we do it to show off, that laying out everything so each donation can easily be seen is akin to blatant advertising.

I disagree. Those pictures are our way of showing the people who contributed those materials exactly where their donation went, who received it, and how happy they made those kids and teachers. It also gives us a chance to document the state of a place for future reference. As to the comments from NGOs we meet along the way, I figure it's just sour grapes, since what we accomplish with almost nothing for funding makes what they do with huge budgets look bad.

With the school supplies delivered and a new wish list of items for next year safely tucked away, Meggi and I returned to the clinic, where we were soon joined by Dr. Ruth. In our wake we left several very happy teachers busily sorting teaching aids, books, posters, pencils, and pens. Judging by the happy sounds from the school playing field, at least one new football was being put to the test.

Back at the clinic, Dr. Celso had finished sorting, distributing, and storing his medical supplies. It was time to visit the tiny island of Hatta.

Since the government water ambulance was broken, again, Dr. Celso suggested we take advantage of our chartered ferry boat for the visit. Once there, he would conduct a clinic and employ some of the small disposable syringes we brought to continue a child immunization program that had been stalled due to the lack of syringes. Dr. Ruth would take the local midwife her resupply kit and spend some time discussing how to use the new equipment, while Meggi and I visited the school. When we arrived at the beach, the rest of Dr. Celso's team was waiting beside two black nylon supply bags we brought two years before. They were packed and ready to go.

CHAPTER 56

The Hatta Break

Located southeast of Banda Neira and Banda Besar, Hatta is a remote island once famous for its giant teak trees, long ago decimated by the Dutch. At one time, those forests provided wood for all sorts of building projects. Currently, a locally inspired project is replanting teak trees on the island, a project we proudly support.

Today Hatta has little of economic interest, other than some of the clearest water and finest underwater panoramas to be found anywhere in the world. That easily explains why, every time we go there, Meggi brings her diving mask and snorkel. The unspoiled reefs are stunningly beautiful, no matter where you look. Long white beaches, swaying palms, and superb diving make Hatta one of our favorite small island escapes.

Historically, Hatta had only one major military incident, when an English warship's captain fired his cannons in a noisy yet harmless manner and caused the British flag to be planted at several places around the island. With no intent to take possession, he simply did it to enrage the Dutch colonists on Banda Neira and Banda Besar. It worked.

Convinced the English had landed in force to occupy Hatta, the Dutch mounted a major armed expedition to oust them. Arriving in full force, with cannons and all, they soon discovered that after purchasing every available vegetable on the island then indulging in a bit of petty looting, the British were long gone. Only their flag remained behind. One unconfirmed rumor has it an empty brandy bottle was found at the base of the main flagpole with a note inside that read, "Happy April Fool's Day."

Hatta Island is one of the most isolated places imaginable. A lost backwater that for several months out of every year is cut off from the other islands by seas so rough that landing small craft there becomes all but impossible. Fortunately, the day of our visit the seas were calm and our local ferry had no problem approaching close enough for us to safely disembark with the many boxes of supplies we brought for the midwife and village school.

While Dr. Celso busied his team with vaccinations and a general clinic, and Dr. Ruth disappeared for a natter with the local midwife, Meggi and I made our delivery to the school. With that mission accomplished, we set out searching for a likely stretch of beach to relax and play tourist for a few hours. Meggi amused herself snorkeling, and I curled up in the shade to finish a book I was reading. The place was so peaceful I soon drifted into a lazy afternoon siesta.

The next thing I knew a young boy was shaking my shoulder and nattering some indecipherable gibberish. The little pest clearly wanted my attention. So I pried open an eye. Squinting in the bright sunshine, I saw Meggi strolling the beach toward where I sat. She was balancing a large collection of loose seashells in one hand and her snorkeling kit in the other. The huge ear-to-ear grin on her face said it all.

Hopping excitedly from one foot to the other, clearly the boy was on a mission. Celso had sent him to locate and retrieve Meggi and me. With the clinic over and the last child vaccinated, the boat was waiting to take us back.

Getting to my feet, I dusted the sand off my bottom and waited for Meggi. Soon the three of us were strolling barefoot down the beach toward where the boat awaited. Two hours after dropping Celso and his team off at Waer, we were back on board *Vega*, with the last of our yearly deliveries completed.

CHAPTER 57

Of Ancient Ships and Kora-Kora Races

As you can tell by now, Meggi and I are both fascinated by archaic ruins, old boats, and maritime history. We often joke that searching out "old stones" is one of our preferred pastimes. There is something about ancient remnants, long ago abandoned by the people who gave them life, that attracts us like two iron nails to a magnet. Call me crazy, if you wish, and you will not be the first, but those places speak to me in some mysterious subliminal manner.

Even though many of the historic sites we visit are fascinating, ships are what attract me the most. Wherever we go, I give the local craft a squint. I relish studying their often-curious shapes and rigging, trying to understand how those forms evolved to suit the job at hand and local sea conditions.

Traditional sailing rigs are even more remarkable. I enjoy following the evolutionary thread where local materials and skills played such an important part in their development from woven palm fronds and rope made from coconut fiber to canvas and more recently plastic awnings with polypropylene cordage.

Seen against that background, you can imagine our delight when a few years ago we arrived in the Banda Islands just in time for the traditional kora-kora races. For over a week before those hotly contested races begin, teams can be seen training in their long, sleek fifty-man canoes. Meggi and I spent hours perched out on *Vega*'s bowsprit watching boat after boat sprint up or down the bay, often at more than fifteen knots.

After that, the races themselves were almost anticlimactic. For me kora-kora will always be hundreds of men all dressed in their everyday kanga and head cloth, paddling those long thin canoes in almost perfect harmony. Once the ceremonial dress comes out, something mystical vanishes. I no longer imagine them setting out to greet, and perhaps help tow in, a newly arrived trading ship, or slipping away at night armed with traditional weapons to raid another island.

The actual races are too modern, too artificial for my taste. Mind you, tourists eat them up with a big spoon. And who am I to say what is authentic or not? When you delve into the tortured history of these islands and their culture, it is amazing they managed to maintain what little they have.

Those kora-kora represent the once dreaded archetypical Bandanese war canoe. The originals carried well over a hundred rowers/warriors and were often arranged like catamarans, with a house suspended between the two hulls. Each of the long thin hulls seen today holds from thirty to fifty rowers. The rest of the crew consists of a captain, two or more lads to toss out any water that gets in, several musicians playing drums and gongs, and a helmsman who sits at the stern steering with a large paddle.

Mind you, with such a mob all busily going at it, there may well be a goat, two chickens, and the cat on board as well. Averaging twenty-two meters in length with a beam of only one and a quarter meters, how those boats fit so many people in such a narrow space without tipping it over always amazes me.

Today, these impressive craft only appear on ceremonial occasions, and when teams come from the surrounding districts to participate in the highly contested kora-kora races. Winning those races is considered an important feat, bringing prestige to the community fielding a successful team and to the individual crew members.

Each boat is brightly painted in its team colors, with the crew tarted up in bright turbans and sarongs to match. Powering their way through the water at up to fifteen knots, the visual effect is stunning. In perfect rhythm, the rowers deliver two power strokes followed by a rest stroke. Their paddles rise and fall in unison. When racing, they often strike a pace that closely resembles the movement of a centipede's feet, an aesthetically pleasing and most impressive feat to watch.

Called *belang* or *orambai*, the Bandanese cargo vessels Europeans saw when they first arrived were more like modest ships. Larger and more full bodied, those trading boats sported one or two masts that originally carried rectangular sails made from platted palm fronds, closely resembling medieval

European square sails. Two large paddles, one on each side of the stern, provided steering. With their high curved bow and stern, slightly reduced in the modern versions, those cargo vessels were strongly reminiscent of Viking longboats. It is a well-known fact that many of them made impressive voyages, maintaining an extensive network of trade routes for thousands of years before Europeans arrived.

One historical Portuguese account, recently confirmed by DNA studies, states that the people of Maluku already had advanced seafaring skills and still communicated with Madagascar in 1645:

> [The Bandanese] are all men very experienced in the art of navigation, to the point that they claim to be the most ancient of all, although many others give this honor to the Chinese, and affirm that this art was handed on from them to the Bandanese. But it is certain that they formerly navigated to the Cape of Good Hope and were in communication with the east coast of the island of San Laurenzo [Madagascar], where there are many brown and Javanized natives who say they are descended from them." (Diogo de Couto, *Decada Quarta da Asia* [Lisbon, 1602])

One local legend tells of a Bandanese *orambai* that sailed on a spice-trading mission to Malacca, where the crew encountered Islam for the first time. Excited by this new discovery, they sailed to the Arabian Gulf and eventually arrived in Mecca. Upon their return, they brought Islam to the islands.

Pushing the historical frontiers back even further, there are several cave paintings in East Timor dated before 9000 BC that clearly depict sailing vessels capable of transporting quite a few people and a respectable amount of cargo. That would have been around the height of the last Ice Age, when two gigantic, now-submerged continents called Sundaland and Sahul were the big thing in Southeast Asia. The boats portrayed in those artworks are remarkably similar to the traditional Bandanese *orambai* in use when the first Europeans arrived.

CHAPTER 58

Fire Mountain

Gunung Api, which means "Fire Mountain" in Bahasa, is the volcano that frequently appears in all those old paintings and drawings you see of the Banda Islands. For over four hundred years, every map showed that volcano erupting, a sign it could be used as a navigational aid. For sure, erupting volcanoes make great landmarks. On a clear day, the plume is visible for twenty or thirty miles, long before the actual island can be seen.

Back in the days when navigation was more a case of guesswork than art form, ships arriving from ports half a world away employed that pillar of smoke by day and the loom of volcanic fire at night to help locate those tiny islands.

After a long and often difficult ocean passage, Gunung Api was the first visible sign of land for most ships arriving fresh from Europe. It would also be the first accurate position many of them would have had for some time. Whether or not it actually did erupt for the old navigators, we know it last popped its top in 1988, destroying three villages. That eruption poured out several massive lava flows that are still visible as huge black scars on the landscape.

If you have never seen a volcano up close and personal as it spits and fumes, take my word for it, the experience is awe inspiring. Most of us are accustomed to thinking of nature, at least geological nature, as something rather placid. That is, until you see a huge mountain blow over five hundred meters off its summit, then enthusiastically spew ash and lava to the four winds. An occurrence that happens all too frequently in Indonesia.

Today Gunung Api still smolders and smokes occasionally. But most people know it for the view from its peak and the century-old cinnamon plantations. Getting to the six-hundred-foot-high summit is a tough climb. But, providing you manage it without suffering a heart attack on the way, the view offers an unsurpassed panorama of the islands.

From high on the crater of Gunung Api, it is easy to make out the enormous rim of an ancient volcanic crater that once exploded, leaving the Banda islands as meagre remnants of its once mighty splendor. Before it went bang, that mountain was one of the tallest in the world. Pretty impressive, considering its base starts some five thousand meters below the surface of the Banda Sea and extends underwater for miles in every direction.

How snakes manage to infiltrate those newly emerged islands is one of life's mysteries worth reflecting on. You see, we have a history with snakes on *Vega*. Twice we had one crawl in via the stern windows to infest our aft cabin. I will give you one guess who had the jolly job of evicting them both.

And then there was the day I returned to Raffles Marina in Singapore and found Meggi halfway up the mizzen mast rigging hanging on for dear life and squealing for help. Several boat boys were gathered around our aft deck brandishing various improvised implements of destruction—a nice way of saying they had everything from brooms to life rings in hand. One clever lad even brought a bright-red fire extinguisher with him. The center of all this excitement was an evil-looking black hooded cobra well over a meter long that had somehow found its way into our dingy, which at the time was peacefully hanging from the davits a good two meters out of the water.

Only minutes before, Meggi had gone aft to get something out of the dingy, and as she moved the floorboards, up rose this harbinger of sudden death with its hood back, tongue flicking obscenely and all. A sight guaranteed to chill any sane person's blood.

Well, Meggi didn't hesitate. With a shriek and a yelp, she shot out of there and straight up the mizzen ratlines. From that august perch, she raised the alarm in a voice that must have had people miles away turning their heads. Of course, all the boat boys came running to her assistance, mostly out of boredom, mind you. It was just about then that I pitched up.

When it comes to snakes, I readily admit to a serious fear of the things. It may be unwarranted and I know most of them are innocent enough. On the other hand, even I know that anything that looks like a snake and spreads a hood like that one did is not of the friendly garden variety. Add the fact I know almost nothing about managing snakes, other than perhaps playing them an Indian flute sonata before scampering up a rope.

It was the fire extinguisher that finally did for the hideous creature. The lad who brought it had more sense than we gave him credit for. As we all watched—from a safe distance—he raced in to fling his extinguisher with deadly accuracy. After that first strike, the mob quickly descended, wielding everything from brooms to hamburgers. The result was a bloody mess of shredded snake in the bottom of our dingy. Luckily, the boat boys agreed to cart away the remains since Meggi refused to climb down until it was well and truly off of the boat. Can't say that I blamed her. She always had been a sensible lass.

CHAPTER 59

The Lost Forts of Gunung Api

Like most adventures, this one began innocently enough over dinner, when our friend Abba Rizal commented on an ancient map of the islands that recently came into his possession. I should mention that Abba is as fanatical about old stones and historical mysteries as Meggi and I. Although, being a native-born Banda Islander, he tends to confine his historical studies to the islands.

"The old chronicles clearly state that at various times there were no less than three fortified emplacements on Gunung Api," he said, lightly slapping his hand against the table for emphasis. "There should be ruins remaining, but no one has any idea where they are."

Abba glanced around the table, then waved his index finger in the air. "Three stone-built fortifications on an island the size of Gunung Api and no one can find them?" He shook his head in disgust and continued. "I have asked all of the old people, the hunters, and even the palm wine tappers. They all know the stories, yet none of them has the slightest idea where even one of those forts might be." Mind you, coming from a man like Abba, that little speech was equal to a tirade in the House of Commons.

More to prevent him knocking over my wine glass than for any other reason, I casually suggested that, if he felt it so important, why not mount an expedition to search for the lost forts of Gunung Api. Then of course Meggi jumped in with what a wonderful idea that was. The next thing I knew we were out on the terrace sipping coffee and poring over old maps. Which, by the way, proved useless.

Even though we were due to leave Banda in a few days, for inveterate "old stone" lovers like Abba, Meggi, and me, this was a challenge not to be ignored. Aside from the fact that it would be great good fun and a bit of innocent adventure, those old forts are an important part of Banda's historical heritage. They needed rediscovering.

Here was a chance for Meggi and me to make a useful contribution while indulging our love of exploration and old ruins. Our friend Abba, who among other things is the duly elected president of the Banda Island Tourist Association, was constantly bemoaning the lack of interesting places for tourists to visit on Gunung Api. An old fort might be just the ticket for an afternoon of carefree snorkeling mixed with ancient ruins.

Having reviewed all the available information, the three of us agreed to mount an expedition the following morning searching for the three lost forts. We decided to investigate the one indicated on Abba's old Dutch chart first. Should that prove fruitless, we would continue our circumnavigation of Gunung Api. Since those defensive fortifications surely faced the sea, our best chance of spotting them would be from the water. If nothing else, the voyage allowed Abba to survey likely new picnic and snorkeling sites.

If we could find even one of those lost strongholds in reasonable condition, it would not be long before the locals cleared away paths and created open spaces where visitors could wander about gawking at the trees and taking selfies. With any luck, excavations and academic research would outpace touristic development. Which of course it rarely does.

Gunung Api is about four kilometers from north to south and one and a half from east to west. Most of that is mountain, with only a few flat spaces along the coast. The volcano last erupted in 1988, spewing ash all over the neighborhood and creating two new craters. One each on its northern and southern sides had a volcanic field day disgorging rivers of lava, while the main crater amused itself ejecting copious amounts of smoke and ash.

You might think finding at least one out of three medium-size stone forts on such a small island would be easy. But I am here to tell you, searching for anything on an island that sports few if any trails or even goat tracks worth following is no simple matter. Especially when the place is shrouded in densely packed undergrowth, with the exception of those lunar-like areas covered by the latest lava spill.

Then again, if there were paths leading to any one of those forts, by now the people living on Gunung Api would know exactly where they were. From personal experience, I can assure you children get into everything.

The night before setting out, we carefully reviewed Abba's material concerning each of the forts. Other than a few mentions in old manuscripts and the single reference we had from an 1800s-era Dutch sea chart, there was not much available. Meanwhile, I went on the internet to download the latest Google satellite photographs, which proved useless due to the thick vegetation covering the island.

We knew that hidden somewhere along that rugged coastline were the remains of one Portuguese and two Dutch fortifications. All the available evidence agreed that at one time they had been there, although none of our references had bothered to document their position. No one currently living on Gunung Api knew where they were, or even if they still existed.

More than one of Abba's friends speculated they had been destroyed by volcanic eruptions, either during the last century or in 1988. This theory seemed to have some credence in that two of them did not appear on our navigation chart. Then again, those forts were also absent from older charts dating from early Dutch days until roughly the mid-1800s. Most likely, their locations were omitted for military reasons.

Of course, the position indicated on our chart for the first fort proved to be useless. Again, we suspected the Dutch of purposely obscuring its position. Either that or documentarians of the day considered stone forts such obvious landmarks they were not worth mentioning. We also faced another problem: the shape of the island had changed since that chart was created.

To make life even more complex, our reference books gave four different names for the objects of our search. Those names are Kota, Batavia, Orange, and Columbia. Even though this posed a problem when asking people living on the island about those ancient ruins, we treated it as another important clue. Perhaps one of those three forts started life as Portuguese before being taken over and renamed by the Dutch.

It was early morning when Meggi, Abba, and I set out in *Vega*'s dinghy on our mission of discovery. Thanks to Abba's wife, Dila, we had a well-stocked picnic hamper packed with culinary delights and several large bottles of nutmeg-flavored drinking water alongside our pile of snorkeling gear. We knew our targets were not big forts, like Belgica or Nassau, but smaller coastal fortifications that Abba estimated were no more than fifty meters on a side, with walls originally five or six meters high.

Finding those fortifications, if they still existed, might pose considerable problems. By now, due to earthquakes from various eruptions, the walls could very well be no more than piles of rubble effectively camouflaged by jungle vines and brush. Our main hope lay in discovering the remains of a man-made boat landing used to supply one or more of the forts. From there, an overgrown path might lead us to success.

Even though in high spirits, we knew such a find would depend on luck more than any skill we might bring to the search. The densely forested coast when seen from our small boat could easily hide such remains, especially walls damaged by past volcanic activity or by age and neglect.

As our five-horse-power Yamaha outboard growled its way across water as smooth as a lake, I realized what a difficult task we had taken on. And how little time we had for such an investigation. Since we were still on the side facing Banda Naira, Abba provided a running commentary on various sites of interest. You see, there are many ruins on Gunung Api. Not the least of which is an entire village abandoned during the last eruption and never repopulated, an eerie place with empty houses and shops, well populated by snakes and spiders yet devoid of people.

Let me tell you, water so clear it seems to disappear is not easy to navigate on. Add to that an overactive imagination and you have visions of hitting a submerged rock with the propeller of our outboard and having to paddle home. Amazing how the thought of such a long row back concentrated my attention.

On the other hand, Meggi was like a kid at the circus, dancing with delight as each new reef or coral garden slid beneath our keel. Hopping from one side of the boat to the other, she chanted a constant litany of, "Look at that, look at this, did you see the?" The way she was continually pointing and gesticulating, anyone seeing us from a distance might think we had a snake loose in the boat.

What appeared as a rather small island on the chart quickly became a lengthy, convoluted shoreline slightly more than eight nautical miles long. A rugged coast where any one of the many small coves and bays might hide some clue to the object of our expedition. Abba and I took turns scanning the shoreline with binoculars. On several occasions, a natural rock formation appeared to be modified by man. Each time, after diligently investigating, we came away empty-handed.

Have I mentioned Meggi is one of those people who is constantly exploring her surroundings, easily distracted by a beautiful coral reef passing under the boat or strange bird hovering overhead? She loves exploring new places. Being a natural-born artist, that woman can spend hours happily looking for beautiful seashells or fragments of old ceramic on beaches. She loves nothing better than ambling among ancient remains or simply wandering aimlessly taking in the sights and sounds of a new place.

That day she was in her element as we cruised through flawless water with pristine coral reefs only a meter or so below. The water was so clear that even at depths of ten or more meters few details were hidden from view. It was this water clarity, and her incessant bottom gawking, that led to our first discovery.

We cruised around the southern end of Gunung Api and about halfway along its western coast, finding only dense scrub forest accented by an impressive lava field, a massive black scar where the separation between verdant green of plants growing in the preexisting rich volcanic soil and the newly minted stone of the lava flow are as distinct as if cut with a knife. A raw, awesome beauty that left us feeling humble in its shadow.

The sheer bulk of lava that flowed from the volcano's side on its way to the sea was breathtaking. The entire island had grown noticeably during the last eruption. If one of our lost forts stood in the path of a lava flow, it was lost forever under a million of tons of rugged volcanic rubble.

Mind you, that did not discourage us from frequent snorkeling stops and the exploration of small beaches. Talk about a paradise for underwater exploration. No wonder the Banda Islands are considered among the top five unspoiled dive sites in the world. One place we found featured a series of three modest stone arches perfectly spaced and just begging to be traversed by inquisitive snorkelers.

CHAPTER 60

Of Broken Bottles and Sunken Ships

Late in the afternoon, we decided to turn back. Having investigated many lovely inlets and coves, including several caves well worth exploring with masks and snorkels, we saw nothing to indicate the existence of fortifications. Although the diversion of snorkeling in one of the world's most pristine marine environments was more than enough to compensate for our effort, it would have been nice to see at least some trace of an ancient fortress.

On the return voyage, we followed the coastline much closer than before, carefully scrutinizing the shoreline for any indication of man-made works where small boats could have landed to resupply a fort. Twice we spotted likely places. But on approaching closer, we soon discovered they were not artificial constructions but mere quirks of nature and light. New snorkeling sites aside, and some of those were spectacular, up until then our expedition appeared to be a failure.

As we entered the southernmost bay on Gunung Api, Meggi spotted the long-abandoned remains of two traditional *prahau*-style sailing ships. Both were firmly aground at the bottom of the bay. With her happily pointing the way, there was nothing else for it but to investigate. So, having more or less given up our search, I steered a course for the derelict hulls.

That bay is basically a shallow mangrove inlet. Arriving at low tide, it took patience to thread a way through the coral heads and jagged black stones that litter the bottom. A roundabout route eventually took us to where those two skeletal wrecks lay rotting in the mangrove mud. Both had clearly been there for ages.

One was all that remained of a traditional Bandanese sailing *prahau*, once the favored long-distance trading vessel from these islands. The other was a disintegrating built-up dugout canoe, a type of local fishing boat where planks are added to the sides, employing wooden dowels as fastenings, a practical system utilized by local boat builders to fashion a canoe larger than available trees allow.

As we came closer to the shore, Meggi began frantically gesticulating from the bow. I thought she was warning me of something on the bottom, which in a way she was. Being the cautious type, I took the engine out of gear and tilted it up. As we began to drift, I realized why she was so excited. Scattered on the seafloor were countless fragments of Old Dutch gin bottles.

Those bottles came out from Holland in two types, either glass or ceramic, each with a very distinctive shape and color. The ones she saw were fired earthenware, beige leaning toward light brown in color. The other type was handblown glass that centuries exposed to the tropical sun had turned almost black. Intact examples of either type are extremely rare.

In a flash, she was over the side wading along beside the boat in search of an unbroken bottle. You see, Meggi is an ardent collector, and one of her dreams has long been to find an unspoiled example of each of those bottle types for her collection. Several times in the past she came close to realizing that ambition, only to find a piece missing when she freed her prospective treasure from the sand or mud. From what I could see, as we approached the two derelict hulls, there were only broken pieces littering the bottom. But that did not deter her search.

While we waited for Meggi to scour the bottom for bottles, Abba and I paddled the dinghy ashore, pulling it up onto a sandy patch between the two rotting hulks. It was a charming little spot. A small sand-and-mud beach tucked under several large overhanging trees. Once we had the boat safely secured to a tree limb, we turned our attention to more pressing matters.

As any man will do after spending hours cooped up in a small boat, we each went in search of an appropriate tree to relieve ourselves. An old ship's rib provided the perfect setting for my immediate purpose. Happily putting it to a use its builder never intended, I reflected on the many derelict ships and boats I have visited over the years.

There is something mystical about an abandoned wooden sailing vessel that calls out, begging to be explored. Perhaps those pleas stem from loneliness and a desire to once again feel the tread of bare feet on her decks and the voices of long-departed sailors.

Sadness and mystique permeate the air around such ships, conveying ghostly reminders of each vessel's past. One can almost sense the halcyon days of fair wind and distant voyages intermingling with the dreams and aspirations of those who once gave her life, the men who once cared for her, spread her sails to the wind, or steered her by a convenient star through the long hours of a tropical night, a steady flow of glowing phosphorescence streaming away arrow-straight in her wake.

Fresh from the builder's yard, with her paint gleaming in the bright sunlight, this abandoned wreck was once someone's pride and joy, until the day she innocently made this final voyage to where, driven far up onto a tiny beach on the highest of tides, she came to rest, abandoned to the depredation of neglect, wood worm, and rot by those who once loved her.

I wonder if her owner felt the sadness that such forsaken vessels evoke. Did she call out to him in unspoken words that with a few repairs and some new paint she would happily continue carrying cargo to distant ports? Her death knell was easy to see in the unpierced stern deadwood. That vessel had never been fitted with an engine. Sail alone and the winds of fortune had powered that boat for her entire life. The things that pass through what I euphemistically call a mind never cease to amaze me.

Abba and I met back at the beach, where we lit up smokes, stretched our legs, and gawked at the scenery until Meggi waded ashore grinning from ear to ear and sporting a handful of broken gin bottle pieces that she stowed in the dinghy. Another excited shout followed when she discovered the beach was also littered with fragments. Distracted by more pressing demands, neither Abba nor I had noticed them.

Within minutes, she was following a trail of broken bottle shards. Like breadcrumbs in a fairy tale, they led her straight into the bushes. No sooner had she disappeared into the undergrowth, presumably to do what Abba and I had just done, when we heard her shouting some incomprehensible gibberish. Uncertain if she was under attack by a heard of sex-crazed baboons or had simply stubbed her toe on a rock, we rushed to her aid.

I distinctly remember snatching up a large stick while wondering what could have befallen her—being Meggi, it could be almost anything. For all her down-to-earth common sense, that woman has the curiosity of a small kitten.

We almost collided when she burst out of the underbrush announcing the discovery of something important. Abba and I eagerly followed her to where she proudly indicated a three-step stairway built to the standard double arm-span width popular with European military engineers of the epoch. A bit more poking around showed those stairs formed part of an ancient colonial track.

Tracing what remained of that wide path, once crudely paved with stone flags, we fought our way through giant spiderwebs and dense clawing foliage to see where it led. Fortunately, stout sticks soon did for the spiderwebs, while Abba's sharp bush knife made short work of the hanging vines and creepers. Between dodging spiders, vines, and other assorted flora and fauna, we almost missed what we were searching for.

Abba spotted it first. About ten meters off of to the right of our path stood a wall of dressed stone partly covered with vines and moss. Roughly five meters high, it looked like something straight out of an Indiana Jones film, minus the bizarre statues and background music.

We soon realized that wall continued to both the left and right of where we stood. Following it, we slowly circumnavigated the outer perimeter of an enclosure. On the side facing away from the ocean stood the remains of an arched gateway. Slots in the outer wall showed where wooden roofing beams had once been lodged. Clearly, we had stumbled on one of the lost forts.

Passing through the ruined gate, we found the interior in surprisingly good condition. Even though overgrown with scrub brush and a few small trees, it was easy to make out the roofless rooms that occupy each corner of the walls. On closer inspection, we discovered half-buried portals leading into large underground spaces hidden below the wide ramparts. Those sea-facing parapets were where cannons would have been positioned.

Having no portable lights, and with spiders as big as your hand infesting the place, not to mention the assortment of resident snakes, we decided to put off exploring those mysterious chambers until another day. Such well-protected spaces would have served to store gunpowder and other important supplies.

Here was a long-abandoned fortification that to our delight was in much better condition than many of the others we had seen on the islands, such as Fort Lonthor on Banda Besar. It was also located some distance away from where the nautical chart indicated.

Abba was ecstatic, repeatedly saying he had lived all his life on the islands yet never knew this fort existed. Of course, being Abba, he quickly began planning a modest pier to bring visitors ashore in the little cove, where to put the picnic tables, and how to clear away a path around the walls. He also quickly agreed that we should report this find to the proper archaeological authorities so they could plan an excavation and perhaps even basic restoration.

Not being able to resist the temptation, we randomly chose a likely spot and with the help of Abba's bush knife dug a small hole. Only centimeters below ground level, we found shards of Chinese porcelain and pieces of what Abba identified as copper nuggets once used for trade. The urge to continue digging for new discoveries was hard to resist. But defy it we did.

Carefully replacing the pieces, we refilled the hole. Our superficial finds strongly suggested the site was undisturbed. Good news for the archaeological team we hope pitches up one day to properly excavate and document the place. Mind you, by the time that happens they might need to dig through a new stratum of touristic detritus.

By counting the gun embrasures, we established that our fort once mounted six large guns. Although the three of us performed a perfunctory search of the surrounding jungle, we failed to find any cast-off cannons. Although that does not mean there are none waiting to be discovered. Our exploration was only superficial. Those missing cannons could easily be hidden under the thick layer of decomposed vegetation. We purposely avoided digging or any other action that might disturb an apparently virgin archaeological site.

Having successfully rediscovered one of the lost forts, a happy crew bubbled over with speculations as the little outboard diligently put-putted us back to *Vega*. What with Meggi rambling on about seashells, spiders, and broken bottles, Abba happily planning how to have the fort cleared and cleaned up for tourists, and me trying not to crash into anything, the return trip went quickly. Later that evening the three of us sat around a table at Abba's historic Cilu Bintang Estate, enjoying another of Dila's fantastic dinners and recounting our great adventure to anyone who would listen.

The following morning we were too busy preparing for our departure to worry about lost forts. Getting *Vega* ready for sea again is nothing like it would be for a small sailing yacht, where basically all you do is pull up the hook, then hoist the sails to be off and gone. We have sun awnings to take down, sheets to be rerun, engine and electronic checks, and a whole list of preparations to complete before we finally cast off the lines.

Take the main engine as an example; I always check the engine oil, coolant, gearbox, and prop hydraulic oil, then grease the shaft bearings as soon as we arrive at a new place, in case of an emergency where we might need to shove off quickly. But I also like to recheck those things before we leave. "In case of a case," as Meggi likes to say.

It was in the midst of such hemi-, demi-, semicontrolled chaos that we received a deputation of Bandanese notables. Arriving unannounced, they asked permission to come aboard in order to speak with Meggi and me before we left. Of course we were happy to meet with our friends, even if a bit flustered at having to delay our sailing preparations to receive them.

Once we had them safely on board, and after the obligatory long-winded greetings followed by coffee, observations on the weather, and exciting news about who had won the latest football match somewhere, they sprung a big surprise on us. Mind you, these were some of the most important civic and political leaders on the islands, come that sunny morning in their formal capacity as important officials.

Grinning like Cheshire cats high on nitrous oxide, they presented us with a lovely framed certificate appointing Meggi and me as official "Good Will Ambassadors for the Banda Islands." It was signed and sealed by Banda's most important dignitaries. Meggi was stunned speechless. Mind you, that in itself made the occasion worthy of a red tick mark on the calendar.

Somehow we muttered and mumbled our heartfelt thanks as we accepted their gift, along with a few thankfully short speeches. Having our efforts on behalf of their communities recognized so thoughtfully was quite an honor. On the other hand, that recognition gave us an "official standing" to gather the materials and other forms of assistance needed by our friends on the islands.

That honor adds to what Baba Eki said to me a few years ago. "You are our voice to the outside world. They may have forgotten us, but you remind them we are still here." When I think about the huge difference between the Banda Islands, where the government is trying to make improvements, and the tiny island of Nila, where that same government abandoned the islanders to their own devices in 1978, the contrasts are stunningly different.

True to form, the breeze jollied us along the whole time we were shaking hands and saying goodbye. Then, as soon as we set out full of excitement at the prospect of getting some sails up and miles behind us, the wind fizzled, forcing us to motor around Gunung Api. At least it had the common decency to fade away before we hoisted all those sails.

There are fourteen sails on *Vega*. Altogether they total a bit over 420 square meters. Setting the whole collection for light weather can be a real "all hands to the braces" effort, complete with a symphony of grunting and groaning, people running about, and sails flapping as they go up. Of course, if all proceeds true to form, just about the time we get the whole lot out and can sit down for a well-earned coffee and a smoke, the wind dies.

Usually what happens is we get a good breeze, watch it for a while to make sure it's stable, then start hoisting sails. As each sail goes up and is sheeted home, *Vega* surges forward a little faster. That encourages us to set even more sail. Just about the time we struggle our way through setting both mains and a jib or two, the wind starts to fall in direct proportion to the rate at which we hoist more sails, until eventually we have every rag on the boat out, including the laundry. Then the wind dies completely and we get to take the whole lot down. And people wonder why sailors are notorious for their profligate use of profanity!

I tell you, that is one rule that never seems to fail. Except of course those odd times when the wind stays true. Then the old girl gets a real bone in her teeth as she happily glides through her natural environment propelled by her favorite power source.

Amazing as it may seem, given a good breeze we can sail at almost twice the speed we motor. That definitely says a lot for modern horses, and of course the efficiency of sail. All 215 of Mister Perkins's finest thoroughbred horses barely propel us along at six or seven knots while consuming fuel at such a frightening rate I can never bring myself to use more than a third of our available power.

The best part is the silence of sailing along exactly as the gods intended for man to move over the water. After all, I am convinced if the gods wanted boats to run on engines they would have made trees with propellers on.

For me, sailing starts when the engine shuts down and *Vega* settles into her happiest pace. The silence that falls over the boat is wonderful and so relaxing after all that *rhumm-rhumm, roar-roar, sputter-sputter, put-put,* and stench.

CHAPTER 61

Farewell, Banda

Departing the Banda Islands is always a sad event. We have many good friends there and always manage to accomplish so much during our visits. I shall never forget the first time we set out from those islands after a few highly memorable weeks.

We bade all our friend's farewell and goodbye, then finally hauled up the anchors and headed for the open ocean. As *Vega* made her way out to sea, we waved until our arms hurt and all the other stuff you do at such times. Passing between Karaka Island and Banda Naira, both Meggi and Jo became all choked up. As we turned the northern tip of Gunung Api, Meggi looked at me with tears in her eyes: "Banda is so beautiful. I don't want to leave."

Jo was just as bad. Imagine the pair of them poised on the aft deck sniffling in three-part harmony and honking into their hankies while going on about how much they loved the Banda Islands. I can't really blame them. I enjoy visiting those islands, seeing the friends we have there, and having the adventures we always seem to find ourselves enthralled by there.

Even after all these years, I still get the same feeling Meggi so aptly expressed on that first of many eventful voyages to the original Spice Islands. There is something magical about those tiny little islands lost in the middle of nowhere that permeates every stone, cave, and crevice. It helps that we always time our arrival during the short dry season, an important consideration for islands that regularly receive over 160 centimeters of rain every year.

For me going around the top of Gunung Api is where one delivery year ends and the next one begins. The moment we stop delivering and start collecting again. Before us lies thousands of sea miles, *Vega*'s annual maintenance, and all the hard work of refilling her with tons of educational and medical supplies.

It will be 1,500 miles until our next stop, our longest sail of the year and usually the most enjoyable. With the wind either slightly before the beam or pouring over the stern quarter, *Vega* slips through the water happily, logging between 120 and 150 sea miles a day. Those are exhilarating times, with perfect weather and reliable sea conditions. The stuff a sailor's dreams are made of.

Once around the northern tip of Gunung Api, we turn south-southwest on the port tack, gliding along at a stately pace between Gunung Api on one side and the islands of Rhun and Ai on the other. Watching those two islands so steeped in history pass down our starboard side, I reflected on what we had accomplished that year.

We achieved a lot for the schools and medical services along our route. Hundreds of elderly people received life-changing reading glasses. But there was still a lot left undone. The requests we carried for next year's deliveries were not long, but every item was important. Behind us someone was waiting and hoping that next year we would pitch up with at least part of his or her wish list. Looking at the requirements for next year, many of the items seemed meaningless, yet for the teacher with no chalk or the midwife with no bandages, every box of paper clips, push pins, or rubber bands is a treasure.

When you consider places like Singapore, Kuala Lumpur, or Jakarta—just to name a few—and all the useful items people chuck out with the rubbish, it's enough to have the Good Fairy in tears. I often reflect on how to make people living in the luxury, one might even say decadent splendor, of a modern city aware of the vast disparity between their way of life and that of someone isolated and forgotten hundreds of sea miles from the nearest small town. That what they spend on one meal at a fast food outlet is enough to purchase eight full courses of antibiotics, or seven pairs of reading glasses, or a year's worth of chalk.

Being able to run down to the corner pharmacy to buy drugs, or visit a properly trained, well-equipped doctor, is a given for most citizens living in big cities. For the people we assist, the ones who fantasize over a simple list of exercise books, pencils, and pens, such luxury seems unreal. An aspiration to strive for, yet so far out of reach it is difficult for most of them to even imagine. On many of the small islands we visited with Dr. Ruth, most people came to her clinics just to say they spoke with the only doctor to ever visit their island. Those are places where having an official nurse would be considered posh.

As the hours slip by like water under the keel, we quickly fall back into the easy rhythm of sea watches. That night I kept watch under a cloudless sky with the stars so close it seemed I could reach out and stir the Milky Way with my fingertips. With the big square running sail drawing nicely, we were making between two and three knots on a breeze that barely managed to fill it, or carry away the smell of cooking from below. The smell of onions frying wafted up from the galley, an aroma that always starts my mouth watering. I firmly hoped that Meggi was making one of those famous sweet-and-sour tuna sauces she picked up from Abba's wife, Dila.

As I went below to fetch a cup of coffee, the boat felt enormous and strangely empty. The tons of boxes and bags that accompanied us for the past several months had all found homes. In our wake, thousands of people's lives had been slightly improved. Perhaps we even saved a few of those lives. Once again, the cabins were spacious and comfortable rather than cramped and cluttered. Even though I knew that within the next few months the boat would fill up again with another load of school supplies, Kits-4-Kids bags, and medical supplies, she still seemed strangely empty.

I often compare our yearly cycle to the way they teach breathing in yoga. We inhale by loading, then there is a pause while we move to our first delivery stop. The beginning of those deliveries is like exhaling. We pause again as we return to the north, where the cycle begins once more.

Dawn hovered under the horizon, casting just enough monochrome gray light to illuminate the long deep-sea waves rolling in a stately procession along our ship's side. I was alone at the helm, watching the last star fade from view when an old sea ditty surfaced through my unfocused thoughts:

Evening red and morning gray are certain signs of a very fine day;

But evening gray and morning red cause a sailor to shake his head.

Have you ever noticed how each morning just before dawn the sea and sky take on a dark, sinister gray color, as if to remind us that somewhere below the horizon loom raging storms and howling gales that only fools disregard—at their peril.

With the gray of dawn rapidly turning pink, I toured the deck, taking in the hundreds of things that can come adrift in the night. Stopping at the main mast, I snugged up a loose topping lift, then coiled the fall back on its belaying pin, before walking forward to inspect the bowsprit. Taking the forestay in hand, I braced against the rise and fall of the bow, noting the set of the headsails. A slight vibration in that stay indicated it would soon need tightening.

Vega felt vibrantly alive. A well-found sailing ship reaching across the Spice Island sea on a steady Southeast Monsoon. The foam racing back from her bow told me we were moving through the water at about six knots. Eyeing the great curving belly of our main square sail, I checked its set, then gave the port tack a slight heave, taking up slack from the night's run. I always find it amazing how much brute power that 120-square-meter sail generates, yet how easy it is to manage.

Glancing aft to where the sun would soon appear, I noted we were still right on course. Not that I expected anything else. A good sailing ship with properly trimmed sails all but steers herself. She may drift off her course a few degrees to one side or the other, but at the end of the day makes good a relatively straight route.

That is something most modern sailors have forgotten. For them, it is all about driving a boat. Bending her to their will, while they chase computer-generated images across cyber-world screens between precise satellite-generated waypoints. They prefer to click buttons rather than build empathy with their boat. Real sailors know the best results are always achieved by teamwork. Sailors trim the sails and set a course. The boat then gets on with devouring sea miles.

Boats will talk to you if you let them, telling you exactly what they need to get on with sailing the seas safely. All you must do is pay attention. Learn to sense that marvelous interplay between wind, sails, water, and hull. If you are constantly fighting her with the rudder, then something is amiss with the trim of your sails or the design of your boat, or perhaps with the guy sailing it.

At three a.m., our last plotted position put us 280 miles south-southeast of the nearest land on our second day running under square sail alone. It seems like only minutes since I stood in the bow watching fiery green phosphorescence erupt around us as *Vega* cleaved the sea, throwing spray out to her sides in sheets of glowing luminosity so bright I am sure I could read medium-sized print by its light. Occasionally, a dolphin came racing along the side, its form outlined in the ghostly liquid green of tropical phosphorescence.

That was then. Now, in the heart of a tropical thunderstorm, squall-driven wind blows a deluge of cold rain horizontally across where I sit. Having changed to fore and aft sails, the *Vega* is rolling and pitching as she slams into the choppy head sea. Rain on the dome and salt in my eyes make it difficult to read the compass. As if that were not enough, every fifth or sixth wave hits the bow splashing upward, where the wind flings it straight back into my face. On a few lucky occasions, I manage to close my eyes and turn away before the deluge arrives.

If you imagine sitting in a thunderstorm with someone throwing buckets of seawater at you every few seconds, that lovely image will be close. Ah, the myriad joys of sailing. To be honest, those times are not fun. Not exciting. And not at all adventurous. They are pure cold wet misery—and I still had three more hours until the end of my watch. Two hours and forty-eight minutes, if you want to be precise.

The only highlight on our horizon is tomorrow's landfall. Providing this line of thunderstorms really does move on as predicted, somewhere in the middle of her next watch Meggi should see a reddish glow reflected from the clouds hovering over an active volcano.

Chapter 62

A Promise Made Good

Meggi first spotted the tiny island of Komba at four in the morning. Even though the island was still below the horizon, she could see glowing fireworks spewed up into the night sky every few minutes and a deep-red glow reflected by the clouds hovering over its crater. Lucky girl, she had clear skies and an impressive fireworks display for her night watch.

Komba volcano belches a billowing column of steam and ash into the otherwise clear air roughly once every twelve minutes. Each thunderous convulsion spews out enormous red-hot stones that cascade down the scree flow before crashing into the sea. Some of those boulders are half the size of *Vega*.

The deep-throated boom and the hissing roar of escaping steam combine with a subsonic rumble to form an unforgettable experience. The sea around the island quivers with each eruption, something I could easily see reflected in my coffee cup. We spent the better part of a morning drifting around in front of Komba, often only a few hundred meters from the scree flow where huge stones tumbled into the sea. An awe-inspiring experience to say the least.

Meggi had just finished reading Patrick O'Brian's wonderful book *The Wine Dark Sea*, for about the fifth time. In that story, O'Brian vividly describes an undersea volcanic eruption throwing stones like mortar bombs. Those red-hot flying boulders caused serious damage to the hero's ship. So naturally, Meggi was often heard muttering that we were too close and what if one of those rocks crashed down on us.

Later that morning, we slowly circumnavigated the island accompanied by several dolphins and a pod of friendly whales. They frequently came within meters of us to closely inspect *Vega*, while I amused myself by taking careful bearings and noting the wind drift. Coming around to the western side of the island put us downwind of the eruption plume. Within minutes our decks were covered in a thin layer of fine volcanic ash. Feeling that gritty ash between my teeth came as an unpleasant surprise.

The western coast of Komba Island is quite different from the eastern side. Where the eastern landscape is stark and lunar-like, the western side is green and lush, sporting the typical vegetation you expect on a small tropical island. There is even a temporary fishing camp tucked into a corner of the small bay, where an interesting shelf of shallow water begged us to come in and anchor for a few days.

Nothing gives you the sensation of really living like standing on an erupting volcanic island in the middle of nowhere. The ground trembles every few minutes and a thin veil of ash constantly fills the air. The intense smell of rotten eggs and a background of roaring rumbling volcano permeates everything. And, trust me, when the whole place gives an unexpected violent shake followed by an almighty thundering roar, you realize exactly how puny we humans really are.

The water was so clear I could distinctly make out details on the bottom ten meters below us. Perhaps that was what gave Dr. Ruth the idea to go snorkeling. After reflecting long and hard for about two seconds, Meggi went looking for her fins, mask, and snorkel. I was soon besieged with a hundred reasons why they should go for an exploratory swim. By then Meggi and Ruth had convinced themselves there were multitudinous wonders that needed staring at, and most likely ancient pirate ships filled with chests of gold, for all I remember.

The upshot is, while I watched the boat—read drifted around in circles—they took the dinghy and went off for a squint at Komba's underwater life. People say it is impossible to yell through a diving snorkel, but I could distinctly hear Meggi's excited shrieks at fifty meters.

Two hours later they were back on board, bubbling over with tales of beautiful sights, and the rumbling, grumbling sound an erupting volcano makes underwater. What impressed them most were the brilliant neon-colored corals and fish seen against a background of pure black sand.

You see, thanks to the volcano, the bottom around Komba consists of coarse black sand. Go snorkeling there and you get all the vibrant electric colors of a pristine marine environment, highlighted against a velvety black backdrop. Judging by how those two were hopping from foot to foot, the effect must be spectacular. It seems the periodic earthquakes even help preserve the local coral gardens by shaking off accumulated layers of silt. It was soon agreed that next year we would go ashore to explore that strange little island lost in the middle of nowhere.

Meggi would not have traded that experience for anything, except perhaps another volcano. One with a big glowing lava flows added for color. There are some moments in life that you simply cherish, and if you ask her, that was one of them.

That visit to Komba Island also confirmed our long-nurtured desire to visit another remote volcano indicated on our charts. With a few minor tweaks, our next delivery route will take us right by there for a closer look. It is not every day you get to see a newly born volcanic island emerge from seven thousand meters of water, the tiny tip of a gigantic undersea mountain that must have been erupting for eons before it finally saw the light of day.

Just after lunchtime, the volcano gave another impressive belch of smoke and steam as we turned away from Komba Island. Returning to our original route, we headed west under a sky so blue that our red sails took on a purplish tint as they filled with the gentle breeze.

There is something magical about the swish and glide of a boat under sail. Hurling along at six knots, *Vega* bravely shouldered aside the waves, advancing through the water with an effervescent flow. Suspended from her tall wooden masts, red sails effortlessly harvested the power of an unwavering monsoon wind. Her stem perpetually sundered the present with the sound of tearing silk, as our little ship bravely sailed into the future.

A frigate bird soared in the updraft from our mainsail, hovering motionless on invisible currents. *Whoosh, splash, sparkle*—miniature rainbows peel away from the bow, announcing a rush of spray that soon races down our ship's side. Streaming out into the past, a foaming wake reveals the gradually dispersing shadow of our existence.

As the boat rolls away from the wind, out of habit I tighten my grip on the fore shroud. From my position halfway up the windward ratlines, the rhythmic creak and groan of lines working through wooden blocks provides a counterpoint to the whistle and moan of wind in the rigging, a musical sound, constantly changing pitch in phase with the roll of the boat. Everyone on board, including the cat, is enjoying another beautiful day at sea.

Speaking of the cat, for Scourge the most fascinating part of life at sea are the flying fish that occasionally land on her deck. Fluttering and flapping, they provide great good fun for a prowling cat and a decent little snack, all delivered within easy reach of her paws. The best part being that flying fish never fight back.

Scourge is a small cat with delusions of being a Bengal tiger. She will fearlessly attack without mercy absolutely anything, as long as the intended victim is smaller than her. Watching Scourge stalk the decks intently menacing her rubber ball with a bell inside, or a fluffy rope end, is almost as much fun as seeing her scamper back to the boat and dive behind one of us at the mere sight of another cat. Being an inveterate wimp, she never hesitates to run at the first whiff of trouble, times when she suddenly becomes the most snugglesome animal imaginable.

Typical of most Asian felines, Scourge has a kink at the end of her tail. The majority of cats you find in Southeast Asia have distorted tails or no tail at all. Since this is an unnatural state of affairs, I decided to investigate. Being such a deeply rooted part of the local tradition, it took a while for me to discover the cause. Everyone seemed to think it so obvious they could not be bothered explaining. In the end I managed to worm it out of a line boy at the Royal Langkawi Yacht Club.

It all started with the way a cat will occasionally stroll around holding its tail straight up in the air and vibrating it. Well, back in the long-forgotten past, some bright tabby hater, with nothing better to do than smoke mushrooms and guzzle palm wine, decided moggies do that to attract and capture a chunk of someone's spirit. Exactly why they would seize spirits, or what they did with them once trapped, remained a nebulous mystery. Seeing the world through delirium, with a herd of gossamer-winged pink elephants orbiting his head, that cave-dwelling ding-dong decided cats with distorted tails were unable to steal souls.

This earth-shattering discovery soon spread throughout Asia, condemning any kitten with a normal tail to extinction. When only mousers with crooked tails survive to breed, well, you get the idea. Not only does our cat have a contorted tail, she likewise sports several different colors, ranging from black to white through various shades of brown, with both long and short fur. Darwin would have loved the little critter.

CHAPTER 63

Pilot Whales and Sunsets

Just off the northern coast of Flores, we hove to in the midst of a large pod of black-and-white pilot whales. There must have been fifty of those delightful small whales all around the boat. I never did figure out if they were feeding or simply enjoying a rest from their annual migration, but whatever their reason the hour we spent among them was magical.

They seemed to be formed into small groups, perhaps families. Occasionally a cluster would approach the boat. Forming a circle of heads poking out of the water, they conversed among themselves, most likely commenting on how the neighborhood was going downhill or perhaps blaming us for the paucity of fish. One would nod its head up and down addressing the group, then another would take up the thread. Trying to explain how funny they looked while doing so is beyond me. You simply have to imagine it for yourself.

With their heads held well out of the water, they would give us the once-over, nodding up and down in our direction to have a better view, then turn back to share the latest gossip, before eyeballing us again.

They really do babble among themselves. Something we could clearly hear from the closer groups. Mind you, when they were not busy inspecting the new neighbors, roughly half of a circle remained on the surface, intently watching us, while the rest went down for a go at the seafood buffet. Then the shift would change, freeing the other half for a quick snack.

With almost fifty of them surrounding the boat as we peacefully drifted along, they made quite a spectacle. Meggi of course was ecstatic, racing from one side of the boat to the other squealing every time something new occurred. She wound up sitting on the main top platform, a privileged position with an exceptional view down through the crystalline water.

Not to be outdone, Ruth, who was every bit as excited as Meggi, found a perch out on the end of the bowsprit. Another position with the widest possible field of view. Once established there, if you ignore the animated arm waving and excited yells, she more or less settled in to follow the action. Jo contented herself with going from side to side to watch a show that lasted until the sun had almost set. Then, as if alerted by some mystical signal, the entire gang slipped below the surface. We waited for another fifteen minutes but never saw them again.

While Jo and Meggi hoisted *Vega's* tanbark-red sails, I went back to my place at the helm. As the fore staysail filled on the starboard tack, I steered back to our original heading. By then, we were well into the Flores Sea on a course taking us almost due west, directly into the gradient orange of another tropical sunset.

I confirmed the set of our sails, then checked the horizon for ships or thunderstorms. The sea and sky remained empty. Meggi came to sit beside me. Taking my hand in hers, she leaned against my shoulder and mumbled something I failed to catch.

Scourge appeared from down below. Without so much as a by-your-leave, she took up her usual station wedged between me and the steering box. I scratched her head and she purred her satisfaction. Then, like a gentle mist, rich with the aroma of night flowers, it came to me. After all the years of searching, at last I had found my place in life. There was nothing else in this world I would rather be doing.

Epilogue

Soft morning sunlight illuminates where I sit with the golden hues of a Malaysian island morning. The air has a silky feeling, deeply scented with the dusty aroma of land and a sharp salty tang from the open sea. Perched by the steering station with a fresh-brewed cup of coffee in hand, I find it easy to savor such a tranquil morning.

Mosques provide the background music, each calling their faithful to the second Morning Prayer. What began with a single clear strong voice quickly became a discordant cacophony of amplified sound as every mosque in town proudly added its own powerful loudspeakers with the volume as high as it will go.

Over the years, while living and traveling in some of the world's most exotic places, I learned to treasure the call to prayer as both a great way to keep track of time and a marvelous background accompaniment to the symphony of daily life. That all-pervading music, ritually repeated five times a day, is a distant echo from the silk routes of Samarkand and the mysterious splendor of *A Thousand and One Nights*. Though I doubt Scheherazade's wardrobe would pass muster these days. It might be considered too conservative.

Depending on which direction I let my gaze wander, this lovely morning presents either an idyllic island setting or something quite different. Just to the west, a few hundred meters off the stern of our 130-year-old sailing vessel, is an uninhabited islet. Golden brown in the morning light, the island is alive with the sound of tropical birds and a million insects. Only the hint of a green tree here and there disrupts its dry-season monotony.

Such a peaceful setting invites exploration. An invitation Meggi readily accepted, taking a cup of coffee, along with her mask, snorkel, and our dinghy for an early morning investigation of this new anchorage. I can just see the tip of her snorkel as she happily delves into every new cove and inlet.

Later, she will return with another collection of shells and driftwood. Face beaming with the honest pleasure of her latest discoveries. An artist from the end of her hair to the tips of her toes, I can easily picture her, bubbling over with tales of brightly colored coral gardens and strange neon-tinted fish.

Looking to the northeast across this lovely bay, I see several fantasy-style *pinisis*, ranging from one very accurate historical replica that really can sail to some rather bizarre concoctions more akin to multistory floating hotels. Most sport strings of colored lights to pick out their rather comical sailing rig at night. Some of those lights even blink, blatantly displaying the inherent lack of taste that universally infests most popular tourist destinations. All gently tug at their moorings, patiently awaiting the next batch of excited vacationers to bring them back to life.

Some distance to the east is a hectic commercial pier where traditional wooden cargo vessels dock. Two older, less refined *pinisis*—both heavily loaded with freight, each in need of a coat of paint and lots of maintenance—are creating quite a stir in the middle of this busy little port. One has gone aground on a shallow mudbank. The other is bustling around trying to free her sister from the mud.

I can easily imagine the red-faced captain of that grounded vessel worrying about his ship and the damage to his "face." His friends of course would never think of watching the drama as it unfolds, each one thankful it didn't happen to them.

In between, colorful swift-moving local fishing boats with their brightly painted high curved bows go about mysterious errands, their lone occupant accompanied by the raucous *pop-pop-pop* of an unsilenced single-cylinder diesel engine, the whole punctuated by a lower deep-throated rummm-rum-mm-rummm from the two struggling *pinisis*.

We just came out of the boatyard five days ago, with *Vega* freshly painted and a few minor repairs all neatly done in preparation for our next deliveries. These few days of peace and tranquility are our reward for once again surviving the annual haul out. In the morning our short break ends. Bright and early, we will pull up the anchor and set sail to begin another year of collecting and delivering. *Vega* will sail more than six thousand miles before we see this snug little anchorage again.

For the next three months we will be constantly on display, selling our T-shirts and spice packages, blatantly mooching and begging for the items needed to fulfill our humanitarian commitments. Tons of school supplies and hundreds of Kits-4-Kids bags will flow into *Vega*. In Jakarta we will load even more school bags and the remaining medical supplies from our lists. By the time we set out for the islands, *Vega* is usually so well stuffed that we must sleep on the aft deck.

Getting our supplies to those who need them most requires a little over five months and many thousands of sea miles. Months of reaching out to some of the most remote island communities on our planet. We make the deliveries, but our friends who provide the items we deliver and the hearty band of volunteers who help crew *Vega* to those distant locations are the real heroes. Me? I just drive the bus.

About the Author

SHANE GRANGER (1948–UNTIL HIS LUCK RUNS OUT) HAS BEEN IN LOVE with the sea since he was seven years old. Having worked as a radio DJ, advertising photographer, boatbuilder, director of museum ship restoration, and bush pilot, he always comes back to the sea.

Shane has traveled over a quarter of a million sea miles, including thousands of miles on a square-rigged brigantine he salvaged in West Africa and once single-handedly sailed across the Atlantic without an engine or functioning rudder. After crossing the Sahara Desert with a Tuareg caravan and being kidnapped by bandits in Afghanistan, his greatest ambition is to find a comfortable niche where he and his partner, Meggi Macoun, can enjoy the healthy benefits of monotony and boredom.

He and Meggi currently live on the historic wooden sailing boat *Vega*. Since 2004, they have logged almost one hundred thousand miles delivering donated educational and medical supplies to remote island communities in eastern Indonesia and East Timor.